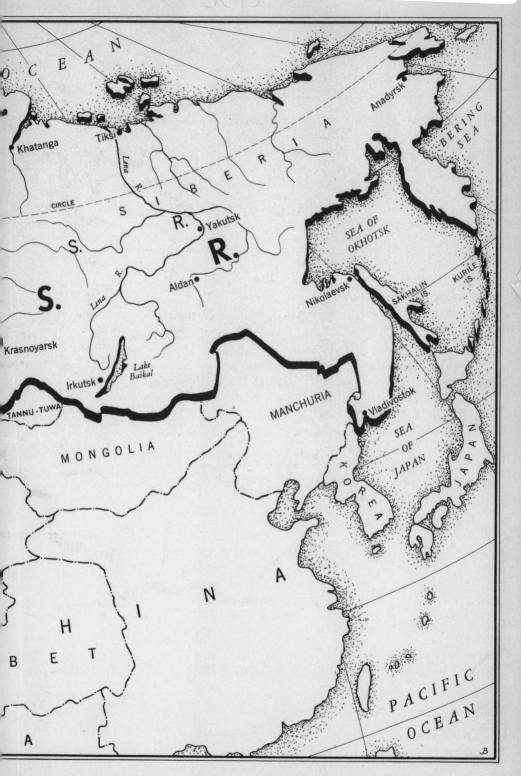

W9-AEW-170

947
St45

O C E A N

Khatanga

Tiksi

CIRCLE

S. S. S R.

Lena R.

Lena

S.

Krasnoyarsk

Irkutsk

Lake Baikal

TANNU-TUWA

MONGOLIA

S I B E R I A

Yakutsk

Aldan

R.

Anadyrsk

BERING SEA

SEA OF OKHOTSK

Nikolaevsk

SAKHALIN IS.

KURILE IS.

Vladivostok

SEA OF JAPAN

K O R E A

MANCHURIA

C H I N A

T I B E T

A

JAPAN

PACIFIC

OCEAN

B

DK4
S8

UNDERSTANDING THE RUSSIANS

A Study of Soviet Life and Culture

EDITED BY

BERNHARD J. STERN

AND

SAMUEL SMITH

New York

BARNES AND NOBLE, INC.

AUG 1961

69675

COPYRIGHT, 1947

BARNES & NOBLE, INC.

MANUFACTURED IN THE UNITED STATES OF AMERICA

Contents

6. SOVIET ART, MUSIC, AND LITERATURE

7. SOCIAL LIFE IN THE U.S.S.R.

8. EDUCATION IN THE SOVIET UNION

9. SOVIET LAW AND JUSTICE

APPENDICES

Introduction

The nations of the world are close neighbors who must now choose between two ways of living. One is the way of prejudice, suspicion, bitter rivalry, attempts to dominate by force, and mutual destruction. The other is the way of understanding, confidence, warm friendship, co-operation, and united efforts to build a decent and peaceful world.

To be a good neighbor requires not only good will but especially understanding. Good will is of course necessary, for envy, fear, and hatred blind the intellect to the truth. But good will is not enough. If democracy, be it American or Soviet in character, means anything to the common people it means that vital policies must be decided by individuals responsible to the common people. The people make the final decisions. And, to make correct decisions, they need adequate knowledge and insight as well as all the facts they can obtain about each other.

This book contains information contributed by people whose appraisals of the Soviet Union are widely respected. Too many of us have been too indifferent and have known too little about our Soviet neighbors. We have known too little about their ideals and ambitions, too little about their ways of working and living, their government, science, education, recreation, and arts, too little about their resources, customs, institutions, laws, and literature. As Dr. Geroid T. Robinson, of Columbia University, has aptly said, "Never did so many know so little about so much."

We have assembled in this volume materials written by outstanding students of Soviet life and culture. Our main purpose has been to provide significant evidence for those who are sincerely eager to learn the truth about the Soviet people. Friendship is a crossroad of many different roads and in the center of that crossroad is mutual understanding. As knowledge about our neighbors grows, perhaps we shall discover how much like ourselves they are; perhaps we shall better appreciate the reasons for their views and policies. The essence of democracy is the right to differ from others. Because differences in customs enrich the lives of neighbors, the Soviet Union has much to contribute to all the world.

No system of society is perfect. The crucial test of any way of life is not merely what it has accomplished in the past but especially the direction in which it is moving. What are its fundamental ideals? What progress is being made to fulfill these ideals? What can we learn from the experiments of our neighbors in the Soviet Union and what can they learn from us? These are basic questions to bear in mind as we evaluate Soviet life and culture through the eyes of the fifty-one authorities who have contributed to *Understanding the Russians.*

UNDERSTANDING
THE
RUSSIANS

* 1 *

Soviet Principles and Goals

FACTS OF SOVIET PROGRESS *

We inherited from the past a technically backward, impoverished and ruined country. Ruined by four years of imperialist war, and ruined again by three years of civil war, a country with a semi-literate population, with a low technical level, with isolated industrial islands lost in a sea of dwarf peasant farms—such was the country we inherited from the past. The task was to transfer this country from medieval darkness to modern industry and mechanized agriculture. A serious and difficult task, as you see. The question that confronted us was: *Either* we solve this problem in the shortest possible time and consolidate socialism in our country, *or* we do not solve it, in which case our country—weak technically and unenlightened in the cultural sense—will lose its independence and become a stake in the game of the imperialist powers.

At that time our country was passing through a period of an appalling dearth in technique. There were not enough machines for industry. There were no machines for agriculture. There were no machines for transport. There was not that elementary technical base without which the reorganization of a country on industrial lines is inconceivable. There were only isolated prerequisites for the creation of such a base. A first-class industry had to be built up. This industry had to be so directed as to be capable of technically reorganizing not only industry, but also agriculture and our railway transport. And to achieve this it was necessary to make sacrifices and to exercise the most rigorous economy in everything; it was necessary to economize on food, on schools, on textiles, in order to accumulate the funds required for building up industry. There was no other way of overcoming the dearth in technique.

Naturally, uniform and rapid successes could not be expected in so great and difficult a task. In a task like this successes become apparent only after several years. We therefore had to arm ourselves with strong nerves, Bolshevik grit, and stubborn patience to overcome our first failures and to march unswervingly towards the great goal, permitting no wavering or uncertainty in our ranks.

You know that that is precisely how we set about this task. But not all our comrades had the necessary spirit, patience and grit. There were com-

* Joseph Stalin, *Leninism: Selected Writings* (New York: International Publishers, 1942), pp. 361-4, 366-9, 371-2, 392, 475-6.

rades among us who were frightened by the difficulties and began to call on the party to retreat. They said: "What is the good of your industrialization and collectivization, your machines, your iron and steel industry, tractors, harvester combines, automobiles? You should rather have given us more textiles, bought more raw materials for the production of consumers' goods, and given the population more of the small things that make life pleasant. The creation of an industry, and a first-class industry at that, when we are so backward, is a dangerous dream."

Of course, we could have used the three billion rubles in foreign currency, obtained as a result of a most rigorous economy, and spent on building up our industry, for importing raw materials and for increasing the output of articles of general consumption. That is also a "plan," in a way. But with such a "plan" we would not now have a metallurgical industry, or a machine-building industry, or tractors and automobiles, or aeroplanes and tanks. We would have found ourselves unarmed in face of foreign foes. We would have undermined the foundations of socialism in our country.

We chose the plan of advance, and moved forward along the Leninist road. . . . Everybody now admits that we have achieved tremendous successes along this road. Everybody now admits that we already have a powerful, first-class industry, a powerful mechanized agriculture, a growing and improving transport system, an organized and excellently equipped Red Army.

Having emerged from the period of dearth in technique, we have entered a new period [May, 1935], a period of a dearth in people, in cadres, in workers capable of harnessing technique and advancing it. The point is that we have factories, mills, collective farms, state farms, a transport system, an army; we have technique for all this; but we lack people with sufficient experience to squeeze out of this technique all that can be squeezed out of it. Formerly, we used to say that "technique decides everything." This slogan helped us to put an end to the dearth in technique and to create a vast technical base in every branch of activity for the equipment of our people with first-class technique. That is very good. But it is not enough, it is not enough by far. In order to set technique going and to utilize it to the full, we need people who have mastered technique, we need cadres capable of mastering and utilizing this technique according to all the rules of the art. Without people who have mastered technique, technique is dead. In the charge of people who have mastered technique, technique can and should perform miracles. . . . Emphasis must now be laid on people, on cadres, on workers who have mastered technique. That is why the old slogan, "Technique decides everything," which is a reflection of a period already passed, a period in which we suffered from a dearth in technique, must now be replaced by a new slogan, the slogan "Cadres decide everything." That is the main thing now. . . .

The slogan "Cadres decide everything" demands that our leaders should display the most solicitous attitude towards our workers, "little" and "big," no matter in what sphere they are engaged, cultivating them assiduously, assisting them when they need support, encouraging them when they show their first successes, promoting them, and so forth. Yet in practice we meet in a number of cases with a soulless, bureaucratic, and positively outrageous attitude towards workers. . . . We have not yet learned [May, 1935] to value people, to value workers, to value cadres. . . .

The Stakhanov movement is a movement of working men and women which set itself the aim of surpassing the present technical standards, surpassing the existing designed capacities, surpassing the existing production plans and estimates; surpassing them—because these standards have already become antiquated for our day, for our new people. This movement is destined to produce a revolution in our industry. . . .

Some people think that socialism can be consolidated by a certain equalization of people's material conditions, based on a poor man's standard of living. That is not true. Socialism can succeed only on the basis of a high productivity of labor, an abundance of products and of articles of consumption, a prosperous and cultured life for all members of society. But if socialism is to achieve this aim and make our Soviet society the most prosperous of all societies, our country must have a productivity of labor which surpasses that of the foremost capitalist countries. Without this we cannot even think of securing an abundance of products and of articles of consumption of all kinds. The significance of the Stakhanov movement lies in the fact that it is a movement which is smashing the old technical standards and is thus converting our country into the most prosperous of all countries.

But the significance of the Stakhanov movement does not end there. Its significance lies also in the fact that it is preparing the conditions for the transition from socialism to communism.

The principle of socialism is that in a socialist society each works according to his ability and receives articles of consumption, not according to his needs, but according to the work he performs for society. This means that the cultural and technical level of the working class is as yet not a high one, that the distinction between mental and manual labor still exists, that the productivity of labor is still not high enough to insure an abundance of articles of consumption, and, as a result, society is obliged to distribute articles of consumption not in accordance with the needs of its members, but rather in accordance with the work which they actually perform for society.

Communism represents a higher stage of development. The principle of communism is that in a communist society each works according to his abilities and receives articles of consumption, not according to the work he performs, but according to his needs as a culturally developed individual.

This means that the cultural and technical level of the working class has become high enough to undermine the basis of the distinction between mental labor and manual labor, that the distinction between mental labor and manual labor has already disappeared, and that productivity of labor has reached such a high level that it can provide an absolute abundance of articles of consumption, and as a result society is able to distribute these articles in accordance with the needs of its members.

Some people think that the elimination of the distinction between mental labor and manual labor can be achieved by means of a certain cultural and technical equalization of mental and manual workers by lowering the cultural and technical level of engineers and technicians, of mental workers, to the level of average skilled workers. That is absolutely incorrect. In reality the elimination of the distinction between mental labor and manual labor can be brought about only by raising the cultural and technical level of the working class to the level of engineers and technical workers. It would be absurd to think that this is unfeasible. It is entirely feasible under the Soviet system, where the productive forces of the country have been freed from the fetters of capitalism, where labor has been freed from the yoke of exploitation, where the working class is in power, and where the younger generation of the working class has every opportunity of obtaining an adequate technical education. Only such a rise in the cultural and technical level of the working class can undermine the basis of the distinction between mental labor and manual labor, only this can insure the high level of productivity of labor and the abundance of articles of consumption which are necessary in order to begin the transition from socialism to communism. . . .

The basis for the Stakhanov movement was first and foremost the radical improvement in the material welfare of the workers. Life has improved, comrades. Life has become more joyous. And when life is joyous, work goes well. Hence the high rates of output. Hence the heroes and heroines of labor. That, primarily, is the root of the Stakhanov movement. If there had been a crisis in our country, if there had been unemployment—that scourge of the working class—if people in our country lived badly, drably, joylessly, we should have had nothing like the Stakhanov movement. Freedom alone is not enough, by far. If there is a shortage of bread, a shortage of butter and fats, a shortage of textiles, and if housing conditions are bad, freedom will not carry you very far. It is very difficult, comrades, to live on freedom alone. In order to live well and joyously, the benefits of political freedom must be supplemented by material benefits. It is a distinctive feature of our revolution that it brought the people not only freedom, but also material benefits and the possibility of a prosperous and cultured life. That is why life has become joyous in our country, and that is the soil from which the Stakhanov movement sprang.

People in our country work for themselves, for their own class, for their own Soviet society, where power is wielded by the best members of the working class. That is why labor in our country has social significance, and is a matter of honor and glory. . . . Here the working man is held in esteem. Here he works not for the exploiters, but for himself, for his class, for society. Here the working man cannot feel neglected and alone. On the contrary, the man who works feels himself a free citizen of his country, a public figure, in a way. And if he works well and gives society his best— he is a hero of labor, and is covered with glory.

In the old days, under capitalism, before the revolution, the intelligentsia consisted primarily of members of the propertied classes—noblemen, manufacturers, merchants, kulaks and so on. Some members of the intelligentsia were sons of small tradesmen, petty officials, and even of peasants and workingmen, but they did not and could not play a decisive part. The intelligentsia as a whole depended for their livelihood on the propertied classes and ministered to the propertied classes. Hence it is easy to understand the mistrust, often bordering on hatred, with which the revolutionary elements of our country and above all the workers regarded the intellectuals. True, the old intelligentsia produced some courageous individuals, handfuls of revolutionary people who adopted the standpoint of the working class and completely threw in their lot with the working class. But such people were all too few among the intelligentsia, and they could not change the complexion of the intelligentsia as a whole.

Matters with regard to the intelligentsia have undergone a fundamental change, however, since the October Revolution, since the defeat of the foreign armed intervention, and especially since the victory of industrialization and collectivization, when the abolition of exploitation and the firm establishment of the socialist economic system made it really possible to give the country a new constitution and to put it into effect. . . . Parallel with this painful process of differentiation and break-up of the old intelligentsia there went on a rapid process of formation, mobilization and mustering of forces of a new intelligentsia. Hundreds of thousands of young people coming from the ranks of the working class, the peasantry and the working intelligentsia entered the universities and technical colleges, from which they emerged to reinforce the attenuated ranks of the intelligentsia. They infused fresh blood into it and reanimated it in a new, Soviet spirit. . . . There thus arose a new, Soviet intelligentsia, intimately bound up with the people and, for the most part, ready to serve them faithfully and loyally.

In 1917 the peoples of the U.S.S.R. overthrew the bourgeoisie and established the dictatorship of the proletariat, established a Soviet government. This is a fact, not a promise.

Further, the Soviet government eliminated the landlord class and transferred to the peasants over 150,000,000 hectares of former landlord, government, and monasterial lands, over and above the lands which were already in the possession of the peasants. This is a fact not a promise.

Further, the Soviet government expropriated the capitalist class, took away their banks, factories, railways, and other implements and means of production, declared these to be socialist property, and placed at the head of these enterprises the best members of the working class. This is a fact, not a promise.

Further, having organized industry and agriculture on new, socialist lines, with a new technical base, the Soviet government has today attained a position where agriculture in the U.S.S.R. is producing one and a half times as much as was produced in pre-war times, where industry is producing seven times more than was produced in pre-war times, and where the national income has increased fourfold compared with pre-war times. All these are facts, not promises.

Further, the Soviet government has abolished unemployment, has introduced the right to work, the right to rest and leisure, the right to education, has provided better material and cultural conditions for the workers, peasants and intelligentsia, and has ensured the introduction of universal, direct and equal suffrage with secret ballot for its citizens. All these are facts, not promises.

Finally, the U.S.S.R. has produced a new constitution which is not a promise but the registration and legislative embodiment of these generally known facts, the registration and legislative embodiment of what has already been achieved and won.

INDIVIDUAL LIBERTY IN THE USSR *

First, what is meant by national efficiency and individual liberty? I mean by national efficiency, maximizing the bodily health, the productivity, the culture, the joyfulness of the whole population, of both sexes and all races; with a particular emphasis on the bearing and rearing of children, seeing that it is on the quality and quantity in race reproduction that the future of a nation depends.

By individual liberty I mean doing what one likes; expressing one's personality in thought, word and act. This depends on two conditions— sometimes conflicting conditions—the absence of restraint and the presence of opportunity. If there were an absence of restraint in the use of the roads there would be precious little opportunity for individuals, especially pedestrians, to reach their chosen destination in safety. Only the most powerful steam-roller could crash through with impunity. And this brings me to the heart of the controversy about individual liberty. Those who possess power, whether it be the ownership of land or capital, or a money making gift,

* Beatrice Webb, "Individual Liberty in the U.S.S.R.," *Soviet Russia Today*, October, 1943, Vol. VII, pp. 8, 28.

or, to cite the most honorable types, the innovating thinker and the creative artist, are obsessed by the notion that it is the absence of restraint which constitutes liberty. Those who have no secure livelihood, and are dependent on others for their continued existence from day to day, that is, the mass of the wage earners and poor peasants, passionately desire the presence of opportunity to live the good life. That seems to them the outstanding meaning of liberty. They want to be given the means for bodily health, for culture, for freedom to choose the profession for which they are most suited, and, in the case of the woman, full provision for bearing children, with the certainty that those children will have the opportunity for a vigorous life and secure livelihood, from infancy to old age.

What are the achievements of the Soviet government in national efficiency? Remember that the Soviet government started with an immense territory, inhabited by 160 millions; the vast majority being poverty-stricken, illiterate and deplorably superstitious. For the first two or three years it was confronted, not only by civil war, but by four invading armies, first the Germans, then the British, French and lastly the Japanese. Hence, a regrettable necessity, it had to create a powerful defence force. Note the word defence. The Soviet statesmen are dead against national aggression. They are, without exception, the staunchest upholders of collective security. Secondly, in the short space of fifteen years they have built up a great manufacturing industry, today in aggregate output second only to that of the United States. Thirdly, they have mechanized their agriculture, thereby not only securing the nation's food supply, but also greatly increasing their harvests of flax and hemp, cotton and tea.

And now—come to the greatest achievement. From the Arctic Ocean to the Black Sea, from the Baltic to the Pacific, they have created a gigantic health and educational system, a universal network of crêches and schools, colleges and universities, clinics and hospitals, research institutes and sanatoria, accessible to the whole of the population, without class or racial discrimination. I do not say that the standard of life of all the people in the USSR is yet as high as that of skilled workers in Britain or America who are in constant employment. There is, for instance, still a conspicuous shortage in leather boots and separate bedrooms. Under the Tsar the mass of the people had neither the one nor the other. But I confidently assert that, during the past twenty years, the standard of health, of education, of technical skill, of culture, of individual enterprise and adventure, and above all *provision for child-bearing* of this vast population, has risen far more rapidly and far more universally than in any other country of the world.

What about individual liberty? This depends, you will remember, on two conditions, the absence of restraint and the presence of opportunity. In so far as maximizing the opportunity for a healthy, vigorous life, with ample provision for child-bearing, for education, culture and a secure old age for all the people, all the time, the Soviet government, considering the depths out of which it started, has accomplished wonders. But what about the absence of restraint? Not the warmest admirer of the USSR can deny that they have diminished this type of individual liberty drastically, in exactly the direction which seems the most essential to the governing class of capitalist democracies. No one is permitted to express his personality by becoming a landlord, a capitalist employer, a trader or a financier. Why is profit making made a crime? Because the Bolsheviks believe that the profit making motive leads inevitably and universally to a corruption and perversion of the economic system; that it divides the community into two nations, the rich and the poor; that it concentrates power in the hands of the wealthy, and keeps the wage earners and the peasants in a state of poverty and dependence; that it produces a disastrous alternation of booms and slumps, with a permanent army of unemployed persons, tragically deteriorating in health and happiness, skill and character. This profit making motive even leads to the destruction of natural resources, and turns forests and fertile plains into sand-swept deserts.

What is the substitute for the profit making motive? The alternative has been discovered in planned production for community consumption. This does not mean the abolition of private property, or having all things in common. On the contrary, there has been and still is a steadily increasing amount of private property in the USSR. But it is distributed among the whole population, it is not heaped upon a class of rich persons. It does not mean the universal engagement at wages, by the state, or the consumers' cooperative movement. More than half of all the families of the USSR are not working for wages at all, but are working with their own instruments of production, either individually or cooperatively, living in their own houses and sharing among themselves their own product; for instance, in the quarter of a million collective farms. But they must not hire labor, or engage in trading, or let their property to rent paying tenants.

. . . Judged by the amount produced, whether in capital or consumers' goods, in railways or canals, in hospitals or universities, in scientific research or holiday resorts, [planned production] has been brilliantly successful. This success is due to there being no enemy party. The general council of trade unions who take an active part in state planning, know that the amount set aside each year as wage fund will be estimated according to the past productivity of the workers. Hence the trade unions have started what is called socialist competition; each individual in each plant competes with other individuals and other plants, in seeking to produce more commodities for the wages to be received. They are all equally anxious to use any method of remuneration, or to introduce any machinery, lessening effort and increasing productivity. What is even more surprising is the device of "patronage." If one factory has beaten another factory in the race for increased production, it is in honor bound to send its best men, and even provide machines to bring the other factory up to the level of production. This sounds romantic. But as a matter of fact, as the wage fund is dependent on the total production of all the workers in all the plants, it is in the interests of each plant to increase the productivity of every other plant. That is obvious. So you get a unity between the personal motive to get more wages, and the public-spirited motive for increased production by the nation as a whole. It is this unifying effect of planned production for community consumption which accounts for the immense progress which the USSR has made during the last ten years. It accounts also for the absence of unemployment. The more that is produced the more leisure will be permitted, the greater the social services available for the whole population; and, what is even more important, the more opportunities will be furnished for maximizing science and giving to everyone the pleasure derived from music, the drama, exploration of the land, the sea, and the air; general culture and the spirit of adventure.

AN INTERVIEW WITH STALIN *

ROY HOWARD: Admittedly, Communism has not been achieved in Russia. State Socialism has been built. Have not Fascism in Italy and National Socialism in Germany claimed that they have attained similar results? Have not both been achieved at the price of privation and personal liberty sacrificed for the good of the state?

JOSEPH STALIN: The term "State Socialism" is not precise. Under this term many understand an order under which a certain part of the wealth, sometimes quite a considerable part, passes into state ownership or under its control while in the great majority of cases the ownership of plants, factories and land remains in private hands.

Many understand "State Socialism" in this way. Sometimes a system is concealed behind this term in which the capitalist state, in the interests of preparation for the conduct of war, takes upon itself the maintenance of a certain number of private enterprises. The society which we have built can in no way be termed "State Socialism."

Our Soviet society is Socialist because private ownership of factories, plants, land, banks, and means of transportation has been abolished in our country and replaced by public ownership. The social organization which we have created can be termed a Soviet, Socialist organization which has not yet been quite completed, but is in its root a Socialist organization of society. The foundation of this society is public ownership: state ownership, namely, ownership by the entire people as well as cooperative-collective-farm property.

Neither Italian Fascism nor German National "Socialism" have any-

* *Roy Howard Interview with Stalin* (New York: International Publishers, 1936), pp. 2–3.

thing in common with such a society, primarily because private ownership of factories, plants, banks, means of transportation, etc., remain untouched there, and, therefore, capitalism in Germany and Italy remains [1936] in full force.

Yes, you are right that we have not yet built a Communist society. It is not so easy to build such a society.

The difference between a Socialist and Communist society is probably known to you. A certain inequality in regard to property still exists in a Socialist society. But in a Socialist society there is no unemployment, no exploitation, no oppression of nationalities. In a Socialist society, everybody is obliged to work and he is remunerated for his labor not yet according to his needs, but according to the quantity and quality of the labor expended.

Therefore, wages still exist and unequally differentiated wages at that. Only when we succeed in creating an order in which people receive for their labor from society not according to the quantity and quality of their labor, but according to their needs, will it be possible to say that we have built up a Communist society.

You say that in order to build our Socialist society we sacrifice personal liberty and suffer privations. In your question appears the notion that Socialist society negates personal liberty. This is incorrect. Of course, in order to build something new, one has to economize, accumulate means, temporarily limit one's requirements, borrow from others. If you want to build a new house, you save money temporarily and limit your requirements, otherwise you might not build your house. This is all the more true when the upbuilding of a whole new human society is concerned. It was necessary temporarily to limit certain requirements, accumulate necessary means, strain forces. We acted precisely in this way and built a Socialist society. But we built this society not for the curbing of personal liberty, but in order that human personalities should really feel free. We built it for the sake of real personal liberty, liberty without quotation marks.

It is difficult for me to imagine what "personal liberty" the unemployed can have who go hungry and cannot find utilization of their labor. Real liberty exists only where exploitation has been annihilated, where no oppression of some peoples by others exists, where there is no unemployment and pauperism, where a person does not tremble because tomorrow he may lose his job, home and bread. Only in such a society is real and not illusory personal and every other liberty possible.

HOWARD: Do you view as compatible American democracy and the Soviet system?

STALIN: American democracy and the Soviet system can exist simultaneously and compete peacefully. But one cannot develop into the other. The Soviet system will not evolve into American democracy or vice-versa. We can exist peacefully together if we do not indulge in too much mutual fault-finding in all kinds of trifles.

HOWARD: A new constitution is being elaborated in the U.S.S.R. providing for a new system of elections. To what degree can this new system alter the situation in the U.S.S.R., since formally only one party will come forward at elections?

STALIN: We will adopt our new constitution probably at the end of this year. The commission for elaborating the constitution is functioning and will soon finish its work. As we already announced, in accordance with the new constitution, elections will be universal, equal, direct, and secret.

You are misled by the fact that only one party will come forward at these elections. You do not see how there can be an election struggle under these conditions. It is evident that election lists will be put out not only by the Communist Party, but by all kinds of public and non-party organizations. And we have hundreds of these. We have no parties standing in opposition to each other, just as we have no class of capitalists and a class of workers exploited by capitalists in opposition to each other.

Our society consists exclusively of free working people of cities and villages, workers, peasants, intellectuals. Each of these strata may have its special interests and express them in numerous existing organizations. But as soon as there are no more classes, as soon as boundaries between classes are effaced, as soon as only a few but non-fundamental differences between various strata of the Socialist society remain—there can no longer be nourishing ground for the formation of parties struggling among themselves for power.

Why will our elections be universal? Because all citizens, excluding those deprived of vote by court, will have the right to vote and the right to be elected.

Why will our elections be equal? Because neither differences in regard to property (differences partly existing) nor differences of race and nationality will cause any privileges or disadvantages. Women will enjoy the right to elect and be elected equally with men. Our elections will be really equal.

Why secret? Because we desire to give the Soviet people absolute liberty of voting for those they desire to elect, those whom they trust to ensure their interests.

Why direct? Because direct elections on the spot to all representative organs, up to the supreme organ, are a better guarantee of the interests of the working population of our boundless country.

Do you think the election struggle will not exist? But it will exist and I foresee a very animated election struggle.

Not a few organizations exist in our country which function poorly. Sometimes it happens that this or that local government or organ has to satisfy one or another of the many-sided and ever-increasing demands of the working population of town and countryside. Have you or haven't you built a good school? Have you improved living conditions? Aren't you a bureaucrat? Have you helped to make our labor more effective, our life more cultured? Such will be the criteria with which millions of voters will approach candidates, casting away those who are unfit, striking them off lists, advancing better ones, nominating them for elections.

Yes, the electoral struggle will be animated. It will proceed around numerous very sharp questions, namely practical questions having first-rate significance for the people. Our new election system will spur on all institutions and organizations and will force them to improve their work. Universal, equal, direct and secret elections in the U.S.S.R. will be a whip in the hands of the population against poorly functioning organs of government.

THE SPIRIT OF THE PEOPLE *

Alexandra Cherkassova is a schoolteacher. She has two children. Her husband died defending Stalingrad. "I remember our first Sundays given up to clearing the streets and factory grounds," she says. "Everyone took part, both young and old. And then one Sunday I got an idea: could not we inhabitants think of something to rehabilitate our city quicker? What if we whipped together volunteer brigades of women and went out every day after work to rebuild and repair the houses? Surely somehow we could find three or four hours a day for the job. True, we were not bricklayers, nor plasterers nor carpenters—but these are made, not born. Our Russian woman isn't the kind to shrink at difficulties. We would try. . . ."

So Cherkassova got together eighteen women. Most of them were, like herself, working in kindergartens. She didn't make a long speech. She said, "For all of us Stalingrad is our life. We cannot look at its ruins without pain. Let's start building."

The others talked it over and agreed with her. But no one could agree where to start. Work was already going forward on the war production plants. An apartment? A bathhouse? A theater? Everyone had a suggestion. Finally someone said, "Pavlov's house!" and there was no more discussion. Pavlov's house was a building which was defended for two months by a handful of men of the 62nd Army. On the facade of the house they wrote: "Motherland! Here some of Rodimstev's guardsmen stood until death. . . . This house was held and kept by the guardsman Sergeant Yakov Fedorovich Pavlov."

The kindergarten teachers and some of their friends called themselves the "Pavlov Brigade" and set about restoring the historic house. There was not a professional builder in the brigade. Everyone had a full-time job in addition to her work in the volunteer effort. "We did not think," Cherkassova admits, "that our initiative would start a whole movement, that it would stir the whole city. Now, of course, I realize that if we hadn't set the

* Richard E. Lauterbach, *These Are the Russians* (New York: Harper & Brothers, 1945), pp. 242–4.

ball rolling somebody else would have done it because everyone had the same desire."

Cherkassova and her brigade wrote a letter to the local paper and asked for more volunteers. Five days later over five thousand Stalingrad citizens were out at the job of rebuilding their city. It was suddenly coming alive again. Some groups were restoring a drugstore, some a school, some filling street craters. But it wasn't all fun. "It was somewhat tough at first," Cherkassova recalls; "there were moments when you just wanted to sit down and weep: five times you would build a Dutch oven and there'd be something wrong every time. Or you had to make a door and you couldn't think for the life of you how to fix the frame. . . ."

Several days later seven thousand turned out, and the number kept increasing until by the fall of 1943 over thirty-five thousand volunteers were giving two or three hours a day. By the winter of 1943–1944 the people of Stalingrad had some place to live, even if it wasn't perfect. There were warm schoolhouses for the kids and enough baths and laundries and dining rooms for all.

All during this period the volunteers had to watch out for hidden mines. A year and a half after Stalingrad's liberation, over three hundred a month were still being discovered. They were hooked to water pails and desk blotters, to phonographs and coffee grinders, even to coat racks so the hanger would explode when used.

During the winter months the building stopped. But the volunteers still gave their two or three hours a day to the task of reconstruction. They spent the time learning carpentry, plastering and other trades. Cherkassova was invited to go to other liberated areas and tell how she had organized things. The central government in Moscow honored her with a decoration. And the volunteer rebuilders of the Soviet Union became "Cherkassovites."

The Soviets are fond of statistics. In an editorial praising Cherkassova one of the Moscow newspapers figured out that she and her brigades had voluntarily contributed 650,000 work days between July and December, 1943, to reconstructing Stalingrad.

The people of Stalingrad have never been alone. Everyone is pulling for them or with them. Nearly every week I read in the Soviet press that some factory or some group of workers had raised money to rebuild Stalingrad, had worked in excess of plan for Stalingrad, had sent furniture or clothing to Stalingrad. We cannot imagine what a terrific driving force this desire to rebuild, rebuild, rebuild can be. In April, 1943, I am told, five hundred members of the Moscow Komsomols volunteered to go to Stalingrad and work; that same month three hundred men and women volunteers reached the Volga city from the Tatar Republic and six hundred construction workers from Kirov also turned up to help Stalingrad arise from the ashes.

* 2 *

The Land and the People

THE SOVIETS' INDUSTRIAL POWER *

Our nearest neighbor outside our own hemisphere sprawls over one-sixth of the earth's surface and is still spreading. Prewar Soviet Russia had an area of 8,174,000 squares miles. Postwar Russia, probably bigger by at least 170,000 square miles, will be nearly three times the size of the continental U.S. One Soviet hand stretches for the North Pole, the other grips the 40th parallel. Its shores are wet by the Pacific and the Arctic and by arms of the Atlantic and the Mediterranean. It crowds two continents and edges toward a third where a man on Alaska's Little Diomede island (sold to us by a czar) can look across a couple of cold watery miles to Chukotski's Big Diomede. Russia's flanks press on a dozen neighbors: Norway, Finland, Poland, and Germany; Czechoslovakia, Hungary, Rumania, and Turkey; Iran, Afghanistan, and China's Sinkiang, Outer Mongolia, and Manchuria. This subplanet has a population of 200 million of three-score nationalities, which normally increases by two and a half million a year. . . .

The Russian soil . . . is suited to almost every agricultural product. Here are wheat and rye and corn; cotton and flax and hemp; the commonplace fruits of temperate zones and the exotic vegetation of the subtropics; rubber plants, tobacco, sugar beets. Men breed cattle, sheep, horses, camels and, through the shadows of one-third of all the world's forest area, trap and hunt mink, marten, fox, sable. In the depths of the North Pacific are multitudes of fish and in inland seas teem others that inexhaustibly produce a luxury of worldwide acceptance in Russian caviar. Under the Russian earth is deposited the world's largest combination of mineral resources—coal and iron and oil; gold and silver and platinum; radium and uranium and industrial diamonds; bauxite and potash and phosphates; manganese, tungsten, copper, nickel, tin, mercury, zinc, lead, molybdenum. How much, nobody knows, but no people in the world can legitimately boast of greater natural riches.

Such riches become available, of course, only by the application of technology and industry—and long after the Western world had begun transforming itself by these forces, Russia continued overwhelmingly agricultural. . . . It was not until the 1890's, after oil was found at Baku and iron found side by side with the coal of the Donbas, that the industrial revolution began to stir in Russia. It stirred but slowly toward a wartime

---

* "What Business with Russia?", *Fortune Magazine*, January, 1945, pp. 153-4.

peak of production in 1916. Being a late starter, Russia did have the advantage of starting with the most modern industrial equipment.

But if Western civilization is industrial, Russia was just entering that civilization when it was thrown back by revolution, invasion, and the chaotic indiscipline that came with a transfer of management and ownership to an unorganized proletariat. Then it started the long hard pull toward what Lenin called communism: "Soviet power plus electrification." By the eve of the first five-year plan, 1928, iron and steel production were no better than back to prewar levels. From then on, although Russia remained predominantly agricultural (percentage of working population employed in industry rose from 5 in 1913 to 20 in 1937), a series of five-year plans produced a phenomenal expansion of the things by which industrial civilization reckons its score: prodigious dams and power plants, new factories, furnaces, mines, wells, highways, railroads, harbors and canals. Russia became the world's largest producer of manganese, the second producer of oil, gold, and iron ore.

All this new industrial might is symbolized by the giant plant of Magnitogorsk, a place in the Ural Mountains that was nameless on the maps of a few years ago. Here are six blast furnaces with a total capacity of 2,700,000 tons annually—which about equals the capacity of the largest American mills except U.S. Steel's Gary—plus twenty open-hearth furnaces, eight rolling and two blooming mills, plants for wire, tank armor, coke, chemicals and chemical byproducts, nitrogen fixation, synthetic rubber, machinery, locomotive repairs.

The plans called not only for the building but also for the nationwide scattering of industry. The old coal and iron mines concentrated in the West were exposed to attack by a powerful enemy. New mines were opened in the Urals and throughout Siberia. By 1938 the Ukraine had lost some of its predominance as Russia's chief iron-ore and coal source—although their production mounted it was being overtaken by that of the East. In the East, too, were set up new important metallurgical plants, machinery industries, and around them new major producers of cement, paper, transport equipment, consumers' goods.

This dispersion of productive capacity was conceived as a part of the development and industrialization of the U.S.S.R., and was pressed on at an increasingly feverish tempo as the Kremlin foresaw that its foreign policy would probably not succeed in forestalling forever a war in the West, to which the older industrial centers would be vulnerable. Then the Germans did come, and the Russians withdrew, according to plan, and fought. Even battle did not wipe out the industrial potential of the West. To escape the invaders more than a million carloads of equipment and materials were somehow evacuated eastward over choked railroads. With the plants went part of the nation, perhaps as many as 20 million workers, foremen, managers. Moscow and Leningrad and Kharkov factories were reassembled in the burgeoning cities of the Urals and even farther east. Don coal miners were transported to the Siberian coal fields of Kizel and Karaganda and even to the Kuzbas 3,000 miles away; iron miners from Krivoi Rog to Bakal and other Ural mines. The grind of the coal-cutting machines and the blast of dynamite were loud in the raw steppe country. By 1942 the Urals were producing more aluminum than had all prewar Russia, and seven or more new blast furnaces were blown in in that region, a safe distance away from the front the Germans were desperately hammering. The industrial cities of the East boomed in the midst of war: doubled was the 180,000 peacetime population of Alma-Ata, in Kazakhstan, the 400,000 of Novosibirsk, halfway to the Pacific, even the 500,000 of the Ural city of Sverdlovsk.

The Far East, too, moved ahead. . . . There is steam up in Russia and its people are going places.

A NATION OF VAST RESOURCES *

World War II has dramatized the immense human and natural potentials of the Soviet Union, officially termed the Union of Soviet Socialist Republics. A sixth of the globe, Russia is bounded on the north by the Arctic Ocean, on the east by the Bering Straits (which separate her from Alaska) and the Pacific Ocean, on the south by Manchuria, China, Afghanistan, Iran, Turkey, and the Black Sea. On the west, the Soviet Union faces Rumania, Poland, . . . and Finland. This immense perimeter of over 25,000 miles encloses more than 8,000,000 square miles.

The land dominates eastern Europe and northern Asia, and confronts, within a distance of less than a thousand miles from its land frontiers, more than half the human race. Its strategic position with regard to air routes is decisive, but, on the other hand, its maritime position is astonishingly small compared to its immense bulk.

In Europe, Russia faces the landlocked Baltic and Black Seas; in Asia, the inland Caspian Sea; in the Arctic, she looks to the icebound ocean. Only in the Pacific, near Japan, does she have some harbors onto the open ocean, which can be used the year round; but these are immensely distant from her industrial centers: here her population is sparse and her industry small.

The river systems of the U.S.S.R., although apparently among the greatest in the world, are curious in that they run either to landlocked or to Arctic seas. The Volga, Russia's greatest river highway, ends in the Caspian Sea which has no outlet at all. The Don and Dnieper rivers flow into the locked Black Sea. The Siberian rivers, such as the Ob, Yenesei, and the

* Sumner Welles, *An Intelligent American's Guide to the Peace* (New York: The Dryden Press, 1945), pp. 111–2.

Lena, however large they may appear on the map, are frozen most of the year. These waterways serve as inland arteries only, and then for only part of the year.

The area of the Soviet Union (over 8,000,000 square miles) is larger than the U.S.A., Canada, Alaska, and Mexico, combined. The population (about 190,000,000) exceeds the total of the U.S.A., Canada, Alaska, and Mexico by 20,000,000. The arable area is enormous: about 900,000 square miles, as against 500,000 square miles in the U.S.A. The climate of the U.S.A., however, is on the whole more favorable to agriculture.

For the most part, the Soviet Union is a vast plain. Her northern area is forested; the southern areas contain the famed steppes (endless grasslands) on which the celebrated Cossacks ride their horses. The Ukraine, the great plain in her southwest, is perhaps the largest single fertile tract in the world, excepting, perhaps, America's Middle West. In Asiatic Russia, called Siberia for the most part, the climate of a large section of the country is too cold for important agriculture. The swampy tundras diffused through Siberia are large and also fairly useless. To the south, in Turkestan, part of the country is a true desert. As it stands, therefore, about 3,500,000 square miles of huge domain of the Soviets may be cultivated intensively some day. The other 4,500,000 square miles can support only a relatively sparse population: mainly foresters, fishermen, and miners. But although geographers think the use of this land is limited, intensive exploration, planning, and irrigation conducted by the Soviet government have indicated possibilities that were lightly esteemed heretofore. The pioneer attitude of the Russians toward these neglected areas recalls the covered-wagon era in American history.

In minerals the U.S.S.R. is second only to the U.S.A., and these resources are widely diffused through the land. She has large deposits of iron and oil, and in many minerals (such as platinum) and fuels (such as peat) she is first in the world. But in relation to the size of the settled area, the U.S.S.R. is not so richly endowed in mineral resources as are some smaller countries in western Europe; and by this test, she is far poorer than the U.S.A. Yet the coal deposits of the Donets basin near the Black Sea are now rivaled by newly discovered Siberian fields, and during World War II, the shift of heavy industry to areas whose mineral resources were formerly little known indicates that many surprises are possible.

The winters are exceedingly cold in most of Russia. Moscow's temperature averages only 13.3° in January and 66° in July—an annual average of but 39°. North of Moscow, the skies are cloudy five days out of six. In the Ukraine (to the south), however, the climate is similar to Ohio's; and farther south the winters are even milder, especially in the beautiful Crimea and the Caucasian-Black Sea coast where semi-tropical vegetation grows and cotton and tea plants flourish. In other words, the Soviet Union, by reason of her extension from 40° to 75° latitude, and her breadth of over 5,000 miles, has almost every variety of climate, with the colder areas predominating.

In the south, the *chernozem* (or black soil), given good rainfall, should be about the best in the world for abundant crops. Most of agricultural Russia has an average rainfall of about 25 inches, fairly well distributed; but the northern and Siberian areas are deficient in rainfall, the average for 4,000,000 square miles being 10 inches or less.

Outside the great central plain, where the population is densest, the mountain ranges rise. The Caucasus Mountains (in the extreme south) are the highest in Europe, and the Pamir plateau, bordering Afghanistan, has been termed the "roof of the world." The Ural Mountains, however, are actually low, hilly, low-strung masses. This range, conventionally separating Europe from Asia, contains considerable mineral and petroleum resources.

The populations of the U.S.S.R. are among the most diverse known, but Slavs overwhelmingly predominate. The "Great Russians," radiating from Moscow (these are the people usually meant by the term "Russians"), constitute the absolute majority. With the "Little Russians" (Ukrainians), and the "White Russians" (in the extreme center-west), and other Slavonic groups, they amount to nearly four-fifths of the population. Tartar influence is strong in the southern desert country; Mongolians are found near China; the Georgians (Stalin is one) are important in the Caucasus, as are the Armenians and Jews. There were numerous German farming colonies, principally about the Volga, who have been recently shifted inland; and, in the newly acquired territories in the west, the Letts, Estonians, and Lithuanians, together with the Moldavians in the south, are significant elements. Many Soviet peoples of mixed origins, such as the Cossacks, have adopted a Russian culture.

Differences in nationality are emphasized by the Soviet government, which regards them as valuable and significant. Native literatures, dress, dance, customs, and cuisines are vigorously encouraged among the more than 150 peoples, under the cultural slogan: "Socialist in content, national in form." Nevertheless, the Russian language enjoys such prestige that it gains despite this nationalist emphasis. The minority peoples are largely grouped into separate commonwealths, corresponding to the British Dominions. But central control is firmer than in the British Commonwealth of Nations.

The population is estimated at 193,000,000 in the territory claimed. This includes the Soviet Union as it existed before 1939, the territories formerly in Poland, Rumania, and Finland in the west, and also the three small Baltic republics. It was estimated in 1943 that if the Soviet population maintains its rate of increase (which though steadily lessening is still impressive), it will have 250,000,000 in 1970, and if the new territories are included, it will have 285,000,000. War losses are assumed in this calculation. It is expected that the population of the U.S.A. in 1970 will be about 160,000,000.

Granting these estimates, the proportion of the Soviet Union's population to that of Europe and the Soviet Union combined will rise from 30% in 1930 to 40% in 1970. If her agriculture and industry increase in proportion, she will be the paramount economic power of continental Europe. Germany (that is, the old Reich, as of 1937), at that time, will not number more than 70,000,000. It is this possibility that may explain the haste of the German assault—a last battle to subdue a people whose impending population superiority as an independent state would be too large to be contested a generation from now.

SOVIET POLICY ON NATIONAL MINORITIES *

Few observers will now take exception to the judgment of the Webbs made in 1938 that the Soviet Union can claim with a high degree of accuracy that it has solved the difficult problem presented by the existence of national minorities in a strongly centralized state. The extraordinary unity manifested by all segments of the population which has enabled the Soviet people to repel the Nazi invaders has been the outcome of a successful minority policy.

Soviet minority policy was not a product of expediency, a matter of arbitrary tactics of maintaining power and extending control. It is rooted in the Soviet philosophy of historical materialism which abjures racial factors as a determining force in history. It was therefore not difficult for the Soviet leaders to conceive of "backward" peoples irrespective of pigmentation and other racial or language differences, as participating as equals in a society where opportunity prevailed for the expression of their talents. . . .

This philosophy might have remained in the realm of theory had it not been implemented by skillful statesmanship on the part of Stalin who immediately after the Bolshevik revolution was appointed People's Commissar for Nationalities. He had given considerable thought to the problem of the nationalities long before the Soviets took power. . . . Already in 1912–13 he had posed concrete questions in terms of actual situations that revealed the complexities of the national problem with which the Soviet leaders had to deal when they came to power. He then wrote:

> In the Caucasus there are a number of peoples each possessing a primitive culture, a specific language, but without its own literature; peoples, moreover, which are in a state of transition, partly becoming assimilated and partly continuing to develop. How is national cultural autonomy to be applied to them? . . .

* Excerpts from Bernhard J. Stern, "Soviet Policy on National Minorities," *American Sociological Review*, June, 1944, Vol. IX, pp. 229–35.

To such questions, Stalin gave basic answers which became the corner-stone of Soviet policy. Among them was the crucial plan of regional autonomy:

The national problem in the Caucasus [he wrote] can he solved *only by drawing the backward nations and peoples into the common stream of a higher culture.* . . . Regional autonomy in the Caucasus is acceptable because it draws the backward nations into the common cultural development; it helps to cast off the shell of isolation peculiar to small nationalities; it impels them forward and facilitates access to the benefits of a higher culture; whereas national cultural autonomy acts in a diametrically opposite direction because it shuts up the nations within their old shells, chains them to the lower rungs of cultural development and prevents them from rising to the higher rungs of culture.

A minority is discontented not because there is no national union, but because it does not enjoy liberty of conscience, liberty of movement, etc. Give it these liberties and it will cease to be discontented. Thus *national equality in all forms (language, schools, etc.) is an essential element* in the solution of the national problem. A state law based on complete democracy in the country is required, prohibiting all national privileges without exception and all kinds of disabilities and restrictions on the rights of national minorites.

The Soviet leaders did not wait long after they seized power to put these ideas into effect. On November 15, 1917, one week after the Bolshevik Revolution, the Declaration of the Rights of Peoples of Russia was issued by a Council of People's Commissars over the signatures of Lenin and Stalin. After recounting in its preface the Tsarist pogroms and the incitement of one nation against another under Tsarism, and pledging that there would be no return to this policy, the Declaration established four basic principles which would motivate Soviet efforts. These were (1) equality and sovereignty for the peoples of Russia, (2) the right of the peoples of Russia to self-determination, to the point of separation from the state and creation of new independent government, (3) abolition of national and religious privileges and disabilities, and (4) the free development of national minorities and ethnographic groups inhabiting the territory of Russia. This Declaraton became the charter for national minorities and the basis of the federal structure later to be incorporated in successive constitutions.

Not satisfied with a formal statement of policy, Lenin and Stalin three weeks later applied the principles enunciated in a special appeal to the Moslems in Russia and in other parts of the old Russian Empire still occupied by hostile foreign forces. . . .

The constitution of July 10, 1918, which incorporated the principles of the rights of national minorities, was operative only in the part of the old Russian Empire designated as the Russian Socialist Federated Soviet Republic. As soon as the counterrevolutionary forces were ousted, the people of one after another of the other areas established Soviet Republics and adopted constitutions, which emulated the principles of the Russian constitution. . . .

In formulating policies on Soviet minorities in 1921 and in 1922, Stalin took account of the differences in economic levels of the respective nationalities. He noted that of the population of 140,000,000 people, Great Russia was most advanced economically, and of the 65 millions of non-Great Russian people, those of the Ukraine, White Russia, a small part of Azerbaijan, and Armenia had in a more or less degree passed through a period of industrial capitalism. On the other hand, 30,000,000 of the non-Great Russian peoples in the population constituting principally Turkic peoples in Turkestan, the greater part of Azerbaijan, Daghestan, and Gorsti, Tatars, Bashkirs, and Kirghiz had had no capitalism, and no industrial proletariat, and were in a pastoral or semifeudal economy. The task of the Russian people was defined in terms of bringing the non-Great Russian peoples up to their economic level, and of encouraging them to develop and consolidate their own Soviet state systems in patterns consistent with the national character of their cultures. Stalin specified that each nationality should man its own courts, administrative bodies, economic agencies, and government by its own local native peoples and conduct them in its own language, and likewise should be helped to establish its native language newspapers, schools, theaters, clubs, and other cultural and educational institutions.

The emphasis was placed upon the development of native leaderships capable of adapting their constructive work to the peculiarities of the concrete economic conditions, class structure, culture, and habits of each particular people instead of mechanically transplanting the economic measures of central Russia, which are adapted to a different and higher stage of economic development.

For the 10,000,000 Kirghiz, Bashkirs, Chechen, Ossets, and Ingushes who had been pushed into unproductive lands by the colonization of Russians under the Tsars, Stalin proposed grants of suitable land and relief from predatory exploitation by colonizers. He stipulated also the fullest possible use of the right of free development for the national groups and national minorities, such as the Jews, who occupied no definite territory but were interspersed among the compact majorities of other nations. He warned against failure to reckon with the peculiarities of class structure, culture, social life, and historical past of the given peoples. These proposals . . . became established Soviet policy.

The Soviet republics concluded a series of treaties with one another during 1920–21 on economic and governmental questions requiring united action and also merged various commissariats. Each republic had originally its own foreign commissariat, and diplomatic representation was not assumed by the Union until 1922 when it became necessary to send delegates to the All-European Economic Congress. The action of the

Supreme Soviet of the U.S.S.R. on February 1, 1944, in adopting the proposal by V. M. Molotov to create People's Commissariats of Foreign Affairs in the various Union republics was evidence of the political, economic, and cultural growth of these republics in the interim period after 1922. When foreign relations were centered in the Union People's Commissariat of Foreign Affairs, these republics benefited from the joint strength that centralization afforded. Twenty-two years later they had gained sufficient stature to benefit from decentralization. Throughout this period they have never lost their identity as political entities as Soviet Republics in a federated union.

This multinational union was established by the first Union constitution in 1924, which . . . remained in effect until the new Soviet constitution was passed in 1936.

The interim between the two constitutions was one of extraordinary development of the national minorities in the Soviet Union. The path was not always a smooth one. It was constantly necessary for Soviet authorities to combat several conflicting tendencies. One was the survival of Great Russian chauvinism which Stalin denounced as in practice leading to "an arrogant, negligent, and soullessly bureaucratic attitude on the part of Russian officials towards the needs and requirements of the national republic." Another was the aloofness and lack of complete trust of the formerly oppressed peoples in the good faith of the Russians, a form of aggressive nationalist counter-assertion which tended to lead to the rejection of proffers of assistance. This overt nationalism of the non-Russian national republics also led in some instances to discrimination against other national groups within their boundaries. . . . In addition there were the middle-class, antisocialist separatist movements as, for example, in the Ukraine and in Armenia, sometimes financed by outside powers, designed to take advantage of Soviet minority policy to disrupt the Soviet Union. These were formidable difficulties to cope with which required vision, vigilance, and tenacious adherence to purposeful and carefully conceived policy.

Of major significance in the success of the national policy were the five-year plans of the industrialization and collectivization program of the Soviet Union. These plans were not narrowly conceived in purely economic terms. They had as their purpose the maturation of the industrial, cultural, and political life of the non-Russian Soviet Republics to bring them up to the level of development of Russia. It was felt that unless this were done, no real equality could be developed. There was no effort to restrain any of the national groups from developing their industries, as had been the practice of imperialist powers in relation to their colonies.. On the contrary, millions of rubles were spent in aiding them to use their natural resources, in developing their water power, in introducing scientific mechanized agriculture on collective farms.

Concomitant with this was a prodigious educational program not merely to eliminate illiteracy, which was widespread throughout the land, but to develop technical skills and to stimulate an interest in modern science, as well as in politics. Among the many pre-literate peoples in the Soviet Union both in the Far North and in the Far East, languages and traditions were recorded for the first time. Special institutes were established for this purpose: the Institute of the Peoples of the North and the Far Eastern Institute, whose purpose it was to make ethnographic studies and to record the native languages. The result was that after the revolution the number of written languages did not decline, but increased. In 1941, books were printed in the Soviet Union in 90 languages. Extraordinary literary creativeness was released among the various national groups from the first poetic efforts in languages which had just received their written form to the stories, novels, poems, dramas which are translated into all the languages of the world. . . .

In addition to the written national literature, oral folklore tradition was stimulated, and the best literature of Russia and the world was translated into the various tongues. Scientific literature is also published in the various languages, and each nation has its university center and technical institution and its crops of scientists.

When the revision of the Soviet constitution was made in 1936, account was taken of economic and cultural advances throughout the Soviet Union. Republics still retained the right to secede and Stalin supported this right at the Constitutional Convention against the suggestion that it be deleted. He urged that since the U.S.S.R. is a voluntary union of republics with equal rights, the right of secession should remain. The congress of Soviets was replaced by a Supreme Soviet, which was bicameral. One chamber, called the Soviet of the Union, is composed of delegates elected by the people, one for each 300,000 inhabitants. The other is the Soviet of Nationalities. To it each republic forming the Union sends 25 representatives, irrespective of the size of its population. Thus the Azerbaijan Soviet Socialist Republic with a population of slightly over 3,000,000 and the Ukrainian Soviet Socialist Republic with a population of 30,000,000, each sends the same number of delegates to the Soviet of Nationalities to promote their interests. The separate ethnographic regions within the constituent republics are given representation in accordance with their stage of development, eleven deputies from each "Autonomous Republic," five deputies from each "Autonomous Region," and one deputy from each "National District."

In 1936 there were 11 Soviet Republics and in June, 1941, when the German army attacked, there were 16, each with a constitution conforming to the structure outlined in the new constitution. Within the sixteen republics there are now nineteen "Autonomous Republics" organized with Supreme Soviets and Councils of People's Commissars but lacking full union status with the right to secede. Fifteen of these are within the Russian Socialist

Federated Soviet Republic. The Autonomous Republics have governmental powers almost identical with the powers of a Union Republic. Stalin has emphasized that their status does not mean that their inhabitants are less cultured or advanced than the inhabitants of a Union Republic, and has pointed out instances where the contrary prevails. The determining factors in the formation of a Republic are the size of the ethnographic group, the fact that it constitutes a more or less compact majority, and the fact that it must be located on a border with the outside world so that if it desires to secede it may join with another contiguous state.

The 1936 constitution also put into the constitution what had long been practice. It declared: "Equality of rights of citizens of the U.S.S.R., irrespective of their nationality or race, in all spheres of economic, state, cultural, social, and political life is an indefeasible law. Any direct or indirect restriction of the rights, or conversely any establishment of direct or indirect privileges for citizens on account of their race or nationality, as well as any advocacy of racial or national exclusiveness or hatred and contempt is punishable by law."

The merit of the new constitution and the national policy which it institutionalizes is seen by the fact that in the midst of a war for survival, the powers of the constituent republics are not abridged but extended. In the Molotov plan of February 1, 1944, . . . not only were the Republics given the right to establish direct relations with foreign states, but national army formations were created to form component parts of the Red Army under their own People's Commissariats of Defense. These are extreme tokens of recognition of the unity of a multinational state.

What of the future? Is the emphasis to be always on separate national cultures? Or is the present cultural pluralism a means to broader unity? The answer was given by Stalin in 1930:

> It may seem strange that we, who are in favor of a fusion of national cultures into one common culture (both in form and in content), with a single common language, are at the same time in favor of the *blossoming* of national 'cultures at the present time, in the period of the dictatorship of the proletariat. But there is nothing strange in this. The national cultures must be permitted to develop and expand and to reveal all their potential qualities, in order to create the conditions necessary for their fusion into a single common culture with a single common language.

The war has strengthened this far-sighted policy of the Soviet peoples. It has accelerated the process toward attainment of a common culture by stimulating an even vaster movement of peoples and industries into previously undeveloped areas than took place before the war, and by welding through mutual sacrifice and unity of purpose peoples of all nationalities.*

* For table listing Soviet nationalities see pp. 222–3.

* 3 *

How the Russians Govern Themselves

WHAT IS SOVIET DEMOCRACY? *

The Soviet people have been continuously taught by Lenin and his followers that their democracy is an extension of the forms and principles developed in the capitalist period of history from earlier beginnings. Lenin wrote that "bourgeois democracy is a tremendous historical progress as compared with Czarism, autocracy, monarchy, and all the remnants of feudalism." He held that a democratic republic is the best form of the state for the workers under capitalism because democratic forms of government are an indispensable condition for the defense of the rights of the people against the forces of reaction. This is the base of Soviet friendship for us and Soviet support of national front democratic capitalist governments in occupied countries.

At the moment [November, 1945] the Soviet press is instructing the people about the elections to the Supreme Soviet next February and extolling the virtues of the Soviet electoral system. These are summarized as "general, equal, direct and secret suffrage" and this is said to be "still an unrealizable dream for most of the people of the world." Especially emphasized is the fact that all persons who have reached the age of eighteen, of all races, nationalities and religions, regardless of educational qualifications, social origins, property status or past activities, now have an equal opportunity to vote by secret ballot in a strictly isolated booth. This includes temporary residents in any locality and all persons in the armed forces anywhere.

Lenin outlined the political goal of Soviet democracy as the direction of the state by the whole people. His phrase that even the cook must share in the government has gone around the world. Step by step the Soviet people have moved toward the goal that Lenin set. The commission appointed to draft the new constitution in 1936 was instructed, after studying all existing democratic constitutions, including those of non-governmental organizations, to frame the most democratic constitution in the world, the one that most fully expressed the will of the people.

* Harry F. Ward, "What Is Soviet Democracy?", *New Masses*, November 13, 1945, pp. 6–8.

Raising the question of how do representative bodies become a genuine expression of the people's will, Lenin answered it by saying: "when the people have the unrestricted right to recall those they elect." Consequently all Soviet representatives are subject to immediate recall at any time on the initiative of a specified number of voters. This also holds for unions, co-operatives and professional organizations whose officers and controlling committees are also elected by secret ballot.

Soviet discussion of democracy emphasizes the fact that from the local to the Supreme Soviets the people vote directly for their representatives without intervening "electors." The same is true for nominations: for the right to put up candidates is secured to all public associations—unions, co-operatives, youth organizations, cultural and educational societies—and is exercised in meetings of workers, farmers, office workers, Red Army men, etc. Additions may be made to the nomination lists by a specified number of citizens. Every organization which has made a nomination, and every citizen, has the right to campaign in meetings, the press, and by other means.

Consequently, a Soviet legislative body has a different composition from those in the capitalist democracies. Workers and farmers are not represented by politicians, lawyers, bankers and businessmen but by persons from their own ranks, including intellectuals who have worked with them at the common task.

They are all chosen on the record of their contribution to the creative effort of the people—a woman on the farm, a worker in the mill or mine, a professor from the university. The result is a functional democracy in which those who are working in the common undertaking also compose the bodies that make and direct the policies.

Functional democracy is being further developed by the increasing participation of the people in the government through auxiliary agencies. Labor and farm organizations quite generally take "patronage" over some branch of the local or national government. This means examining, assisting and reporting on its operations, proposing improvements, securing needed dismissals and providing replacements. This is one of several procedures designed to prevent the disease of bureaucracy—which is the deadly danger of socialist democracy.

A kindred preventive measure is the continuous discussion by all workers of each of the Five Year Plans, which provide the economic bases for the social advance of each period. Section by section, in each factory, mine, farm and transportation unit, the workers propose their production goals, check, recheck and amend them from time to time. This unites experts and workers and fuses the lives of all the people in the common creative endeavor. Early in my study of Soviet incentives I found that really to understand how and why things were being done I had to go beyond executives and general meetings and sit down with the small groups which gathered to discuss production after the whistle blew or after they came in from the fields.

When it is understood that the objective of all this planning is not merely production but more physical well-being and more cultural development for more people, then it becomes clear that Soviet democracy is a way of life and not merely the form of government to which our accepted definitions limit it. It is the people learning to meet together all their common needs, to share together all the burdens and risks of life, to achieve together a higher form of human living.

From the beginning Soviet leaders and people have agreed with us that the basic principles of democracy are freedom and equality. In his report to the First Congress of the Third International concerning the new Soviet state Lenin described its purpose as attaining "true democracy, that is freedom and equality." Ask Soviet youth what they mean when they say: "Now we have socialism. Some day we will get Communism," and they reply: "Some day production will be so increased that distribution can be according to need instead of according to effort. Then everyone will be free to develop all his capacities." That is, more equality of opportunity.

By historic circumstance, and on principle, the order of development of the basic democratic principles has been different in the Soviet Union from ours. . . . Lenin said that all talk of universal suffrage, the will of the whole people, and the equality of all voters would be a mere formality as long as economic inequality remained. He contended that if the people, without any previous training in political democracy, could gain economic power, the people's political power must follow. So the first objective was to transfer economic power from the few to the many by nationalizing the economic process. The next was to organize it in such a way as to develop democratic procedure. The severest critics of the Soviet Union have to concede its progress in realizing equality of opportunity for women, for children and youth, and for the many national groups which compose the Union.

Nor can they successfully deny that under the new constitution more political democracy is being continuously achieved.

The main obstacle that hinders many Americans from understanding Soviet democracy as a developing process is the erroneous idea that the Soviet Union is a totalitarian state ruled by the small minority who compose the Communist Party. The Soviet view of the state is the opposite of the totalitarian concept which makes the state the be-all and end-all of human existence and so puts absolute power in the hands of its controllers. Communist philosophy holds that the state is by nature repressive, and therefore evil, and expects it to gradually disappear as the peoples of the world learn to control together all their affairs.

In fact the Soviet system is a non-party state because the Communist Party is not a political party in our sense of the term. It is a leadership organization designed to guide the people through the first stage of a new form of society, and expected by Lenin to disappear as the capacity for leadership spreads throughout the people. It endeavors to avoid the corruption that waits upon the exercise of power by public examination of candidates and periodical "cleansings" of careerists and petty dictators. From intimate observation of local institutions and acquaintance with non-party people in critical periods I can testify to a far greater transfer of leadership to the non-party masses than is recorded in the rising proportion of non-party representatives in the Soviets. How else can the achievements of the Five Year Plans, the war, and the present rebuilding be explained? That Party representation is as high as it is under the present secret voting indicates the degree to which the most capable and sincere people have been drawn into acceptance of the heavy duties that come with membership. The political forms that will in due time express an established socialist economy have not yet begun to appear.

"But there is no freedom of discussion or the press, certainly not in opposition to the system." I remember in 1924 expressing amazement to an intellectual at hearing a man criticizing the government on a street corner in Moscow. "Oh, but you don't understand. He's a worker," was the reply. In later years I saw peasants and intellectuals enjoy the same freedom of criticism. In common with others who have mingled freely and at length with the Soviet people I can say that I know no land where there is more political discussion (over 36,000,000 people attended meetings discussing the new Constitution and sent in 154,000 amendments), and no land where so many of the people express themselves at such length in their press, from the wall newspapers in local institutions to the papers and magazines of their national organizations. The Orthodox Church, for example, now has its own printing plant.

It is a democratic principle that freedom of expression stops at the point where the peace and security of the nation and the stability of the chosen form of government is endangered. People who have only recently been through a revolution against repression, especially in Eastern Europe where opposing opinions and direct action are usually united, draw the danger line finer than we do, with our long stability and security. In this matter of the press as well as the kind of governments of occupied Europe the core of the difference between us and the Soviet people is whether democratic freedom includes freedom for fascist groups, their financial backers and collaborators, to destroy democracy.

THE ROLE OF THE COMMUNIST PARTY *

The Communist Party differs in many respects from Western concepts of a political party. It has no monopoly of the right to nominate, nor of the membership of even the highest elective bodies, while its members form a minority in the lower legislative organs. It regards elections as a demonstration of public unity on issues, rather than on men, and does its utmost to secure unanimity on candidates through "primaries" which take the form of public mass meetings, even when this means withdrawing its own candidates in favor of individuals who are not Party members, or, as is more generally the case, advancing no candidate of its own when a non-Party person is obviously what we would call the "logical candidate." For these reasons, and because of the well-remembered fact of recent history that all other parties placed themselves beyond the pale by armed rebellions which come under the heading of treason by any definition, it is regarded by the populace, in my experience, not as a monopolist political party preventing the emergence of others, but as the organization of the most public-spirited and, in fact as well as in theory, most self-sacrificing citizens.

In peacetime, members of the Communist Party took the toughest pioneering jobs in opening up the Urals and Siberia. In wartime they were called out of the ranks to form the rear guard during the retreats of 1941 and 1942, and are often the first over the top in the offensives today [1944]. Where many observers are impressed by the fact that the membership of the Communist Party forms so small a proportion of the adult population, the thing which has struck me most is that it is by far the largest active-membership voluntary political organization on earth, and that it has grown continually. During the war, despite the death of "hundreds of thousands" (*Pravda*) of Party members, the over-all membership has reached the all-time high of 4,600,000, by comparison to 3,400,000 before the war. Admissions to membership on the eve of Hitler's attack, in May, 1941, were 35,179 members and 16,617 probationary members. In August, 1943, the corresponding figures were 110,038 and 201,135.

The elections held under the new Constitution have been regarded with scepticism in certain quarters because of the unusually large proportion of the electorate participating. However, if the graph of participation in elections be followed, the percentage participating in the most recent elections will be found to represent not a jump, nor a static high figure, but the culmination of a continuing upward swing. The percentage of the electorate voting has risen as follows: 1927—50.2%, 1929—63.5%, 1931—70.9%, 1934—85.0%, 1937—96.8%.

* William Mandel, "Democratic Aspects of Soviet Government Today," *American Sociological Review*, June, 1944, Vol. IX, p. 262.

THE SYSTEM OF GOVERNMENT *

The new Constitution adopted by the Extraordinary Eighth Congress on December 5, 1936 defines the fundamental rights and political liberties of the citizens of the USSR.

The new Constitution invests the citizens of the Soviet Union with broad political rights and democratic liberties: it guarantees their right to work, to rest and leisure, to education, to maintenance in old age, sickness and loss of capacity to work, and the right to unite in public organizations, as well as inviolability of person and home and privacy of correspondence.

All Soviet citizens enjoy equal rights, irrespective of their nationality or race, property or professional status, sex, education or social origin.

A distinguishing feature of this Constitution is that it does not confine itself to defining the formal rights of citizens, but stresses the guarantees of these rights, and the means by which they can be exercised. It does not merely proclaim democratic liberties, but insures them by legislatively providing material means for their enjoyment.

The Constitution establishes that the Soviets of Working People's Deputies constitute the political foundation of the USSR, and that all power belongs to the working people of town and country as represented by the Soviets of Working People's Deputies. In other words, the Soviets are organs of State power and the working people of the USSR—workers and intelligentsia—directly administer the affairs of the State through the Soviets.

The Soviets—from the Supreme Soviet of the USSR, as the highest organ of State authority, down to the rural Soviets as organs of State authority in localities—are the true vehicles of State power.

The Soviets of Working People's Deputies are democratic organs. They are elected by all citizens of the USSR—men and women who have reached the age of 18, irrespective of race or nationality, religion, education, residential qualifications, social origin, property status or past activities—with the exception of insane persons and persons who have been convicted by a court of law and whose sentences include deprivation of electoral rights.

Elections are by electoral areas, on the basis of universal, equal and direct suffrage and secret ballot.

The composition of the membership of the Soviets and the fact that no limiting qualifications are placed on the right of people to vote is a vivid practical demonstration of the principles of Soviet democracy.

The number of deputies elected to all the Soviets—the Supreme Soviet

* P. Tumanov, "The Constitution of the U.S.S.R."; S. Osherov, "The Two-Chamber Legislative System of the U.S.S.R." and "The Union of Soviet Socialist Republics"; in Embassy of the U.S.S.R. *Information Bulletins,* December 7, 1944, January 28, 1945, and September 27, 1945.

of the USSR, the Supreme Soviets of the Union and Autonomous Republics and the rural Soviets—in the years 1938–1940 exceeded 1,400,000. Between 98 and 99 per cent of the electorate took part in voting, and some 20 million persons, representing public organizations and working peoples' societies sat on the electoral commissions which supervised the elections.

The Constitution establishes equality of suffrage for men and women, and women hold an honorable place in all Soviets. There are 227 women in the Supreme Soviet of the USSR, 1,525 women in the Supreme Soviets of the Union and Autonomous Republics, and 456,673 women in the local Soviets. In other words, over 458,000 women have a direct share in the administration of the State, which represents 33 per cent of the total number of deputies. [In February, 1946, 277 women were elected to the Supreme Soviet].

The Constitution declares that equality of rights of citizens of the USSR, irrespective of their nationality or race, in all spheres of economic, State, cultural, social and political life, is an indefeasible law. Any direct or indirect restriction of rights of, or conversely, any establishment of direct or indirect privileges for, citizens on account of their race or nationality, as well as any advocacy of racial or national exclusiveness, or hatred or contempt, is punishable by law.

The equality of the nationalities of the USSR is vividly reflected in the national affiliations of the deputies to the Supreme Soviets. National equality is also reflected in the fact that the Supreme Soviet of the USSR consists of two chambers: the Soviet of the Union and the Soviet of Nationalities. Both chambers have equal rights; both have equal right to initiate legislation, and the members of both chambers are elected for a term of four years. The Soviet of the Union is elected on the basis of one deputy for every 300,000 of the population. The Soviet of Nationalities is elected on the basis of 25 deputies from each Union Republic, eleven deputies from each Autonomous Republic, five deputies from each Autonomous Region, and one deputy from each National Area, irrespective of size or population of the Republic, Region or Area.

The present deputies to the Supreme Soviet belong to 64 different nationalities; deputies to the Supreme Soviet of the Russian Soviet Federative Socialist Republic to 37 nationalities; deputies to the Ukrainian Soviet Socialist Republic to 8; deputies to the Byelorussian Republic to 9; to the Azerbaijan Republic to 16; to the Georgian Republic to 11; and to the Uzbek Republic to 19.

The same diversity of national make-up characterizes the Supreme Soviets of other Union and Autonomous Republics. For example, the national affiliation of the deputies of the Turkmen Soviet Socialist Republic is as follows: 123 Turkmen, 69 Russians, 11 Uzbeks, 7 Ukrainians, 3 Kazakhs, 3 Jews, 2 Tatars and 1 each from the Azerbaijanian, Armenian, Byelorussian, Georgian, Kirghiz, Mordovian, Turkish and Chuvash nationalities.

The make-up of the local Soviets is similarly multi-national. Deputies to the territorial and regional Soviets belong to 51 different nationalities; to the district Soviets to 83 nationalities; to the city Soviets and city district Soviets to 68; to the rural Soviets to 85.

An interesting feature is that the proportion of deputies to local Soviets belonging to each nationality is roughly equal to the proportion of the total number of members of that nationality to the total population of the USSR. For example, Russians constitute 58.4 per cent of the total population, while the number of Russian deputies to local Soviets constitutes 55.5 per cent of the total number of deputies. Corresponding figures for the Ukrainians are 16.6 per cent and 17.6 per cent; Georgians, 1.3 and 1.6 per cent; Turkmen, 0.5 and 0.6 per cent, and similarly for the other nationalities.

The Stalin Constitution thus binds the multi-national peoples of the Soviet Union.

The Soviet of Nationalities reflects the specific interests and peculiarities of the customs and needs characteristic of each nationality, which have to be safeguarded in drafting, discussing and adopting laws.

Each chamber of the legislature elects a chairman and two vice chairmen who preside over the sittings and direct procedure. Joint sittings, which are held by agreement of both chambers, are presided over by the chairmen of both chambers alternately.

Certain questions must, according to the Constitution of the USSR, be settled at joint sittings of both chambers, each chamber voting separately. In this way, for example, are elected the Presidium of the Supreme Soviet of the USSR, the Council of People's Commissars of the USSR, the Supreme Court of the USSR, the Special Courts of the USSR, and the Procurator of the USSR.

All these authorities are responsible and accountable to the Supreme Soviet of the USSR, in other words, to both chambers.

Any member of either chamber is entitled to put questions to, and receive answers from, any People's Commissar.

Each chamber sets up its permanent legislative, foreign affairs and budget committees.

The equality of the two chambers is also guaranteed by Article 47 of the Soviet Constitution, which lays down procedure in the event of disagreement between the Soviet of the Union and the Soviet of Nationalities. In such cases the question at issue is referred to a conciliation commission formed on a parity basis.

If the conciliation commission fails to agree, or if its decision fails to satisfy one of the chambers, the question is considered a second time in both chambers. Failing agreement, the Presidium of the Supreme Soviet must dissolve the Supreme Soviet and call for new elections. Such a case has never yet occurred.

The two-chamber system was first introduced in 1924, soon after the formation of the USSR. Under the first Constitution, the Soviet of Nationalities was one of the two chambers of the Central Executive Committee of the USSR, the supreme Government authority which was elected by the All-Union Congress of Soviets. . . .

This two-chamber system, under which one of the chambers is constituted on national lines, and both are equal and elected on identical democratic principles, has contributed not a little to strengthening friendship and cooperation between the nations of the USSR, within a single federal State.

The Union of Soviet Socialist Republics (USSR) is a federal State, the members of which are the Union Republics. Each Union Soviet Socialist Republic is a sovereign state comprising a distinct nationality, although in some cases small compact minorities are included. All of the Union Republics are equal members of the federation, in which they are voluntarily associated for the purpose of mutual economic and political assistance and for common defense against alien attack.

The USSR consists of 16 Union Republics: the Russian Soviet Federative Socialist Republic (RSFSR), the Ukrainian, Byelorussian, Azerbaijan, Georgian, Armenian, Turkmenian, Uzbek, Tajik, Kazakh, Kirghiz, Karelo-Finnish, Moldavian, Estonian, Latvian and Lithuanian Soviet Socialist Republics.

Having united in their common interest, the Union Republics voluntarily limited their own sovereignty and correspondingly ceded to the Union certain rights which are defined in Article 14 of the Constitution of the USSR. . . . [See Appendix, pp. 206-7.]

Each Union Republic exercises state authority independently and retains all sovereign rights, which are protected by the USSR and by numerous legal and actual guarantees. Each Union Republic, for example, has its own constitution, adapted to the specific features of the Republic, drawn up by itself and not requiring the ratification of the Union. To every Republic is reserved the right freely to secede from the USSR. Territorial boundaries may not be violated. Inhabitants, while citizens of the USSR, are also citizens of their own Republic. Each Republic may make its own laws provided they are not at variance with the All-Union law. It has its own budget, which is the economic foundation of its sovereignty.

The growing strength of the Union, thanks to the common efforts of the Union Republics, made it possible recently, at the height of the war with the fascist aggressors, to enlarge the sovereign rights of the Union Republics. They have been empowered to enter into direct relations with foreign states, to conclude agreements with them and exchange diplomatic and consular representatives with them. Each Union Republic moreover now has its own military formations, which are component parts of the Red Army.

Political power in the USSR falls into three categories; the first within the exclusive jurisdiction of the USSR; the second within the jurisdiction of the Union Republics; the third exercised jointly by the organs of the USSR and the organs of the Union Republics on a basis of mutual agreements and cooperation.

The organization of state authority in a Union Republic is as follows: The highest organ of state authority and the sole legislative body is the Supreme Soviet of the Union Republic, which is elected by its citizens on a basis of universal, equal and direct suffrage and by secret ballot, for a term of four years. The collective president of a Union Republic is the Presidium of its Supreme Soviet, elected by the latter in each term of office. The government of the Union Republic is its Council of People's Commissars, appointed by the Supreme Soviet of the Union Republic. Each commissar and his commissariat has charge of some branch of administration. Justice in a Union Republic is administered by its own judges. The highest judicial body is the Supreme Court of the Union Republic, the judges of which are elected by its Supreme Soviet.

Each Union Republic has its own capital and a distinctive emblem and flag. Within some of the Union Republics there are autonomous Republics and regions, each comprising a compact national minority.

SOVIET ELECTIONS *

A primary feature of the democracy of the Soviet State system is the fact that all Government bodies, from the lowest to the highest, are elective.

Elections in the USSR are universal—in the real sense of the term. There are no restrictions whatever on the right of suffrage. The right to vote is enjoyed by all citizens who have reached the age of 18, irrespective of race, nationality, religion, educational qualifications, social origin, property status or past activities. Neither are there any residential qualifications. A citizen living in a locality temporarily has the right to take part in the elections on an equal footing with permanent residents. Women enjoy the same rights as men. The franchise is extended to all persons in the Armed Forces. The only exception is made in regard to insane persons and persons deprived of electoral rights by a court sentence.

Elections in the USSR are equal. Each citizen has but one vote, and all citizens participate in the elections equally.

Elections in the USSR are direct. All Government bodies, from village and town Soviet to the Supreme Soviet, are elected by direct vote of all citizens.

The voting at elections is secret.

The principles enumerated above apply both to national and municipal

* N. J. Kupritz, "The Soviet Electoral System," Embassy of the U.S.S.R. *Information Bulletin*, October 13, 1945, pp. 2–4.

elections, as well as to the elections for both chambers of the Supreme Soviet of the USSR.

The Soviet of the Union, or the Chamber representing the interests of all the multi-national peoples of the USSR inclusive, is elected on the basis of one Deputy for every 300,000 population.

The Federal Chamber, or the Soviet of Nationalities, reflects and takes care of the specific interests of the various nationalities of the USSR. Each of the 16 Union Republics constituting the USSR is represented in this chamber by 25 Deputies. Other nationality units forming part of the Union Republics are also directly represented in this chamber: Autonomous Republics by 11 Deputies each, Autonomous Regions by 5 Deputies each and nationality areas by 1 Deputy each. There is no difference in the qualifications of candidates for the Soviet of the Union and the Soviet of Nationalities.

Both chambers of the Supreme Soviet of the USSR are elected for the same term (four years) and the elections take place at the same time. The USSR has no individual president elected independently of the popular representative bodies. The president of the Soviet Union is a collegium—the Presidium of the Supreme Soviet of the USSR, elected at a joint session of the two chambers, and accountable to the Supreme Soviet of the USSR.

The legislative bodies of the Union and Autonomous Republics—their Supreme Soviets—consist of one chamber each, and are elected for a term of four years. The basis of representation is established by the Constitutions of the respective Republics. The Supreme Soviets of the various Republics likewise elect their Presidiums. Members of the Soviet legislative bodies may not be prosecuted or arrested without the consent of the respective Supreme Soviet and, in the period between sessions, without the consent of its Presidium.

The same democratic principles operate in the case of the election of local Government bodies, Municipal, District and Regional Soviets. All such bodies are elected for a term of two years, and the basis of representation is established by the Constitutions of the respective Republics.

Elections are so organized and conducted as to insure the fullest possible exercise of the democratic principles of the Soviet electoral system. Lists of voters are drawn up by village, settlement and town Soviets and are conspicuously posted where everyone can read them. The lists must include all electors living (permanently or temporarily) in the city, village or settlement at the time lists are prepared and who will have reached the age of 18 before election day. Complaints of any inaccuracies are filed with the respective Soviets, which must act on such complaints within three days. A petition against the decisions of a Soviet is filed with the People's Court of the particular locality, which must examine it also within three days at an open session, to which a representative of the Soviet is summoned. The decision of the Court is final. There is no room for any sort of "gerrymandering," for any manipulation of election districts. Electoral areas are formed strictly in accordance with the size of the population from which the Deputy to each Soviet is elected.

Elections are held by precincts, formed to make it as convenient as possible for the voters to cast their ballots. An average precinct covers an area with a population of from 500 to 2,500. In the two largest cities of the Soviet Union, Moscow and Leningrad, an election precinct includes a population of 3,000. Separate precincts may be formed in hamlets or groups of hamlets with a total population of 300 to 500. In remote places inhabited by tribes of hunters or mountaineers, 50 to 300 may constitute a precinct. If there are at least 50 voters in each case, precincts may also be formed in military units, in long-distance trains, in hospitals (with the exception of wards for infectious diseases), in lying-in hospitals, sanatoriums, homes for invalids, and also on board ship, if there are at least 25 voters among the passengers and crew.

Election committees made up of representatives of public organizations and confirmed by the Soviets see to it that the elections are conducted strictly in accordance with the law, decide on the type of ballot boxes and ballots to be employed, count the votes, establish the results of the elections, register the elected Deputies and supply them with certificates of election, and submit all the documents of the elections to the credential committees of the respective Soviets.

Candidates are nominated for electoral areas. The right to nominate candidates is secured to a public association: party organizations, trade unions, cooperative societies, youth organizations, and cultural and educational societies. This right is exercised both by central and local organizations and by general meetings of workers, farmers, office employees and Red Army men. The electoral area committees register and enter all legally nominated candidates on the ballots, which are printed in the language or languages of the population of the given electoral area. A candidate may run for any Soviet only in one electoral area. Every organization which has nominated a candidate and every Soviet citizen has the right to campaign for a candidate at mass meetings, in the press and by other means.

Elections are held in the course of one day, which is the same for the entire USSR in the case of elections to the Supreme Soviet of the USSR, or for an entire Republic, in the case of elections to the Supreme Soviet and other Soviets of the particular Republic. No campaigning is permitted in the premises of the election precinct committee on the day of the elections. Sick and aged persons who find it difficult to walk to the election precinct are provided with means of transportation at Government expense.

Voting is secret, each elector personally casting his ballot in a strictly isolated booth. The voter leaves on the ballot the name of the candidates for whom he wants to vote, crossing out the rest. Votes are counted first by the precinct committees and then by the electoral area committees.

Representatives of public organizations and the press have a right to be present at the counting of the ballots. The candidate who receives more than half of all votes cast is considered elected. If none of the candidates polls an absolute majority of votes, a second election is held within two weeks, the contestants being the two candidates who polled the highest number of votes. If less than half the number of voters of a given electoral area have cast their votes, new elections must be held within two weeks.

The electoral rights of citizens are fully protected by Soviet laws. An attempt—by means of violence, deceit, threat or bribery—to prevent a Soviet citizen from exercising his right to vote or be elected is punishable by imprisonment for a term of up to two years. Forgery of election documents or deliberate miscounting of votes by an official representative of a Soviet or by a member of an election committee is punishable by imprisonment for a term of up to three years.

The functions of Soviet voters do not end with the election of Deputies. The Soviet Constitution accords the electorate the right of recall, which enables them to exercise control of the activity of individual Deputies and of whole Soviets. It is the duty of each Deputy to report to his constituents on his own work and the work of the Soviet of which he is a member, and he may be recalled at any time by a majority vote of his constituents.

POLITICAL RIGHTS OF SOVIET WOMEN *

In granting women the right to economic independence and education, the Soviet State laid the basis for the political equality of women in the USSR. The Soviet woman has equal rights with men in running the affairs of the State.

This political equality is guaranteed, first of all, by the election laws. Universality and equality are the rule in Soviet elections. Any citizen of the USSR of either sex, who has attained the age of 18, has the right to vote in the elections of Soviet Deputies of the Working People to all Government organs, from the village or city Soviet up to the Supreme Soviet of the USSR.

Elections to representative bodies are completely democratic and free. In addition, every effort is made to guarantee the participation of the entire voting population. The election laws provide the maximum of convenience for the voter. If, for example, a voter is ill and confined to a hospital, he may still participate in elections, since voting booths are set up in all hospitals. If a voter is ill or infirm, he may be brought to the election center at public expense, or a member of the election commission is sent to his home with a portable ballot box.

Freedom of the vote is guaranteed by secret balloting, freedom in cam-

* Alexander Askerov, "The Soviet State and the Woman," Embassy of the U.S.S.R. *Information Bulletin,* March 8, 1945, p. 3.

paigning for candidates, and the composition of the election commissions. These commissions are composed of representatives chosen by civic bodies, and by general meetings of factory and office workers and collective farmers at their place of occupation. The election commissions decide all questions of voting procedure; in other words, the people themselves control the elections without interference on the part of Government officials.

A number of women were included in the first central election commission for elections to the Supreme Soviet of the USSR, which consists of two chambers: the Soviet of the Union and the Soviet of Nationalities.

In the 1937 elections to the Supreme Soviet of the USSR, 189 women deputies were elected, or 16.5 per cent of the total number of deputies. In 1938, 848 women were elected to the supreme Soviets of the Union Republics. Altogether, there are more than 1,700 women deputies in the parliaments of the Union and Autonomous Republics of the USSR.

Figures for the elections to local Soviets in 1939 are even more striking. Elections were held to the Soviets of six territories, 97 regions, 21 areas, 3,572 districts, 1,301 cities and city districts, and 63,183 rural localities. The number participating in the elections was 92.8 million, or 99.21 per cent of the total number of voters. In all 1,281,008 deputies were elected, including 422,279 women, or 32.9 per cent of the total.

For the various Soviets the results of the elections were as follows: Soviets of territories—158 women elected, or 24.35 per cent of the total number; Soviets of the regions—2,254 women elected, or 28.65 per cent; Soviets of areas—266 women elected, or 28.18 per cent; Soviets of districts—42,049 women elected, or 32.39 per cent; Soviets of cities—36,268 women elected, or 37.42 per cent; district Soviets in cities, 18,142 women elected, or 39.27 per cent; Soviets in rural localities—323,142 women elected, or 32.37 per cent.

The elections in the Union Republics of Central Asia are of particular importance, since it is well known that in this part of the country, in Tsarist times, women had no rights whatever and were the property of their husbands or fathers. Following are the figures on the number of women elected to local Soviets, and the percentages of women deputies to the total number (the average percentage of women elected in the entire Soviet Union being 32.20 per cent): in Turkmenia, 3,619 women were elected, or 34.2 per cent of the total number; in Uzbekistan, 13,853, or 33.98 per cent; in Tajikistan, 4,173, or 32.97 per cent.

These figures show how great is the progress made in the Eastern Republics of the Soviet Union. In the Alma-Ata district of Kazakhstan alone, 85 women were elected chairmen of village Soviets. Eight women are vice chairmen of Executive Committees of Regional Soviets for the Kazakh Republic.

Besides the many deputies to the Soviets, a number of women also fill leading Government posts. In the Chuvash Autonomous Soviet Republic, Z. Andreyeva, a Chuvash woman, was elected Chairman of the Presidium of the Supreme Soviet. In the Yakut Autonomous Soviet Socialist Republic, the same post is held by S. Sidorova, a Yakut citizen of 40 who was one of the first women of Yakutia to receive a higher education. Her indefatigable labor for the Republic won her the highest office in its Government. Since 1938 she has been a leader of Yakutia, which has a population of 200,000 and a territory of 3,000,000 square kilometers, with enormous deposits of gold, platinum, salt, coal and oil.

In 1942, two women were chosen, respectively, to head the Commissariats of Social Welfare and Justice in Uzbekistan. Khamzina, Commissar of Justice, has had a most interesting life. To this woman of the East, the Soviet power brought freedom, opportunity for education and the right to become a civic leader. In a country where, according to the old laws, women did not have even the right to appear as witnesses in court, Khamzina became public prosecutor and finally Commissar of Justice. Today she is a member of the Department of the Central Prosecuting Attorney of the Russian SFSR.

The number of women promoted to Government posts in the Soviet Union is constantly growing. This is one of the surest proofs of the triumph of true popular democracy.

SOVIET FOREIGN POLICY *

For the accomplishment of Russia's main post-war task, which is reconstruction, a long peace is indispensable, and experience has taught Russians that another word for peace is security. They are determined to rid their frontiers of any menace of invasion—today and tomorrow and "for at least fifty years," some have told me. That is the first objective of all Soviet foreign policy, in Europe as well as in Asia.

Just as we want pro-American governments near us, and do not want hostile regimes, so the Soviets want friendly governments on their frontiers. But they fear insecurity more intensely than we do because they have not got two oceans nor even an English Channel protecting them from the Continent, and because their neighbors are not potentially incapable of invading them. If wars had been bred on our frontiers for generations, and if the last two of these wars had cost us over twenty million casualties, as they have Russia, we would doubtless take very decisive measures to immunize ourselves against a recurrence of the disease. It is improbable that we would permit Russia to tell us what measures were or were not justified.

Yet I do not see any reason to doubt that the Soviet leaders believe that a system of collective security would offer them the best possible environment for peaceful development. Long before this war Russia sought to establish the principle that "peace is indivisible." Soviet Foreign Commissar

* Edgar Snow, *People On Our Side* (New York: Random House, 1945), pp. 244-7, 251-4.

Litvinov tried for years to give the League of Nations a blood transfusion by proposing formation of an anti-aggressor front, not only for Europe but also for Asia, and the enforcement of a program of collective security. The world knows that the Anglo-French answer was the appeasement policy toward fascism, which led to this war. It is likewise not forgotten that the U. S. Congress refused to legitimatize Wilson's brain child, which was the League, refused to take part in enforcing peace on the new map of Europe which Wilson had helped to draw, and retreated into isolationism.

Soviet leaders today remain skeptical of the willingness and ability of Anglo-American governments to devise and support measures to eliminate war in Europe and to control its causes. Until there are convincing demonstrations to the contrary, Russia will remain in a position to safeguard herself by her own means, against a third war and against another interruption in her internal growth. Much as the Russians need our co-operation, they say, in effect, that they do not intend to wait for Congress to make up its mind whether and how it will preserve peace on the Soviet Union's frontiers. But in so far as concrete measures are proposed for establishing world security the Soviet leaders say they are eager to join in enforcing them. It must be admitted that thus far they have assumed every responsibility that we have offered to share with them.

After Russia was invaded she subscribed to the terms of the Atlantic Charter, renounced any intention of territorial aggrandizement and promised the right of self-determination to countries liberated from Axis control. In October, 1943, the Tripartite Conference at Moscow affirmed the will of Britain, Russia and the United States to continue wartime collaboration into the peace and it also discussed "economic co-operation and the assurance of general peace." It envisaged a post-war "system of general security" and pledged that the Allied armies would not occupy the territories of other states, except for aims commonly agreed upon in the declaration "and after joint consultation," and it promised to confer later to secure post-war disarmament.

At Teheran the meeting of Stalin, Churchill and Roosevelt "shaped and confirmed our common policy," at the end of 1943, not only in war but in peace. "We recognize fully," said these three men to whom the earth looked for guidance and promises, "the supreme responsibility resting upon us and all the United Nations to make a peace which will command the good will of the overwhelming mass of the peoples of the world and banish the scourge and terror of war for many generations." They also surveyed the "problems of the future," and announced their determination to organize the world as a "family of Democratic Nations," dedicated "to the elimination of tyranny and slavery, oppression and intolerance."

In addition to such declarations the head of the Soviet government, Josef Stalin, on various occasions reiterated Russia's firm resolution not to seek territorial advantages. As early as November, 1941, he declared: "We have not nor can we have such war aims as the seizure of foreign territories or the conquest of other peoples, irrespective of whether European peoples or territories, or Asiatic peoples or territories, including Iran. . . . We have not nor can we have such war aims as the imposition of our will and our regime on Slavic and other enslaved peoples of Europe who are waiting for our help. Our aim is to help these peoples in their struggle for liberation from Hitler's tyranny and then to accord them the possibility of arranging their own lives on their own land as they themselves see fit, with absolute freedom."

And in April, 1944, Foreign Commissar Molotov reaffirmed this principle when the first concrete case arose as the Red Army surged across the frontier of Rumania: "The Soviet government declares it does not pursue the aim of acquiring Rumanian territory or of altering the existing social structure of Rumania."

As for the rest, it cannot yet be stated in more concrete terms what was decided at Moscow and Teheran. Very likely understandings were reached which would render academic some of the questions which exercised American commentators between Cassino and the major invasion of the Continent. It seems certain, for instance, that it was conceded all around the table that, while national boundaries of the three powers would not be expanded through aggression in this war, neither would any power be expected to give up sovereignty in territories where it was established before the power acceded to the Atlantic Charter.

It is just as "natural" to expect the Russians to rely upon pro-socialist elements in extirpating fascism in territories entered by the Red Army as it is for us to expect Anglo-American armies entering France or Italy to rely upon elements there which believe in capitalist democracy. Everywhere in Europe there is, beneath the surface of the national war against fascism, a certain amount of struggle for dominance going on between adherents of two different systems. The Red Army could no more set up a pure capitalist system and make it work than General Eisenhower could be expected to set up a Communist system in France or Germany. It is all very well to say that neither army will interfere in the internal politics of the occupied countries, but in practice such a thing as a political vacuum can never long exist. What actually happens is that during the period of military occupation the authorities favor one element or the other element to assist it, and naturally they tend to encourage adherents of the system most familiar to them and which signifies stability to them.

The test of Russia's pledge not to seek territorial aggrandizement, and to give other states the freedom to choose their own form of government, will not come during the period of occupation but after the war, when the Red Army withdraws to within its own national boundaries. The test will be whether Russia uses any form of coercion to include the states of Eastern

Europe inside her national boundaries, or whether, having disarmed the fascists in the Balkans, Austria, Poland and Germany, she confers with Britain and America on the methods whereby political power is to be transferred to the inhabitants, as she has promised to do, and abides by decisions secured through such consultations.

Aside from that, anyone with a sense of *Realpolitik* can see, however, that Russia's actual power position in Eastern Europe may give her the main influence and responsibility there for at least a generation ahead. Perhaps Russia could not avoid that position even if she wished to, any more than, say, the United States could avoid enforcing the Monroe Doctrine. Small nations wedged in between big neighbors have to lean one way or the other, and just as the Low Countries fall into the British orbit, so Eastern Europe is Russia's special concern. The community of interests which exists cannot be altered by creation of a larger federation of nations, although it can be stabilized by it.

The Soviets recognized that fact when they enacted the constitutional change granting the Union Republics "autonomy" in foreign relations with other states. Essentially what this measure accomplished was an increased flexibility in the machinery of Soviet diplomatic policy as it affects frontier relationships. Among other things it may in practice mean that the Communists in Soviet Karelia may handle matters affecting Finland, that the Soviet Baltics and the Ukraine and White Russia may seek close direct ties with Poland and Prussia, that the Ukraine may do similarly in the case of Rumania, Hungary, Austria, Bulgaria and Yugoslavia. Very wide explorations could take place in this way without embarrassing Moscow's relations with Britain and the United States. Mutual-defense pacts and economic pacts might be made; cultural, scientific and military missions exchanged; political bodies organized. Eventually these neighbor states might voluntarily and democratically merge into some new regional grouping of their own, or simply into a larger federation of democratic nations in Europe, if one is organized, or into the U.S.S.R. itself, if no international structure proves practicable.

But the key to Russian security in Eastern and middle Europe is not seen by the Russians to lie in control of any of the smaller countries, but in the industrial heart of the region, which is Germany. Historically every great invasion of Russia since the Middle Ages has come from Germany or has had its support. Russian Communists repeatedly told me that when Nazism and its roots are plucked out, fear of aggression will vanish from the map. We may take it for granted that the Soviets will do the job of extirpation at least as far as Berlin. . . .

All this means that Russian foreign policy works according to a plan with concrete objectives and consisting of two parts. One part concerns her vital near-interests, in the regions adjacent to her national territory. There she seeks to build up a wide belt of friendly states prepared to co-operate with her in every field of diplomacy. The other part concerns her broad international interests. There she concedes to other powers the same rights of regional security as she demands for herself. At the same time she subscribes to the endorsement of such practical proposals as promise to maintain general peace and international co-operation.

INTERNATIONAL COOPERATION *

The Second World War differed from the First World War in many respects—first of all in the number of nations participating in it and also in the number of human victims and in the material damage caused. Fourfifths of the population of the globe in one way or another took part in the last World War. The number of mobilized in both belligerent camps reached over 110,000,000 people.

It is almost impossible to name a country which was really neutral in these years. Having allowed a Second World War—that is, not having in time taken measures against aggressive forces of fascism who launched this war of unheard-of scale—mankind has paid an incalculable price in human life and devastation of many countries. War was imposed upon our people, who declared a great patriotic war only in reply to aggression. Hitlerite Germany attacked the Soviet Union not only with the aim of seizing our territory and destroying the Soviet state. Hitlerism had as its aim the destruction of the Russian people and all Slavs.

One cannot forget what tremendous material damage has been caused us by the German invaders and their allies in their rule over Soviet territory during many months. For all this, first of all the main war criminals must answer. German fascist invaders completely or partially destroyed or burned 1,710 towns and more than 70,000 villages in our country. They burned or destroyed more than 6,000,000 buildings and rendered homeless about 25,000,000 people. Among the destroyed towns and those which suffered the most are the main industrial centers of the country—Stalingrad, Sevastopol, Leningrad, Kiev, Minsk, Odessa, Smolensk, Kharkov, Voronezh, Rostov on the Don, and many others.

The Hitlerites destroyed or damaged 31,850 industrial undertakings which employed nearly 4,000,000 people. The Hitlerites devastated and ransacked 98,000 collective farms, including most of the collective farms in the Ukraine and White Russia. They killed or drove off into Germany 7,000,000 horses, 17,000,000 heads of large-horned cattle and dozens of millions of pigs and lambs. The direct loss alone caused to the national economy and to our citizens has been assessed by an extraordinary government commission at 679,000,000,000 rubles.

We cannot forget all this. We must demand from the countries which started the war at least partial reparation for the damage caused. One

* V. Molotov, *Address to the Moscow Soviet*, November 6, 1945.

cannot deny the justice of this demand by the Soviet people. There can be no argument on the justice of this wish of the Soviet people.

However, among us there are no partisans of a policy of revenge against defeated peoples. In our relations to defeated peoples we do not satisfy our feelings but we make new aggression more difficult and . . . the aggressor should find himself in the greatest possible isolation.

We must not be guided by the wrongs of the past but by the interests of safeguarding peace and security among nations in the postwar period. Undoubtedly the interests of safeguarding a firm peace demand that peaceloving peoples should possess adequate armed forces. In any case, this applies to those countries which bear the main responsibility for the guarantee of peace. The interests of safeguarding peace have nothing in common with a policy of an armament race among the great powers. This policy is preached abroad by some particularly fierce partisans of a policy of imperialism.

In this connection we must speak of the discovery of atomic energy and about the atomic bomb, use of which in war has shown its enormous destructive force. Atomic energy is not yet tested, however, in the field of prevention of aggression or in the field of peace.

On the other hand, there can be no technical secrets on a large scale at the present time which could remain the property of any one country or any narrow group of governments. Therefore, the discovery of atomic energy must not encourage either enthusiasm for the use of this discovery in a game of foreign power politics or indifference regarding the future of the peace-loving nations.

There is also no little talk of the creation of blocs and grouping of states as a means of defending definite foreign interests. The Soviet Union has never taken part in a grouping of powers directed against peace-loving states. In the West, however, such attempts occurred, as is known, more than once.

The anti-Soviet character of such groups in the past is well known. In any case the history of blocs and groups of western powers is witness to the fact that they served not so much to bridle the aggressors as, on the contrary, to foster aggression, first and foremost on the part of Germany. That is why vigilance in this respect on the part of the Soviet Union and other peace-loving states must not weaken.

Establishment of peace throughout the world did not and could not bring back the pre-war situation between nations. For some period Germany, Italy and Japan will no longer be among the great states playing the lead in international life. [This will include] the period during which there operates an allied and united control of these countries, directed against a resurgence of aggression of these powers, but a control which does not hinder the development and rise of these countries as democratic peaceloving states.

Of no small significance for the future of Europe is the fact that several fascist and semi-fascist states have taken the democratic road and are aiming to establish friendly relations with the Allied powers. It seems clear that not only should one not impede these states, but it is imperative to co-operate in consolidating their democratic beginnings. . . . It is impossible not to notice that in the camp of the Allied powers also the war has wrought no small changes. As a rule reactionary forces are now pushed back from their previous positions, clearing the way for old and new democratic parties.

In several European countries fundamental social reforms have been carried out, such as liquidation of the feudal land-owning system which has outlived itself and the distributing of land to small-holder peasants, thus depriving the reactionary fascist forces of their strength and stimulating the rise of democratic and socialist movements in these countries.

Some countries now have on their agenda such important economic reforms as nationalization of heavy industry, an eight-hour day and other measures, which bring in a new spirit and confidence to the growing ranks of the democratic movement in Europe and beyond the confines of Europe.

Some organs of the reactionary press make attempts to attribute these daring democratic reforms mainly to the increased influence of the Soviet Union. The lack of foundation of such arguments is obvious. Everyone knows that problems of such nature were successfully solved in the foremost countries of Europe even earlier. This does not mean that the forces of fascism are completely liquidated and that one has no longer to contend with them.

We have all read the Crimea declaration of the three powers regarding liberated Europe, in which it was stated: "the establishment of order in Europe and the reconstruction of the national economic life must be achieved in such a way as to allow liberated peoples to destroy the last vestige of Nazism and Fascism and to create democratic institutions according to their own choice."

A great deal remains to be done in order to achieve correct fulfillment of the declaration. However, there is no doubt that in spite of all the negative consequences of the war with fascism, which ended in victory, it has in many respects helped to clear the political air of Europe, and has opened new ways to resurrection and development of anti-fascist forces as never before in the past.

Such a situation beyond doubt corresponds to the interest of peace-loving states and it is to be hoped that among the peoples of Europe the consciousness of the necessity to wipe out the last traces of nazism and fascism will be strengthened. The Soviet Union was always true to a policy of consolidating normal relations between all peace-loving nations.

During the war years, the Soviet Union established friendly relations with Great Britain and the United States, with France and China, with Poland, Czechoslovakia and Yugoslavia, and with almost all these countries it now has long-term agreements of alliance and mutual assistance against any possible new aggression on the part of those states which were the main aggressors in the World War. On our part, everything is being done to normalize and establish good relations also with other countries which have done away with the policy of enmity and mistrust of the Soviet Union. To this end we are also working to extend trade and economic relations of our country to an ever-widening circle of foreign countries. Cultural ties are also being strengthened.

The strength of the Anglo-Soviet-American anti-Hitler coalition which came into being during the war is now undergoing a test. Will this coalition be just as strong and capable of arriving at common decisions under the new conditions when new problems of the postwar period are forever coming to light?

A new international organization has been created in this year, that of the United Nations. It was the creation of the Anglo-Soviet-American coalition which has thus taken upon itself the main responsibility for the result of its further work. It is clear to us that the United Nations Organization must not be similar to the League of Nations, which proved itself totally incapable of counteracting aggression and organizing the forces of resistance to aggression.

Nor must the new organization become the tool of any one of the great powers, since the claim to be the leading party by any one of the powers in world affairs is as unfounded as a claim to world domination. Only the common efforts of all powers who bore on their shoulders the brunt of war and have ensured the victory of the democratic countries over fascism, only such co-operation can assist in the success of the work of a new international organization for the creation of a lasting peace.

For these, good wishes are not sufficient. The influence of such co-operation in the interest of the freedom-loving nations must still be demonstrated. The Soviet Union has been, and will be, a reliable factor in the defense of peace and the security of the nations and is willing to prove it both in words and deeds.

* 4 *

The Work of the People

ECONOMIC PLANNING IN THE SOVIET UNION *

Since 1928, the initial year of the first of the three Five-Year Plans, the Soviet Union has been converted from an agricultural country into one of the world's foremost industrial powers. In those fifteen years hundreds of billions of rubles were invested in the national economy. Thousands of modern mills and factories were built, mines were sunk, railways laid, rivers harnessed, power stations erected, and sea and river ports opened. Instead of being concentrated in a few limited areas, chiefly in the north, center and south of European Russia, as it was in tsarist times, industry is now distributed all over the Soviet Union, including Siberia and the Soviet Republics of Central Asia, once so backward.

This vast expansion proceeded not haphazardly, but strictly according to plan. The program of capital development is an integral part of national-economic planning in the Soviet Union. Such a program is practicable because not only all the land, but all the industries of the USSR, except for cooperatively-run establishments, are owned by the State. The country is therefore able to develop in accordance with its needs, making full use of resources.

For practical purposes, the various branches of industry are administered by Government departments, or People's Commissariats; for example, the People's Commissariats of the Iron and Steel Industry, of the Chemical Industry, the Textile Industry, the Railways, of Heavy, Medium and General Machine-Building, of Electric Power Stations, and so on. Each People's Commissariat, besides operating its particular branch, provides for enlarging its existing plants and erecting new ones. But in planning capital developments, the People's Commissariats are not independent or autonomous. If they were, the national economy might be thrown out of balance, with certain branches of industry expanded at the expense of others and to the detriment of the whole.

Plans for industrial development, like the national-economic plan as a whole, are coordinated by the Government through the State Planning Commission, known as Gosplan. In drafting their plans for the coming year the People's Commissariats are guided by the long-term plan for the

* A. Fineberg, "How We Organize Our Economic Planning," Embassy of the U.S.S.R. *Information Bulletin*, October 27, 1945, pp. 4–5. Boris Braginsky, "The Latest Five-Year Plan," Embassy of the U.S.S.R. *Information Bulletin*, October 3, 1945, pp. 1–2.

development of the national economy, drawn up by Gosplan and sanctioned by the Government and legislature. The long-term or "perspective" plan usually covers a period of five years, though before the war a fifteen-year plan was being worked out. The perspective plan . . . gives a general outline for the development of whole sections of industry over a given period of years, without going into great detail or earmarking funds and materials.

The operational plans are the yearly and quarterly plans. They originate in the People's Commissariats. Each industrial enterprise, besides its production plan, draws up an annual plan of capital expansion (erection of new shops, acquisition of new plant and machinery, building of houses for employees and so on), and submits it to the appropriate board of its People's Commissariat. The boards, which administer the various sub-branches of a particular industry, examine these plans, amending, adding to or rejecting them as they deem fit, and collate them into a general plan, which also provides for the building of entirely new plants.

The plans drawn up by the boards of each People's Commissariat are then integrated into a general plan for the whole Commissariat, and submitted to Gosplan. The vast, complex task of compiling the grand plan of capital development on a countrywide scale for the coming year is done by Gosplan. Gosplan is guided first by the perspective plan and the special instructions of the Government, next by its knowledge of the progress of each industry and its needs, as well as of the country's available and prospective financial resources, supplies of materials, machinery and manpower. Naturally, in compiling the current annual plan, the perspective plan is modified to suit the actual state of affairs and to meet any new needs which may have arisen.

An essential feature of Soviet planning is the determination of the location of new factories, railways, power stations and other industrial enterprises, for on the proper placing of these enterprises depends the rational and efficient development of the national resources.

The national plan of capital development, as finally coordinated by Gosplan, is submitted to the Government for endorsement, after which Gosplan sends the approved plan of development to each People's Commissariat. The Commissariats in turn present the plans to their boards, and the boards direct them to the individual enterprises or capital development departments. The plan indicates the volume and cost of capital construction (including the acquisition and installation of machinery) to be undertaken by each branch of industry and by each large construction job in the ensuing year; it states where the new factories, railways, mines, etc., are to be constructed, what the work is to cost, and what plants or sections of plants are to be completed and put into operation in the given period. For greater convenience, each annual plan of capital development is divided into quarterly ones, each of which, after the first, is subject to modification in accordance with the progress made in the early part of the year.

Every industrial and transport People's Commissariat has its capital development department, whose business it is to see that the plan of development endorsed by the Government is carried out. It has under its control building-construction organizations and machine-installing organizations, with appropriate staffs of engineers and skilled workers. A People's Commissariat may either undertake its building jobs itself through its own building organizations, or else contract the work out to the "trusts" of the People's Commissariat of the Building Industry, which specializes in all branches of industrial construction.

But the functions of the People's Commissariat of the Building Industry are wider. It exercises technical control of all industrial building in the Soviet Union by establishing and endorsing construction standards. It works out standard designs for industrial structures. Its trusts hire out building machinery and transport facilities and also manufacture materials and parts. The chief producer of building materials and maker of standard prefabricated components, however, is the People's Commissariat of Building Materials.

Since the industries of the Soviet Union are State-owned, their profits are State revenue. They are credited to the Treasury through the Industrial Bank (Prombank), and constitute a fund for the further development of the economy. Amortization of existing industrial structures and plant is a first cost on production, and is recovered by an increase in the selling price of the products. This too is paid into the Treasury through Prombank, and is earmarked for industrial renewal and expansion. These funds are supplemented, if necessary, from other sources of Government revenue. The appropriations for capital development are made in the annual State budget, itemized for each of the People's Commissariats, in accordance with the plan of capital construction endorsed by the Government. The funds are credited, quarter by quarter and month by month, to the accounts of the People's Commissariats and Prombank.

Prombank handles all the financial and banking transactions connected with industrial building in the USSR. Founded in 1922, and known originally as the Trade and Industrial Bank, it is today a vast organization with offices, branches and sub-branches all over the Soviet Union—in fact, wherever industrial construction is being carried on—and that is in practically every corner of a country which embraces one-sixth of the territory of the globe. Like all the banks of the Soviet Union, Prombank is endowed with wide powers of supervision and control. It is, so to speak, trustee and guardian of the national economic plan, as far as capital development is concerned. It was Lenin who first insisted on this function of the banks in a planned society.

As I have said, all that part of the proceeds of industry and transport which is earmarked for capital development is paid into the exchequer through Prombank. Through it, too, pass Government appropriations for capital development. The capital development departments of all the industrial and transport People's Commissariats keep their accounts with this bank, as do all building contracting, machinery installing and geological survey organizations. Thus every payment and settlement connected with capital investment is transacted through this one bank, which is at one and the same time a vast clearing-machine and a faithful reflector of the state of industrial development in all its aspects throughout the USSR.

All construction organizations have their own working capital in the form of machinery, stocks of material and working funds adequate for the performance of a given volume of work. The Government appropriations are paid by Prombank at stated periods for work actually performed in accordance with the plan. Hence, if a construction organization tends to waste funds in building up excessive stocks of machinery and materials, it very soon finds itself in financial straits, and Prombank will bring pressure to bear to correct this.

The diversion of funds to purposes not envisaged in the current plan of capital development will also automatically put an enterprise into financial difficulties and cause the bank to intervene. The bank by this means enforces what we know in the USSR as "plan discipline" and "financial discipline." Similar automatic signals direct attention to other irregularities. For example, the plan lays down the estimated cost of each item of construction work, which can be adhered to only if materials are acquired at Government-fixed prices, if labor power is not used wastefully and if overheads are kept within reason. Application to the bank for funds in excess of the physical volume of work actually performed will indicate that these provisions have not been complied with, and the bank will exercise its disciplinary powers. This procedure is known in our country as "estimate discipline."

Prombank's powers of control are correspondingly wide. Without interfering in the actual management of the construction job, it may investigate the building site, estimate the volume and cost of work actually performed, have inventories made of stocks of material and machinery, and examine all books, invoices and other documents. It reports any irregularities to the People's Commissariat concerned, or to the Government, and if necessary exercises financial pressure to have them corrected. It will be seen that the role of the Prombank as an instrument of planned economy is a very important one. Prombank is the sentinel of the public interest. Upon it largely depends the effectual, economical and orderly utilization of the huge national investment in capital expansion. Its powers were reaffirmed and reinforced in 1938 by a decree of the council of People's Commissars.

Now that the war is over and the Soviet Union is engaged in peacetime activities, the Government has instructed all planning organizations to prepare Five-Year Plans for the restoration and further development of the economy during the period 1946 to 1950.

The first and most important work is the complete rehabilitation of the economy of regions that suffered from enemy action. After the First World War the chief industrial countries of Europe required ten or eleven years to bring their industrial output up to prewar standards. The destruction and losses of the USSR in the second war greatly exceed those of the First World War. Total damage to industry and collective farms and to property of individuals amounts to the sum of 679,000 million rubles, in 1941 prices.

The rehabilitation of industry, agriculture and transport will not be merely a reproduction of what existed before the war. Rebuilt factories will be better equipped and have larger quantities of machinery; they will make use of the technical experience gained during the war, and new and more highly perfected technological processes will be introduced. All this means that factories will greatly exceed their prewar output.

Reconversion of the national economy is another essential project. During the war the Soviet Union converted thousands of enterprises to the manufacture of war materials. These factories are now to return to the production of civilian goods, and in addition, many war factories will be converted for making equipment for industry and transport.

According to the new Plan all the regions of the USSR are to undergo further expansion. The Urals, the Volga Basin, the Far East, Siberia and the Central Asian Republics greatly increased their industrial production during the war. Many new factories were built and their output increased each year. These regions will serve as a base during the first years of the new Five-Year Plans for the speedy restoration of the ruined economy of the southern and western sections of the country. Machine tools and locomotives made in Moscow, Gorky, Saratov, the Urals and Siberia will go to the Ukraine, Byelorussia and the Baltic Republics.

In general, restoration of the economy of the Republics affected by the German invasion occupies an important place in the Plan. The young Soviet Republics of Lithuania, Latvia, Estonia and Moldavia not only have to heal the wounds caused by war, but they have to raise their whole economy to a higher technical level. With this aim in view measures will be taken to encourage local industries and industrial cooperatives.

The Ukrainian Republic, speedily reestablished, will be a huge coal and iron center as well as the breadbasket of the USSR. The Dnieper power station will begin to provide current in 1946; the iron and steel foundries of the South are already sending out metal. These mills will soon be completely rebuilt on modern lines—in fact, the whole economy of the Ukraine will be based on the latest technical ideas.

Soviet planning has always included cultural as well as economic development. The new program calls for an extensive increase in domestic building, especially in the eastern regions, the rebuilding of dwelling houses and municipal undertakings in the liberated regions, the rebuilding of hospitals, libraries, theaters, schools, sanatoriums and other such installations. The output of consumers' goods will be developed at top speed in plants formerly used for war production.

CITY PLANNING IN THE SOVIET UNION *

Many soviet cities will present very different appearances in postwar years as compared with cities of today, some of which still have the cobble-stone streets of Czarist times. The popular concept that all cities "just grow" or gradually evolve from one circumference containing a heterogeneous group of houses, office buildings, industries, and businesses to a larger circumference will not hold true for many future cities in the U.S.S.R.

The time, energy, skill, and expense which the Russians intend shall go into the planning and rebuilding of important cities will amaze even a veteran in the field of municipal planning. More than 1,000 architects and engineers are reported to be working on government-approved building projects for some 140 municipalities. About 70 major war-shattered cities are in need of reconstruction, and in all cases they will be built where they were before—no city site will be completely abandoned.

Supervision over all matters concerning architecture in the U.S.S.R. has been delegated to the Committee on Architectural Affairs, which was created September 30, 1943, to raise standards of architecture in the country and to solve the tremendous problems arising from wartime destruction. Among its extensive powers is the approval of all city and town plans, as well as those for individual buildings. Organizations engaging in architectural work also are under its jurisdiction.

The Committee exercises control over the quality of construction, and works out model plans and standards for the mass production of buildings and houses. Research and the introduction of new types of building accessories and equipment are also within its domain. The Committee submits to the Council of People's Commissars plans for the largest cities, projects involving the production of building materials and equipment, and plans for conducting experimental construction. General directives on planning the reconstruction of cities also are issued by the Committee.

Although the Committee on Architectural Affairs does the planning, the Commissariat for Construction will handle the actual reconstruction of the various Soviet cities. The Commissariat was formed in 1939, its chief task being to handle industrial construction. It is equipped to meet nearly all of the problems regarding construction and reconstruction, and in general almost any building job, no matter how complex, may be assigned to it. The Commissariat has its own facilities for producing such items as brick,

* Frances M. Coston, "Soviet Union Planning Unusual Reconstruction," *Foreign Commerce Weekly*, May 19, 1945, pp. 10–11, 44, 47.

cement, and lumber, and it supplies most of the steel bridges for all organizations of the Soviet Union.

Many construction trusts operate under the Commissariat for Construction, some of which specialize in certain types of building. In Moscow, for example, most of the housing projects are built by a special construction trust operating under the city government of Moscow (Mossoviet). In many places the building industry operates on a 24-hour schedule, with two shifts of 11 hours each, and 1 hour between shifts.

The responsibility for the centralized administration of urban economy in the Russian Socialist Federated Soviet Republic is delegated to the Commissariat of Communal Economy. In addition to its usual functions—the development and maintenance of electric power, urban transportation, garbage-disposal facilities, water supply, and other public utilities—it has assisted in rebuilding houses and providing homes for people in the war-torn areas. During August, September, and October, 1943, the Commissariat repaired dwellings to the extent that a total of 3,500,000 square meters of housing space in the devastated areas was again put into condition for occupancy.

Each of the 70 important cities to be reconstructed will have a complete "brigade" in charge of its reconstruction. A chief architect, appointed by the Committee on Architectural Affairs, will head the group which will be composed of economists, transportation experts, sanitation experts, and other representatives of all branches of economy and civic affairs.

Every effort will be made to preserve the historical atmosphere and background of the cities; the planning program must harmonize with the former city plan and architectural style. What is left of the destroyed sections of cities will be utilized wherever possible—but not at the expense of beauty or convenience. The rebuilding also must be coordinated with the country's general economic scheme, and every chief architect must know what industries will be located in his city immediately following the war and for several years thereafter, as well as the number of workers to be employed.

A bird's-eye view of a reconstructed Russian city will note a descending roof line from the center to the outskirts. The taller buildings, which will be entirely out of the skyscraper class will characterize the central zone of the city. Usually these will be four- and five-story structures which will level off gradually to one- and two-story buildings in the medial zone, finally reaching the peripheral zone which will consist only of one-story individual homes built by the people who live in them. Some space will be devoted to parks and green areas, and most of the one- and two-story dwelling units will have gardens. Where necessary, new thoroughfares will be built and entirely new transportation facilities provided.

One of the chief aims of the reconstruction program is to reduce overcrowding. In most of the municipalities living space will be allotted at the rate of 9 square meters of space per person. When conditions permit, this will be increased to 12. However, high officials, Army officers, scientific workers, artists, engineers, and outstanding workers in Moscow and other crowded centers will receive a higher-than-average allotment. Living space in some of the apartment houses will vary according to the size of the family and the status of its head.

All construction and reconstruction in Moscow, Leningrad, and some of the other cities will follow the general lines started in 1935 when the Ten-Year Plan was inaugurated. This plan required every city to control its physical development by a master plan approved by the Executive Committee of the Provincial Soviet (Council). Such plans have limited the population of Moscow to 5,000,000 and that of Leningrad to 3,500,000, whereas it is expected that Stalingrad's population, now estimated at 300,000, will increase to 450,000 during the next few years.

Postwar building plans being formulated throughout Russia call for many prefabricated and individually built houses. In addition, many two-story multifamily dwellings will be built by the government. Among the principal building materials used in these postwar dwellings will be wood, brick, plywood, cinder block, and gypsum. Cinder block will be used particularly in the Donets Basin, and gypsum in the Ukraine.

Individual construction will depend upon individual initiative, the supply of local raw materials, and handicraft methods, and will play an important role in Russia's reconstruction program. (In Stalingrad, for example, 20,000 plots of land had been assigned prior to December, 1944 to individual home builders.) Workers who wish to build their own homes will be allocated a plot of land by the factory or enterprise for which they work. Money will be loaned to them, technical advice made available, and assistance will be given in procuring materials. They will be offered standard designs suitable for their needs. The worker, himself, may do the actual construction with the assistance of specialists such as bricklayers or stone fitters who will be furnished by the enterprise, or he may hire some or all of the work done.

In contrast to individually constructed homes are the prefabricated houses scheduled to comprise a large portion of Russia's future dwellings. These houses will be manufactured by State-owned factories located near the sources of raw materials, and will be transported as whole units or in sections on flatcars to their destination. Erected and owned by the State, they will be relatively permanent structures, usually of one story, and will accommodate from one to three families.

Two-story apartments also will be erected by the State on a large scale. While these will not be entirely prefabricated, mass-production methods will be employed and certain parts of the dwellings will be factory-made.

Although the designs of the individual homes, prefabricated homes, and two-story multifamily dwellings will be standardized, they will not present a uniformity of appearance. Different color schemes, various systems of decoration, certain variations in design, and numerous other devices will be employed to break the monotony.

Today the Soviet Union is continuing its plans for the reconstruction of many of its important cities, and is capitalizing on the opportunity which resulted from wartime destruction, to make finer, more beautiful, and more completely utilitarian cities than those of prewar years.

THE DECENTRALIZATION OF INDUSTRY *

In prerevolutionary Russia, urban development remained very limited outside a few large centers. To the east and southeast vast areas, despite their rich untapped mineral resources and agricultural promise, remained thinly populated, and urban development at a low level. With limited transport facilities, interregional trade was bound to be restricted, and only such areas as happened to be near both urban concentrations and sources of fuel and materials were capable of becoming industrial centers. Two-thirds of the large-scale industry that in 1914 existed within the 1939 frontiers of the U.S.S.R. was concentrated in a few large cities of the west—the St. Petersburg and Moscow districts, and the Donetz basin in the Ukraine. By contrast, in Siberia, Central Asia and Kazakhstan, composing three-quarters of the whole territory of the country, there were only 6 per cent of such industrial plants. Eighty-seven per cent of all coal extraction was centered in the Donetz district, although it had only a half of the total coal reserves; 97 per cent oil production came from the Caucasus (largely because this was accessible for export markets via the Black Sea); and the Donetz and Dnieper region smelted three-quarters of the pig-iron. The textile industry was almost entirely located in the central and northwest district (83 per cent of linen, 85 per cent of wool, and 99 per cent of cotton) to which the raw material generally had to come by a 2,000 mile railway haul.

Other regions that were as rich in natural resources, and often richer, were unexploited or their mineral wealth even unexplored. The Kusnetsk Basin in Western Siberia, which rivals the Don Basin in its coal resources, produced less than 3 per cent of the total output of the country—under 1,000,000 tons per annum; while the Altai foothills, which are now thought to contain a third of the coal reserves of the U.S.S.R., were then unknown. The Urals, which have since been proved to be such an important source of rich and low cost ores, smelted only one-fifth of the pig-iron, and the central provinces near Moscow, which was the chief seat of such metal-using industry as existed, produced only 5 per cent of the pig-iron. Non-ferrous metallurgy was almost non-existent; and reliance here was placed on import. Heavy industry, accordingly, presented a picture of mineral re-

* Maurice Dobb, *Soviet Economy and the War* (New York: International Publishers, 1943), pp. 52–63.

sources unexploited, some of the lowest cost locations for extraction and smelting unused, and finishing processes separated from pig-iron and steel smelting.

Light industry clustered round Moscow and Petersburg and a few larger urban centers in the west, or else was undeveloped in face of foreign imports, which though coming from a distance had a price advantage over Russian products, owing to the backward state of subsidiary and primary industries in Russia.

In the First and Second Five-Year Plans considerable changes were made in the direction of shifting the location of industry towards those centers which had the greatest natural advantages with respect to access to materials and to power. But the changes made up to 1937 were regarded as still insufficient; and one of the central features of the Third Five-Year Plan lay in its intention to carry this process much further. For example, the ten-year period 1928–37 saw a remarkable increase of coal production by four times. But though the Donetz Basin in 1937 was producing three times the 1913 tonnage figure, it was producing no more than 60 per cent, instead of 87 per cent, of the coal output of the whole country. The districts which have grown with special rapidity as coal-producers are Siberia, the Urals, the Far East, the Caucasus and Kazakhstan. These districts were in 1937 producing about a third of the total coal output, while Siberia and the Urals alone had an output equal to the output of the Don Basin in 1913.

The Third Five-Year Plan intended that the five districts just mentioned should be responsible in 1942 for over 40 per cent of the total coal output. Of these newer districts the two most important are the Kusnetsk basin in Siberia and Karaganda in Kazakhstan. The former, which now stands second to the Don Basin, is today the fulcrum of a whole chain of neighboring industries—ferrous and non-ferrous metallurgy, engineering, chemical works, and power stations—in a group of towns of half a million inhabitants. Karaganda, which was formerly hidden in the desert steppe, is designed to become the third coal center of the U.S.S.R., although its output is still much smaller than Kusnetsk. It possesses good coking coal; and it is conveniently situated near the iron ores of the southern Urals and the copper ores of Lake Balkash. The Moscow area is another center which has expanded its relative weight, for rather different reasons. Its coal deposits consist of brown coal unsuitable for most industrial uses; and local industries, of which there has always been a high concentration, had to import high-calorific fuel from a distance—Donetz coal and Baku oil or coal from abroad via the Baltic. Inventions in coal-dust-burning (as well as the development and utilization of neighboring peat supplies) now reduce the reliance on Donetz coal, and have enabled local supplies to be used for industry and for the coal (and peat) burning electricity stations which serve the central regional grid. Meantime, the famous Don Basin remains supreme, even if its lead no longer goes unchallenged; and the intention before the war was to specialize this district to coking coal and to anthracite production which was being developed at the eastern end of the basin.

Other fuel and power sources present a similar picture. Of the output of electrical power one-half is in areas outside the Moscow, Leningrad and Donetz electricity districts. There has also been an important regional specialization of the basis of electricity generation itself.

In addition, there are the giant hydroelectric schemes of the Dnieper, the central Volga, the Caucasus, the Angara, and the Yenisei. In oil production Baku and Grozny in the Caucasus still lead, and continue to account for 80 per cent of total oil output. But a beginning has been made with the development of a "second Baku" in the southern Urals, with pipe-line connections to Ural industrial towns as well as to neighboring agricultural (and oil-consuming) centers of the Middle Volga region.

The planned output for this field in 1942 was to be about one-quarter of the combined Baku and Grozny output in 1937. Moreover, while there was a refinery plant for only 62 per cent of the crude oil output in 1913, this capacity has risen to 92 per cent of output today. The figures of oil consumption by regions throw an interesting light on the shifting emphasis of economic development towards the east: whereas the eastern area consumed only about one-sixth of the oil produced fifteen years ago, it now consumes between a quarter and a third.

In ferrous metallurgy a similar tendency is evident, if in a rather less pronounced form as yet: 95 per cent of prewar Russia's pig-iron came from the Dnieper-Donetz district and the Urals. By 1937 this percentage had fallen to about 81 per cent, despite an enormous increase of output during the period of the First and Second Five-Year Plans. Of the country's steel these two districts now produce rather less than three-quarters. The important new center to be developed over the decade, so rapidly that it now yields one-tenth of the Soviet pig-iron and steel, is the Kusnetsk Basin with its first-class coking coal. This center lies, however, more than one thousand miles to the east of the Ural ore deposits. The problem of joining ore and coal together has been tackled by the formation of the Ural-Kusbas combine, which has blast furnaces and steel works located both at the Kusnetsk coal and on the rich magnetic ores of Magnitogorsk. Coal travels west to the Ural blast furnaces, and on the return journey the low-cost ores of Magnitogorsk travel east to feed the Siberian works. (Attempts are apparently now being made to reduce the dependence of Ural plants on Kusnetsk coal by developing local Ural deposits.) Farther east still on the Amur River, which marches with Manchukuo, both coking coal and ore have been discovered, and the Second Five-Year Plan has seen the construction of the first smelting works here to feed the shipbuilding needs of the Pacific coast. Under the Third Five-Year Plan, of the new blast furnaces to be put under construction three-quarters were to be in the eastern regions.

In pre-1914 Russia, the third iron-producing area was the so-called Central Region, comprising the Moscow and Voronezh districts. This produced no more than 5 per cent of the country's pig-iron, although together with the Petersburg district it was the largest center of engineering activities. It was, therefore, an importing area for semi-finished iron and steel, as it was for fuel. To repair this deficiency, the blast furnace and steel furnace capacity of this region has been very greatly increased, on the basis of local ores (supplemented from the newly prospected Kursk deposits to the south), pyrites and scrap; so that its relative weight in total iron and steel output has actually increased slightly (to 8 per cent of total pig-iron and 17–18 per cent of total ingot and rolled-steel production).

The picture that we have, therefore, is a planning of development in the direction of a greater balance in each of the main areas between primary production, finishing plant, and metal-using industries; in the central European area by expanding primary production, and in other areas by expanding the capacity of finishing processes more rapidly than that of primary production. For example, in Siberia the production of mining equipment was being developed at Novosibirsk and Irkutsk; wagon-building at Stalinsk; in the Urals tractors at Cheliabinsk, machine-equipment, wagon-building and heavy electrical equipment at Sverdlovsk, Diesel-engine works at Omsk; while agricultural machinery is made at Tashkent and flour-milling equipment at Semipalatinsk in the steppes of Kazakhstan. The center and northwest remains an importing area for pig-iron and semi-finished steel, and the Urals and the Ukraine exporting areas; but the disparity has been reduced. The process was apparently being supplemented by a greater standardization of products and a movement towards greater specialization in the output of the various districts. According to the organ of the State Planning Commission, this specialization had not yet been carried far enough and the Third Five-Year Plan designed to improve upon it. It was stated that there was still too little "division of labor between the southern and the eastern metallurgical industry; still great confusion in the location of metal supplies. For example, the Novo-Kramatorsky machine-building factory in the Donetz basin obtained its raw iron in 1938 from Magnitogorsk in the Urals. The Ural railway-wagon works at Nizhny Taghil got only 40 per cent of its metal from the eastern factories and the remainder from the southern and central areas. The electrical machine-building factories are chiefly in Moscow, Leningrad, and Kharkhov, but iron for the dynamos and transformers is supplied by the Verchne-Isetsky works 2,000 kilometers away."

The locational pull of raw materials towards the east is also strikingly evident in non-ferrous metals, and also chemicals, which are virtually new and infant industries nurtured by the Five-Year Plans. During the Second Five-Year Plan nearly three-quarters of the capital invested in the former was located in the raw material regions of Kazakhstan, Central Asia, and the Urals. Up to the middle thirties the Urals region led in copper mining and smelting. But Kazakhstan has recently been the more rapidly developed of the two, to form the basis of one of the largest combined copper plants in the world—the Kounrad combine. Tin-mining was being developed in Eastern Siberia and Central Asia, zinc-working in the Urals and Kazakhstan, and the working of chromium ores and nickel in Kazakhstan. Similarly the Urals (with its powerful synthetic-ammonia plant at Bereznikov and potassium works at Solikamsk), Kazakhstan (with its combine at Aktiubinsk to work local phosphorite deposits), Turkmenistan (with sulphur works in the desert) and Tadjhikistan (with fertilizer works near Tashkent) were the most rapidly developing regions of the chemical industry, even though the Ukraine and the central region continue to supply the bulk of the output.

The net effect of these changes in heavy industry should be transport-economizing, since it brings production nearer to its raw materials, and by securing greater specialization and a better balance between the various stages of production in each region saves unnecessary cross hauls of semi-finished products (as, for example, still exists to an unnecessarily large extent in the British iron and steel industry despite a decade and a half of "rationalization"). Since the products of heavy industry are usually "weight-losing" in course of production, transport is saved by these changes even if the finished products have to be transported to their markets over a wide area.

This transport economy is a particularly important consideration in a country with such a vast land area and such a relatively underdeveloped railway network. During the First Five-Year Plan transport proved to be a crucial "bottleneck," and its backward development seemed to be a limiting factor on the growth of industry. To overhaul the transport system in so vast a country within a short space of time would have involved an enormous rate of investment quite beyond the powers of any but a country that was already rich; and it would have placed enormous demands on heavy industry to provide the rails and equipment needed for construction. It is not surprising, therefore, that at first railway development lagged behind transport needs. In 1937 the railway goods traffic was five times heavier than it had been in 1913.

Meanwhile the mileage of railway track in operation had only increased by less than half. The net result was that the volume of goods traffic per mile of railway during the closing years of the Second Plan was as much as three times greater than in 1913, and on the more frequented lines it was even heavier. Much of this, of course, represented a taking up of the "slack" of previously underused capacity. But there is little doubt that in addition it not only increased the burden of replacement and repair but caused serious congestion and transport delay as well.

In the closing years of the Second Five-Year Plan greatly increased allocations were made for repair and replacement, and more intensive use of the permanent way was aided by the introduction of modern signaling devices, automatic interlocking, and the electrification of block stations. By an increase in the tractive power of locomotives (which in number had only grown by 42 per cent) and in the number and loading capacity of wagons, the carrying capacity of railway equipment was raised in 1937 to two and one-half times that of 1913. By the end of the Second Plan period there were signs that "the rate of increase in transport material began to surpass the demands of freight and passenger traffic"; and under the Third Plan the capital to be invested in railway development was nearly double that of the previous quinquennium. But even when these developments have been completed, the vital importance of so planning industrial location as to economize to the maximum in the demands laid by industry on transport will remain.

Light industry presents us with a somewhat different picture than heavy industry; and since its pace of growth in the past decade has been much slower than that of heavy industry the changes to be seen are less striking. Unlike heavy industry, light industry is more often attracted to its markets than to its raw materials; since its products are less often "weight losing" in production, they often represent a process of assembly of materials from diverse sources, and often they are perishable or need to be adapted closely to local requirements. Soviet planning intends that a large number of consumers' industries should be decentralized to the extent of making each of the main regions virtually self-sufficient in these products. This is the intention, for example, with respect to such industries as tobacco, sugar, tinned foodstuffs, flour-milling, beer, confectionery, furniture, clothing, bricks, and in agriculture vegetables and the chief dairy and meat products.

In his speech to the Eighteenth Congress of the Communist Party, M. Molotov added to this list glass, cement, and chemical manures as things in which each economic region must strive after the maximum self-sufficiency during the period of the Third Five-Year Plan. By such decentralization two separate ends are served. Transport costs are, again, saved by causing the needs of each region to be supplied from within this region by industries which tap either local sources of raw materials or else a number of scattered sources. Secondly, the social disadvantages of a too narrow specialization of each region (of which we have in this country [England] heard much in recent years in connection with the distressed areas) are avoided.

Among the light industries textile production apparently occupies a midway position. The traditional textile districts of Leningrad, Moscow, and Ivanovo-Vosnessensk remain the chief centers; but a certain amount of decentralization has taken place, at least so far as to redress the anomaly of cotton-growing areas sending away cotton and receiving back cloth from an industry located two thousand miles distant. Some of the most important of the new textile mills constructed in the 'thirties have been located amid the cottonfields of Central Asia (at Tashkent, Askhabad, Ferghana, Stalinabad, and Khojent), and also in Armenia; and it was intended that the mills put under construction in the new regions under the Second Five-Year Plan should have a capacity equal to one-fifth of the textile output of the country, and that the mills of Central Asia should supply the local demand of that area by the end of the decade. Western Siberia was also to have its cotton combine, which was to draw its raw cotton via the Turksib railway on the return journey of trains that traveled to Turkestan with Siberian timber and grain. Similarly, in the paper industry it was intended that there should be some decentralization, but mainly in the direction of the timber regions of Karelia, the Urals, and Siberia.

The social significance of these giant economic changes is graphically epitomized in the results of the Soviet census of 1939. This brings into relief two sharply marked tendencies: a striking increase in the urban population and an even more rapid urbanization of the formerly backward agrarian (sometimes nomad) Asiatic regions. Since the previous census of 1926 the total population of the U.S.S.R. increased by 15.5 per cent; but while the rural population *decreased* by 5 per cent, the urban population doubled and now constitutes almost a third of the total. But the urban population of Kazakhstan and Turkmenistan was more than trebled.

THE EXPANSION OF HEAVY INDUSTRY *

Soviet heavy industry built up before the war was able during hostilities to increase its output fifty fold, as compared with 1913. Every modern type of machine, machine tool and industrial equipment was produced.

On the eve of the First World War the machine-building and metal-working industries of Russia accounted for only 10.5 per cent of the country's total industrial output. Having primitive machine-building plants and lacking certain important branches of the industry—such as the making of machine tools—tsarist Russia was not in a position to produce complex machines and the more important types of armaments. Three-quarters of all machine tools, as well as important categories of industrial and agricultural raw material and a large proportion of coal, were imported from abroad, notwithstanding the country's own vast natural resources. This technical and industrial backwardness of tsarist Russia materially affected the supply of armament and equipment to the Russian army in the First World War.

A radical change in the country's economy took place in the period of Soviet rule. In 1938, the beginning of the Third Five-Year Plan, more coal was mined and iron smelted in the eastern regions of the Soviet Union than in the whole territory of tsarist Russia in 1913. At the outbreak of

* S. Turetsky, "Heavy Industry in the War Years," Embassy of the U.S.S.R. *Information Bulletin,* September 8, 1945, pp. 1–3.

the Second World War the Soviet Union possessed adequate resources of all major strategical material to wage war on a modern scale. In the decade preceding, the output of aluminum, molybdenum, wolfram, sulphur, nickel, copper and other strategical raw materials had increased enormously.

In 1914, on the eve of the First World War, aluminum, nickel, antimony, molybdenum, wolfram and bismuth were not produced at all in tsarist Russia. Nor were sulphur or barium salts. At that time large deposits of only 14 out of the 86 known elements were mined in Russia; all the rest were obtained from abroad as manufactured products.

Thanks to the Five-Year Plans, the Soviet Union not only ceased to be a backward industrial country but its production facilities were distributed evenly all over the country. At the outset of the First World War nearly one-half of Russia's industrial output came from the central and north-western provinces, chiefly from Moscow and St. Petersburg. The vast industrial potentialities of the Urals, the Volga region and Siberia were undeveloped.

The creation in the years of peace of new industrial centers in the eastern areas, the industrialization of the Union Republics and the complete development of industry created the possibilities for the organization of an efficient munitions industry in the first period of the recent war. Actually, however, the building of a war industry was handicapped by severe difficulties encountered by no other country. Owing to the German occupation of important industrial regions in the west and south of the European part of the USSR, the metallurgical, fuel, power and food resources of the country were drastically diminished. Some of the largest metal-working plants were located in German-occupied regions and in the immediate vicinity of the front.

In 1941, in the course of a few months, hundreds of big plants had to be evacuated from the war areas. They were all re-erected and started up again deep in the country's hinterland early in 1942. Hundreds of thousands of workers were employed at these transplanted factories. The cost of the machinery evacuated and later reassembled exceeded the value of all the production facilities used for the armed forces of tsarist Russia in 1914–1916.

Not only was the machinery of the removed plants one of the chief sources of the mass production of munitions during the war, but it is now playing a large part in the rehabilitation of regions devastated by the German occupation. The increase in the output of heavy industry in the eastern areas in the second year of the war was several times greater than the total output of similar branches of industry all over Russia in 1915–1916, the second year of the First World War. In 1943 the output of the Chelyabinsk Region alone increased 3.5 times compared with the prewar year of 1940.

The conversion of factories from civilian goods manufacture to munitions and the transfer of large quantities of machine-building equipment to the eastern regions made possible a considerable expansion of the production capacity of the munitions industry very early in the war.

A number of complex organizational and economic problems had to be solved in order that the increased industrial facilities of the eastern region could be effectively exploited.

Materials and labor power had to be assigned in accordance with a strict plan; iron and steel, fuel and power had to be expanded in the eastern regions and facilities and labor had to be employed far more economically.

Roughly, within a year after the outbreak of war, the economic and manpower resources had been redistributed. The output of war industries had been increased several times over, while at the same time the expenditure of raw materials and fuel per unit of output had been considerably decreased. This will give some idea of the scale and efficiency of the planned allocation of resources and their improved utilization.

The production of immense quantities of armament, ammunition, machinery and other equipment for the Red Army could not have been maintained if the old norms of the expenditure of labor, metal, fuel, raw materials and power per unit of output had been adhered to.

New and perfected production methods, technical inventions in the manufacture of aircraft, tanks, armament and ammunition, and a plentiful use of substitutes resulted in an economy during the war of millions of tons of metal and billions of hours of labor.

The progress made in the technical and production efficiency in the major branches of Soviet industry during the war would have required 10 or 15 years in ordinary times.

Up-to-date methods of casting were widely introduced in the manufacture of shells, mines, tank bodies and motors. Stamping was greatly perfected in making tanks and artillery as well as in other branches of war industry. At the beginning of 1945 over 95 per cent of all the casting in the tank-building factories was done in coquilles and with machine molds, whereas before the war three-quarters of the castings of tanks were done with hand-made molds in sand. In the last months of hostilities 90 per cent of all hot forgings in the tank-building factories were handled by power hammers and all parts made of thin sheet metal were stamped on presses.

In the period of 1941–1944, the expenditure of metal in the production of the major types of armament had decreased 30 to 35 per cent, while the combat and tactical properties of weapons were considerably improved.

If the expenditure of metal per unit of output had remained at the pre-war level, several million tons of additional coal and ore would have had to be mined annually and this would have involved extra labor, large capital investments and many more hundreds of thousands of carloads in railroad freight.

Preliminary estimates show that in the three years 1942–1944 the economy obtained from the reduced expenditure of metal in the metal working industry compared with 1942, made it possible to produce additional war goods greatly exceeding in value the total munitions output of prewar Russia.

The utilization of labor on some of the more important types of munitions decreased during the war to one-third or one-fourth the prewar standard.

These systematic advances of the first year of war were extended to other manufacturing branches of heavy industry in 1943 and to the extracting branches in 1944.

By 1944 the new efficiency had become general. From every ton of fuel consumed at the power stations in that year, 15 per cent more electricity was produced than in 1940. For every ton of coke consumed in the blast furnaces of the big steel plants in 1944, 10 per cent more pigiron was smelted than before the war. The blast furnaces themselves were exploited much more effectively than in 1940. In 1944 the Kuznetsk iron and steel works averaged one ton of pigiron per day from every 0.8 cubic meters of useful space of the blast furnace, as compared with the usual 1.1 to 1.2 cubic meters, a very noteworthy achievement.

In 1943 the steel works and power stations of the Urals saved over 200,000 tons of coal. In 1943–1944 the power stations of the most important industrial areas of the country showed an economy of 800,000 tons of coal. In the Urals the reduction in 1944 made it possible to generate an additional 220 million kilowatt hours of electricity.

The metallurgical, oil refining, coke and chemical and other important branches of heavy industry changed the character of their products to meet the needs of war. The value of output per unit of raw material employed increased. By the increased use of high-grade steels, the value of output in the iron and steel industry per ton of pigiron increased in 1944 compared with 1940 by over 30 per cent. In the oil industry, owing to the increased portion of the more valuable light fractions obtained (aviation spirit, etc.) the value of the product per ton of crude oil increased from 15 to 20 per cent.

Some idea of the economies effected in the Soviet munitions industry may be obtained by the following figures. One of the factories in the first three years and four months of war produced medium-sized shells to an amount equal to one-half the number of such shells turned out by all tsarist Russia in the First World War, and at the same time reduced costs, compared with the prewar equivalent, by 1,100,000,000 rubles. The ordnance plant, during the war, economized 2,800,000,000 rubles.

In the period 1942 to 1944 the cost of production of the main types of munitions was reduced 45 to 60 per cent. Large cuts were also achieved in the cost of army clothing and equipment. The total economy effected in Soviet industry during the war is estimated at 50 billion rubles. As the cost of production diminished, the Government lowered the prices of war goods as much as 50 per cent and more in many categories of armament and ammunitions. The saving was equivalent to the cost of waging the war against Germany for 150 or 160 days. This ameliorated the financial burden of the war and helped to balance budgets and to preserve the stability of the currency.

In connection with the Soviet Union's war expenditures, it should be borne in mind that part of its raw materials and foodstuffs was received from its Allies.

In his message to the President of the United States, June 12, 1945, Joseph Stalin said: "The agreement by which the United States all through the war in Europe supplied the Soviet Union on a lend-lease basis with armament, strategical materials and food, played an important role and greatly contributed to the successful consummation of the war against the common enemy, Hitler Germany."

The Soviet Union's very large war expenditures were chiefly covered by the country's national income.

The ever increasing scale of offensive operations of the Red Army, bearing the main burden of the war in Europe, consumed a considerable part of the national income and an even greater proportion of the national revenue. But nonetheless the Soviet Union was able to make great economic and cultural gains. In 1944 alone the Government appropriated 95 billion rubles, or 38 per cent of total expenditures, for the purpose of economic and social and cultural development. In the past two years the Soviet Union spent tens of billions of rubles on economic rehabilitation in the former German-occupied regions.

On May 1, 1945, on the eve of the defeat of Germany, Stalin said: "Despite the fact that the Soviet Union for four years has been waging a war on an unparalleled scale demanding colossal expenditures, our socialist economic system is gaining strength and developing, while the economy of the liberated regions, plundered and ruined by the German invaders, is successfully and swiftly reviving."

Now that Hitler Germany has been vanquished, new and much greater potentialities exist in the Soviet Union for rapid progress in all branches of industry and culture. There is no fear in the Soviet Union that the production facilities will not be fully utilized, just as there is no threat of crises or unemployment.

The vast resources which the USSR had to divert to the war with Germany now have been released and can be employed for increasing the national wealth, for developing heavy industry, for raising the output of consumers' goods and improving the standard of living of the people.

SOVIET FINANCES *

The structure of the finances of the USSR naturally reflects the major distinguishing features of the Soviet economic system; its functions reflect the basic aims and objects of the Soviet State. These distinguishing features are so considerable that although the financial terminology employed is often the same, a superficial comparison of the finances of the USSR with that of other countries might easily lead to serious misunderstandings.

One might cite an example which rather strikingly illustrates the difference between the finances of the USSR and other countries. In other countries the State budget absorbs 50 or 60 per cent of the national income only in time of supreme national effort, when the country is engaged in a big war, for example. In order to attain such a record absorption of the national income, the country in question has to increase taxation considerably and to float loans which virtually exhaust the capital market.

The Soviet budget, on the other hand, even in peacetime normally absorbs a good half of the national income. Moreover, it borrows not from the capital market, which is non-existent in the USSR, but from the citizens in general, whose savings from their earnings in field, factory and workshop, although modest individually, in the aggregate total a quite considerable sum.

However, while the Soviet budget annually absorbs roughly half of the national income, the direct revenue from general taxation and loans does not exceed 10 per cent of the total. Consequently, 90 per cent of the budget revenues were derived from another source. This source is mainly the State-owned industries, State farms and machine and tractor stations, State trade and transport and other forms of socialist enterprise.

Inasmuch as the implements and means of production in the USSR may not be privately owned, it will be clear how vast is the direct economic basis of Soviet finances.

Earnings of the State-owned enterprises come under the disposal of the State finances. On the eve of the war 90 per cent of these earnings passed directly into the budget, while the remaining 10 per cent were left at the disposal of various branches of industry whose finances, in their turn, constitute an organic part of the general State finances.

As to cooperative bodies, only a small part of their earnings is extracted for State revenue, as the policy is to allow the greater bulk of these earnings to be reinvested by the cooperatives in their own enterprises, collective farms, and producing societies.

From this it will be seen that funds which in other countries go to replenish the loan market, in the USSR constitute current revenue of the

* Mikhail Bogolepov, "Soviet Finances" Embassy of the USSR *Information Bulletin,* October 20, 1944. Also articles on Soviet banking, in *Information Bulletins,* May 22, 1945 and November 13, 1945.

State. Balances to the account of State enterprises with banks, all of which are also State-owned, run into billions of rubles, but they do not and cannot include any free funds of enterprises derived from their earnings, except for their daily cash balances. Enterprises are obliged to conduct all their accounts with their clients and budget through the State bank, which for this purpose has thousands of branches all over the country. The bank also handles the revenue and expenditure budget.

Earnings of State enterprises are defined as the difference between the cost of production of their products (factory cost) and the prices which are fixed by the Government. It will therefore be clear that the financial policy of the State, of whose revenues the earnings of State enterprises comprise an overwhelming part, is organically bound up with the Government's price policy.

. . . The annual national economic plan always provides for a definite reduction in the cost of production. This is made possible by a steady rise in the productivity of labor, due in its turn to continuous improvement of production technique, training of skilled workers, and traditional socialist competition among the working bodies of the factory, mine, and collective farm. The manager of every enterprise has a special fund at his disposal for the encouragement and reward of achievements in socialist competition.

Reduction in the cost of production results annually in an immense increase in financial revenue. In time the reduced production costs lead to a reduction in sale prices, particularly of goods intended for industrial use, which in the end is tantamount to a reduction of State investments in industry. The improved efficiency of the defense industries in wartime has made it possible to considerably lower the price of armaments and thus to reduce the war expenditure.

The fact that all earnings of the national economy pass into the State budget largely predetermines the character of State expenditure. In fact, the major part of budget expenditures go to financing the national economy, and is an item varying from 50 to 65 per cent of the total expenditure from year to year. These funds are employed to increase the basic and working capital, to build new enterprises and reconstruct old ones. The remaining part of the budget expenditure goes to social and cultural needs, administration and defense.

Expenditure for social and cultural measures, schools, hospitals, social security, health resorts, child welfare institutions, etc., exceeds the budget revenue derived from the general public in the shape of taxation and loans. For example, in 1940 the expenditure for social and cultural measures totaled 40,900 million rubles, while revenue from general taxation and loans totaled only 19,500 million rubles. The difference is covered by revenue derived from State enterprises.

Another distinguishing feature of the Soviet budget should be noted.

While called the budget of the USSR, it represents the consolidated budget of the Union, as such, of the 16 constituent Republics and of the local government bodies (Soviets). Each of these budgets is independent and is indorsed by the government body concerned. If any of these budgets, however, cannot be balanced, it does not mean that the item of expenditure considered necessary under the government national economic plan is excluded from it. In such cases the necessary funds are provided out of the budget of the Union.

It is this policy that has made possible the steady economic and cultural development of the formerly backward eastern and southeastern regions of the country. When the Germans invaded the Soviet Union and industrial enterprises had to evacuate from the central and western parts of the country, this policy compensated the Soviet people a hundredfold.

The budget for 1945 [see also Appendix, pp. 225–6] is balanced in the total revenue and expenditure of 307.9 billion rubles. It is a budget designed to finance the final victory in the Great Patriotic War, the rehabilitation of the German-devastated regions, and the further development of the national economy and cultural life of the country.

The supreme effort made by the Soviet people for victory was reflected in the scale of financing the first three and a half years of war—that is, to the end of 1944—during which period a total sum of 420 billion rubles was provided for this purpose out of the budgets. In the 1945 budget, appropriations for war financing amount to 137.9 billion rubles, or 45.1 per cent of the total budget expenditures for all purposes.

The Soviet economic system has stood the severe test of war. It is sufficient to say that the budget for 1944, which was estimated for a revenue and expenditure of 249.6 billion rubles, actually yielded 268 billion rubles; while expenditures amounted to 263 billion rubles, showing a net excess of revenue over expenditure of five billion rubles. This sound state of finances was due to an increase in the total revenue of that year of 58 billion rubles as compared with 1943, and to the patriotic spirit displayed by the Soviet people in oversubscribing Government loans.

The chief source of national revenue in the Soviet Union is turnover and taxes on profits of State-owned enterprises. In the 1945 budget these two items are expected to yield more than half the total revenue. The profit tax on State enterprises is estimated to yield 27.6 billion rubles as compared with 24.4 billion rubles in 1944. Taxation and the Fourth War Loan are expected to yield 45.3 and 25 billion rubles respectively.

Another indication of the soundness of Soviet finances is the steady growth of balances in savings bank accounts.

As Zverev pointed out, the 64.6 billion rubles which the 1945 budget allocates for financing the national economy represents an increase of nearly one-third over last year. This is one of the most striking features of this year's budget. The greater bulk of this item—over 35 billion rubles—will go to finance industry; a little over nine billion rubles to agriculture; almost an equal sum to transport and communication services, and about three billion rubles to municipal services and housing.

New iron and steel, machine-building, power and other plants have sprung up in the Urals, Siberia and Central Asia during the war. Construction work will assume a still wider scope in 1945, for which period the budget provides 40.1 billion rubles for capital investment as compared with 29 billion rubles in 1944. Nearly half this sum is earmarked for rehabilitation work in the liberated regions. The Germans destroyed factories, collective farms, railways, houses, schools and hospitals in the areas which they occupied. However, the Nazis were mistaken in their belief that the Soviet people would be unable to restore their ruined economy.

The first results of their efforts are already visible. Compared with 1943, the total coal output of the country increased by 30.6 per cent, of which 18.6 per cent was accounted for by the rehabilitated mines of the Donbas, which for two years had been in the hands of the invaders. Large quantities of iron and steel have already been supplied by the rehabilitated plants in the South. Over 2,000 machine and tractor stations have resumed operation in the liberated areas, helping collective farms to raise bigger harvests.

But of course much still remains to be done. One of the major tasks in the capital development of 1945 will be to restore and reconstruct the heavy industries and, in the first instance, the coal mines and iron and steel plants of the liberated regions. Large funds are also to be appropriated for the rehabilitation of transport services, agriculture and housing.

. . . The 1945 budget allocates 66.1 billion rubles, or 22 per cent of the total expenditures, for education, health, social and cultural services. There will be an increase of 2,800,000 pupils in primary and secondary schools this year as compared with 1944. The number of students of universities and higher technical schools will increase by nearly one-third and will approximate the prewar figure.

A 50 per cent increase as compared with last year is provided for the financing of scientific institutions, which is indicative of the attention science receives in the USSR.

Large appropriations are provided for child welfare institutions. The welfare of mother and child is given great attention by the Soviet State. The number of mothers receiving grants from the Government increased by nearly 50 per cent in the second half of 1944. Grants to mothers of large families and unmarried mothers in 1945 will be 500 million rubles more than in 1944.

Care of disabled soldiers is one of the prime concerns of the Soviet Government and the public. Under the Constitution every citizen has the right to social maintenance in sickness, old age or loss of working capacity. This provision of our fundamental law finds practical expression in the 1945 budget which allocates 18 billion rubles, or two billion rubles more than in 1944, for social maintenance, including pensions and grants to soldiers and their families.

A noteworthy feature of the 1945 budget is that for the first time since the outbreak of war the budgets of all Union Republics are included. . . .

The increase of budget expenditures is largest in the case of the Republics liberated from the Nazis, because of the vast scale of rehabilitation work which must be undertaken.

The basis of the present banking and currency mechanism of the Soviet Union was laid at the end of 1921, when the State Bank of the USSR was founded and authorized to issue banknotes. By a separate law passed at the same time, the new bank of issue was endowed with the monopoly right to acquire both home-produced and imported gold, as well as other currency metals and foreign currency.

The foundation of the State Bank was the first step toward the reform of the currency, which was completed in 1924, when, in addition to bank-notes of comparatively large denominations (the lowest being 10 rubles), treasury notes of smaller denominations were introduced. Both forms of currency circulated freely and were exchangeable at par, and both were legal tender. Subsequently, when the currency had been definitely stabilized, the State Bank took over the treasury issue, maintaining the regulation cover for the joint issue. The State Bank thus became the sole repository of currency reserves and the responsible regulator of the entire currency system.

Once the currency had been firmly stabilized, it became possible to proceed to introduce a more effectual organization of short-term and long-term credit. Of the two, short-term credit was the more important problem to tackle, for on its solution the regulation of the production process and to a large extent the stability of the currency depended.

In the first ten years or so of its existence, the State Bank was only one of the banks engaged in economic financing. There were other smaller banks which had been especially formed to finance specific branches of industry. Furthermore, in addition to bank loans, there was a system of financing by bills of exchange drawn by one business concern on another. The existence of this system naturally interfered with the utilization of the banks as instruments of rigid control over the financial activities of business organizations.

Accordingly, in 1930, steps were taken to reform the whole credit system. The reform was based upon two underlying principles: (1) All short-term financing was an exclusive prerogative of the State Bank, and (2) bills of exchange were abolished and no business firm had the right to grant credit to another. All short-term financing thus became bank financing, concentrated in the State Bank, of which all the business organizations in the country became the direct clients. The other banks were converted into exclusively long-term financing institutions.

Simultaneously there was begun the gigantic undertaking of reconstructing the working capital of business enterprises. Its effect was to set limits to bank financing. Every enterprise was assigned definite working funds essential for the fulfillment of its production program. These funds formed part of its assets and were at its full disposal and management. They were originally provided out of the State budget or out of the accumulated profits of the given enterprise, or from both sources. And it is from either or both of these sources that further working capital is provided when the production program of an enterprise is increased.

But although producing enterprises now had sufficient working capital to insure normal operation, nevertheless the need for funds arises which they are unable to meet, and which it would be inexpedient for them to meet, out of their working capital. This applies chiefly to expenses involved in purely seasonal production processes, or in the accumulation of seasonal stocks of raw material, fuel, semi-manufactures and the like. These sporadic and purely seasonal expenses are financed by the State Bank, thus obviating the freezing of capital which would result if working funds were maintained at a level sufficient to cover seasonal demands.

Furthermore, the State Bank finances producing enterprises to the full value of finished goods between the time they leave the factory and the time they are delivered and paid for. Thus working funds are not tied up while the goods are in transport.

Lastly, the Bank comes to the aid of a producing enterprise when, as a result of deviations from the production program by which the level of working capital was determined, or from other causes not depending on the client (transport difficulties, for example), working capital proves inadequate. If the deviations from the production program, however, are due to the fault of the enterprise, the Bank refuses to supply additional credit, and the financial difficulties of the enterprise become the object of investigation by the competent Government authorities.

As bank loans are provided on the basis of an analysis of the borrower's financial and economic position, they have become one of the most valuable and effective forms of control by the Government over the activities of State enterprises.

But there are branches of industry whose production processes are not subject to seasonal fluctuation—or vary only to an insignificant degree. This would render them practically immune from the control of the Bank. As many of these branches—machine building, for example—are of great importance to the country's economy, an experiment was recently made in reconstructing the working capital of these non-seasonal industries. A certain part of their working capital is contributed by the Bank, in the form of repayable, or revolving credits. Whenever a particular enterprise is constrained to utilize any portion of this part of its working capital it automatically comes under the control of the Bank.

The conditions under which the Bank grants loans are not governed by hard and fast rules, but are based upon a review of the general conditions prevailing in the given branch of industry. As interest rates in a planned economy do not play the role of a regulator of credit, they remain stable at one level year after year, thus guaranteeing the stability of the credit system and the profits of the bank. These rates at present vary between two per cent and four per cent, depending on the nature of the loans.

The State Bank finances the economy of the country to an amount of many billions of rubles annually. The funds for this purpose are chiefly derived from the free resources of the economy itself, which all flow into the Bank as the sole bank of settlement in the country. Every producing enterprise and business organization is obliged to maintain its cash balances with the State Bank and to make all payments, with the exception of minor sums, through the Bank. Enormous funds are thus constantly flowing into the Bank, leaving a huge and constantly growing aggregate deposit on account.

The economic nature of these deposits should be noted: they consist of the cash resources of the enterprises and organizations of the national economy. Their earnings and profits, as we have mentioned in another place, go into the State budget.

The chief item of the State Bank's resources consists, of course, of the deposits on the accounts of producing enterprises, business organizations, collective farms, etc. But another item of no inconsiderable dimensions is the account of the State budget, which in times of peace, besides the usual cash reserve, is swollen by the large excess of revenue over expenditure.

These resources of the State Bank are further supplemented by the Bank's own funds, which are derived from budget assignments and from its own profits, part of which is paid into the budget, while part remains with the Bank.

Like every bank of issue, the State Bank has another source of funds in the note issue. Its revenue from this source, which depends on the growth of the currency in circulation, is determined not by the Plan for Financing the National Economy, but by what is known as the Bank's Cash Plan. This plan is based upon an estimate of the dynamics of cash transactions, as determined chiefly by retail trade, the wages fund, tax payments, savings, etc., from which the currency policy to be pursued is deduced. The currency in circulation is accordingly expanded, contracted, or left stable. The State Bank's Credit Plan receives revenue from currency issues as a corollary of the Cash Plan. If the sum should prove inadequate to balance the Credit Plan, the budget, that chief fountainhead of financing of a Socialist economy, comes to the rescue.

The State Bank is responsible for the proper drawing up of the Cash Plan, and by virtue of this it is the regulator and guardian of the internal currency of the country.

The position with regard to foreign exchange rates of the Soviet currency unit was simplified by the laws of 1926 and 1928, which prohibited the import and export of Soviet money. In 1936 fixed exchange rates of the ruble were established in respect to the principal foreign currencies. In 1938 the ratio of one U. S. dollar to five rubles, thirty kopeks was laid down as the basis of these fixed rates.

It should be noted, however, that these fixed rates are chiefly intended for the purpose of internal accounting of foreign trade operations, as, for example, when a Soviet industrial enterprise, having received machines or other goods purchased abroad, has to record the transaction in its books in Soviet currency.

In the multiform transactions with the outside world, on the other hand, it is the practice to conduct all operations in foreign currency. All accounting with foreign countries is conducted through the State Bank, which, through its bank correspondents abroad, effects settlement with foreign clients in foreign currency, while conducting accounts in Soviet currency at the fixed rates of exchange with its Soviet clients—the organizations which exercise the monopoly of foreign trade.

THE WAGE SYSTEM IN THE U.S.S.R.*

The Soviet Union is a Socialist State. In it is realized the principle *"from each according to his abilities, to each according to his labor."* Conforming to this principle, wages in the Soviet Union are paid in accordance with the quality and quantity of the worker's labor. The wage systems are planned to stimulate the fulfilment and overfulfilment of norms of output, and so that the workers will have an interest in raising their qualifications.

The main wage systems are: direct piecework, progressive piecework, time work, time work with payment of bonuses, and fixed salaries. In the case of direct piecework, the worker is paid according to the rates per unit of production for the quantity he produces, and the rate remains the same, irrespective of the quantity produced.

Under the system of progressive piecework, where the worker overfulfills the norm by not less than 10 per cent, he gets an increased rate per unit for what he produces above the norm. In machine building, for example, the increase for quantities over the norm is 30 per cent. In some branches of industry it is as much as 150 to 200 per cent.

When the norm is overfulfilled by more than 10 per cent, the rate of pay is increased for quantities produced above 10 per cent. In machine building [the increase is] 50 per cent, and in some branches of industry—for example, metallurgy—as much as 300 per cent.

Workers in branches of labor in which norms cannot be established are

* N. Rytikov, "The Wage System in the U.S.S.R.," Embassy of the U.S.S.R. *Information Bulletin*, May 22, 1945.

paid on a time basis. In cases where the workers can influence the quality of output of the machinery they handle, a bonus is paid in addition to the fixed wage: it may be up to 30 per cent of the basic wage. Especially wide-spread is the system of paying a bonus to workers for saving electric power, fuel and materials.

Engineers and technicians are paid fixed salaries according to the posts they occupy; they also receive bonuses for fulfilling and overfulfilling plans. Office employees, both in industrial enterprises and institutions, as a rule receive fixed salaries.

The Soviet trade unions take part in working out all wage systems, which come into force when they have been approved by the People's Commissariats concerned. The trade unions supervise their application through the wages departments attached to the central committees of the unions, and the wages commissions, consisting of voluntary trade unionists, attached to the primary trade union bodies.

The piecework and progressive piecework systems are the most wide-spread in Soviet industry, as they stimulate labor productivity. . . .

As is generally known, there are in every enterprise trades which are decisive for the fulfilment of the output plan, and other trades of an auxiliary nature. In the iron and steel industry, for example, there are in the open hearth shop steel makers, trimmers and auxiliary workers. The fulfilment of the production plan depends directly on the highly skilled labor of the steel maker.

The labor of the trimmer can easily be calculated and his quotas fixed. He does not influence output directly, and is less highly qualified than the steel maker. As for the auxiliary worker, no qualifications at all are necessary for his labor.

Wage rates in each of these categories are consequently based on the importance of each in the production process. The steel maker's basic rate is five times that of the auxiliary worker. Moreover, the steel maker receives additional pay for overfulfilling the plan, according to a scale which increases as output increases. The trimmer is paid under the piecework system, and the auxiliary worker under the time-work system.

The quality of labor is taken into account in fixing the salaries of office employees. In the case of teachers, physicians, agronomists and other professional workers, additions to the basic salaries depend on educational qualifications and experience.

In discussing wage systems in the USSR it is necessary to remember one very important point: it is that under the Soviet system, wages are by no means the only benefit that is received by the worker in return for his labor.

In the Soviet Union the product of labor is social. It forms part of the wealth of society. This product goes partly to further the expansion of production, partly to the defense of the country, to the upkeep of the State apparatus, to the formation of insurance and reserve funds, and partly to wages. But a considerable part of the social product is used by the State to improve the material well-being of the people, and to raise their cultural level.

Soviet factory and office workers are provided with free medical aid, educational facilities, State social insurance, sanatoria and rest homes, maintenance in illness or old age, and other social and cultural benefits. Rent constitutes no more than 7 or 8 per cent of earnings (and for many population groups the percentage is much less).

In general, workers in the Soviet Union have every incentive to make their labor more productive, and to improve their qualifications.

THE MOVEMENT FOR LABOR EFFICIENCY *

A movement toward efficiency methods—utilization of mechanical devices to the fullest possible extent and the elimination of waste and of lost motion —was started in the coal-mining industry of the Soviet Union in August, 1935. Begun by the initiative of a coal miner named Aleksei Stakhanov, it was enthusiastically adopted by other coal miners and later in many other industries, including agriculture.

In order better to understand the importance of this efficiency movement it should be remembered that when the Soviet regime was established nearly 80 per cent of the population consisted of peasants, largely illiterate and without technical training not only in manufacturing industries, but also in agriculture, in which most of them were engaged. Industries were undeveloped. What little machinery there was was out of date. Although the country possessed untold natural resources, they were similarly undeveloped. Ways of communication and transportation were meager and in poor condition. The [First] World War and the following revolutions and counterrevolutions destroyed much of those meager productive facilities which were in existence before the war.

It was necessary for the new regime to start from the bottom to build up industries under the slogan of industrialization of the Soviet Union; to train and educate the immense backward masses of the peasant population for production and distribution; to develop natural resources; and to construct roads for transportation and establish ways for communication.

This program entailed much effort, sacrifice, and a very low standard of living, notably during the prosecution of the first 5-year plan (1927 to 1932). It was necessary first to build up industries for production of capital goods, leaving the development of production facilities for consumers' goods for the second 5-year plan (1933 to 1937). The resulting deficit in consumers' goods led to the introduction of ration cards for the entire population. As

* U. S. Department of Labor, Bureau of Labor Statistics, "Movement for Labor Efficiency in the Soviet Union," *Monthly Labor Review*, March, 1936, pp. 624–6.

time went on and conditions improved, however, the ration-card system of food distribution was abolished and free trade reestablished.

One of the greatest difficulties confronting the authorities was the lowering of the cost of production or, in other words, increasing of productivity of labor. In order to stimulate workers toward greater efforts in their learning and work, various methods have been applied, such as the introduction of piecework, payment of efficiency bonuses, establishment of minimum standards of output, wage scales adopted by collective agreements, rewards for proper handling of tools, supplements for saving material, and titles and orders awarded to those workers who especially distinguished themselves in efficiency.

The Soviet authorities repeatedly have emphasized the need for greater efficiency. Stalin gave a now famous slogan for it when in his public address on May 4, 1935, he stated: "The cadres (labor forces) decide everything!"

The results of all these measures are shown in the present-day efficiency movement. Although this new efficiency movement in the Soviet Union embodies no new scientific ideas, it is noteworthy because apparently it was initiated and is being maintained and developed by the workers themselves. That the old records of output are now being broken in various industries and occupations all over the Soviet Union has been revealed by reports coming to the central offices in Moscow.

The coal-mining industry was on a low level as regards labor productivity. When Stakhanov became a miner his initial output was about 5 or 6 tons per shift, which was a normal figure for that industry. After a course in coal mining, involving instruction in the use of the power machine for undercutting the coal, he increased his output to 12 or 13 tons per shift. Under the procedure followed at that time, the miner had to clear away the coal and do his own timbering as well as the cutting of coal, and only about two-thirds of the shift time was utilized in the actual cutting of the coal. Thus the mechanical mining equipment was idle a considerable share of the time.

Through some changes in working procedures, by utilizing the services of two assistants for clearing and timbering and by devoting his own time exclusively to cutting, Stakhanov was able to increase the output for the group to 102 tons per shift, then to 175 tons, and finally to 227 tons per shift.

In one mine the standard output had been 7 tons per machine per shift and the number of workers employed (both underground and surface) was 117. The total output of the mine was about 250 tons per shift. Adoption of Stakhanov's methods raised the output to 335 tons per shift. At the same time the total number of workers engaged was decreased to 98.

. . . Stakhanov described his method as involving the following: A better division and specialization of labor; continuous use of cutting machines and other mechanical devices; and better planning of processes to eliminate time lost while waiting for other work to be done. The method involves no extra effort on the part of the workers, as has been testified by all workers who have followed his method.

Coal mining in the Soviet Union is remunerated on the piece basis, at a specified rate per ton, and with a progressively increasing supplement for all output above the standard.

HOW THE TRADE UNIONS WORK *

The role of the trade unions with regard to wage fixing has important differences from the role they fill in a capitalist country. From the nature of the case it seems inevitable that this should be so. In the first place it must be remembered that the whole social situation is very different where, in place of the traditional capital-labor problem, with a class of owners getting their income from profit confronting a class of hired persons who live by selling their labor power for a wage, capital is owned by the state, and the managers are responsible, not to private shareholders, but to the community. Secondly, in a socialist planned economy it seems hardly conceivable that wages could be left to be settled by the free play of bargaining, for the simple reason that the level of wages, determining as it does the level of consumption (and hence the scale of production not only of the consumption good industries but also of the investment good industries), is one of the crucial elements in the whole plan, and to leave it to the chance play of bargaining—to leave it as in part an unknowable factor when constructing the plan—would be to make any complete planning of economic life virtually impossible.

In fact, one could put it the other way around: once the key constituents of an economic plan have been decided upon, such as the rate of investment, the volume of employment, and the distribution of labor and materials between consumption good and investment good industries, the general level of real wages (what the wages can buy, as distinct from money wages) is *ipso facto* determined. All that bargaining about the money wage can subsequently do . . . is to adjust the share of particular groups of workers —modify the distribution of the total between workers in different industries or in different grades—without altering the total itself. What the total of available consumption goods shall be must necessarily be a policy decision to be taken simultaneously with and as one aspect of the complex of decisions which constitute an economic plan. This policy decision as to what is to be the size of the consumption cake for any year will depend in turn on the decision as to what proportion of the available resources of manpower and materials is to be devoted to new construction work to yield fruit in

* Maurice Dobb, *Soviet Economy and the War* (New York: International Publishers, 1943), pp. 75–84.

the future; as it will also depend on such objective factors as the amount and efficiency of existing plant and equipment, the available labor supply and its productivity.

This is not to say, however, that the trade unions will not perform an important function as participants in the discussions which precede the final determination of the plan, and as representatives or advocates of the immediate interests of the workers in discussions of alternatives, in which other (*e.g.,* more long-term) considerations must play a part. This the Soviet trade unions certainly do. In the months preceding the determination of the plan for any year it is customary for the All-Union Central Committee of Trade Unions to go into joint session with the chief economic departments of the government to discuss and determine the general wage policy for that year.

The general decision that is taken in consultation between the Central Committee of Trade Unions and the economic organs of the state includes, in general outline, the standard wages to be paid in the various industries; the determination of this being also an essential element in the plan, if the latter is to embrace financial, as well as real, elements, and hence to include estimates of cost of production and of prices. But even when the general shape of wage policy, regarding not only the general wage level but also wage relativity between industries, has been determined, a great deal remains to be done by way of implementing it, in handling the details of its application. This is done by the negotiation of a collective agreement between the trade union of a particular industry and industrial managements (boards of industrial trusts), and further by the negotiation of more detailed agreements between the lower units of trade union organization, the factory committees, and the managements of particular enterprises.

While these collective agreements are fairly standardized in their general form, they vary considerably in their detail with the special circumstances of an industry or factory. These agreements fix the time-rate scales for various categories of workers, the classes of workers to be paid on a piece-rate basis, and the relationship to be maintained between the normal earnings of piece workers and time workers. The conditions under which overtime is permitted, and the payment for overtime, are stipulated; also the conditions under which workers can be transferred between jobs in different wage categories, and the conditions of engagement and dismissal. The agreements that are made between the factory committee in an enterprise and the individual management generally include provisions governing training, working conditions, including safety measures and accident prevention and the provision of working clothes, and welfare work, including canteens, washing accommodation, and also perhaps a factory club and sports field, and workers' housing.

An interesting clause in most agreements binds the management to give proper consideration to proposals made either by production conferences of the workers or by individual workers, and to award premiums for inventions and improvements that are successfully adopted.

On its side, the factory committee generally undertakes to co-operate with the management in enforcing labor discipline, in overcoming absenteeism and bad timekeeping, "to mobilize the workers for fighting theft and for the protection of socialist property," to co-operate in the enforcement of measures of accident prevention and to provide for the efficient running of the factory canteen, dining room and crèche.

It has sometimes been stated that trade union membership in the U.S.S.R. is compulsory, in the sense that it is a condition of employment. But this is not in fact correct: the Labor Code of 1922, and its supplementary regulations (which among other things defined the legal status of trade unions) laid it down that membership of a union was not to be a condition of employment. At the same time, trade union membership carries certain important privileges, and it is open to a trade union or factory committee to include in a collective agreement a clause which ensures that *preference* in employment should be given to trade unionists, that is, that if trade union members are unemployed, they shall be engaged for a job for which they are suitable before non-members are taken on. This preference clause is in fact very frequently embodied in collective agreements; and when there still existed an unemployed reserve, prior to 1930, the clause had considerable effect. Since 1930, however, when unemployment has yielded place to labor scarcity and the demand for labor has continually outrun the supply (the total number of wage and salary earners in employment more than doubled between 1928 and 1938), this preference clause has lost much of its effect. On the other hand, membership of a trade union is laid open by the Labor Code to all persons who are subject to a contract of service. This includes the technical staff of a factory, but excludes anyone "personally possessing the right to engage or dismiss" (*i.e.,* managers, in any private concern) and also members of co-operative associations of producers, like industrial co-operatives or collective farms (though not collective farmers who take on supplementary work, such as building, for wages).

The Labor Code of 1922, after defining a trade union as any body which is registered with the Central Committee of Trade Unions and is accepted by it for affiliation, laid down certain legal rights for such bodies in relation to the management of industry. The management of an undertaking was not only prohibited from hindering the activities of the factory committees, and dismissing committee members, but was required to afford them certain facilities such as premises in which to meet, "free access to all persons on the business of the committee," and to all trade union representatives "unrestricted right of entry to all workshops, departments, laboratories, etc." Certain matters were also defined as ones in which a trade union had a legal right to joint control with the management. These included matters of overtime and the fixing of output standards as bases for piece rate payment and bonus system, and the "rules of employment" (which include disciplinary fines). In cases of dismissals of workers it was required that notice should be given to the factory committee in advance, and the factory committee was given a right of appeal against the management's decision.

Russian trade unions are organized on the industrial principle, *i.e.,* their frontiers generally correspond to the administrative units under which industry is organized, the union which covers a particular branch of an industry embracing workers of all grades employed there from unskilled laborers to the clerical and technical staff. Originally in the early 'twenties there were no more than twenty-three unions, each of them covering some group or congeries of industries, like the Metal Workers Union or the Agricultural Workers Union. Later these were subdivided; and today there are more than 160.

The basic unit of the union is the meeting of union members in a factory, which elects annually its factory committee (sometimes in larger factories there are separate shop committees or even shift committees). For each district or region there is a regional committee, elected by a regional congress of delegates from the various factories belonging to a certain industry in that district. On a national scale, each industrial union holds periodically a national delegate conference which elects a central committee of the whole union; while for the trade union world as a whole there is an All-Union Central Committee elected at a general Trades Union Congress, which generally meets in alternate years and consists of between 1,000 and 2,000 delegates. . . . At the end of the 'thirties, trade union membership stood at over 22,000,000, or 84 per cent of all wage and salary earners. The trades where union membership is weakest are those such as agriculture and building, which contain a large number of migratory and casual workers.

For dealing with disputes that may arise, either over the interpretation of some existing agreement or in the discussion of a new one, fairly elaborate machinery has been developed, in which the trade unions participate at each stage together with representatives of the management. At the lower end of the scale there are specially constituted Disputes Committees in each factory, composed equally of representatives of the factory committee and of the management. These are competent to deal with all internal factory questions involving the interpretation or detailed application of an existing agreement. It is usually stipulated in the agreement made between the factory committee and the management that when there is a disagreement on such questions as the piece-rate payable for a certain job, the worker has no right to cease work or to refuse to perform the work assigned to him until the matter in dispute has been referred to the Disputes Committee.

Secondly, there are special labor sessions of the People's Court (courts comparable to the local bench in this country), at which one of the three members of the bench must be a trade union representative. Only this court is competent to hear a charge against the management infringing the

Labor Code or the terms of some collective agreement; but in all other disputes over interpretation the aggrieved worker has the option of being heard before this body as an alternative to the Disputes Committee of the factory.

Thirdly, at a higher stage there are district conciliation boards, set up as *ad hoc* bodies to deal with a specific dispute and composed of a representative of each of the two parties to the dispute with an impartial chairman. These are intended to deal with questions of a more general character than those handled by the Disputes Committee of a factory, and disputes to which the trade union itself is a party and not merely a particular individual. It is competent to deal with any matter only by agreement of both parties; and any disagreement involving changes in existing agreements or the interpretation of an agreement which raises a question of principle, can be referred only to such a board and is outside the competence of a People's Court or a factory Disputes Committee.

Finally there are arbitration courts, composed again of representatives of management and trade union, with an impartial chairman. These bodies also have jurisdiction over questions which involve the alteration as distinct from the interpretation of an agreement; they are competent to hear a case at the request of either party alone (the consent of *both* parties, with certain exceptions, being unnecessary); and they are empowered to deliver a binding award.

In the early days of the Revolution, a good deal of discussion took place as to the proper role of trade unions in the new society. The question at issue was whether the unions should become state organs or should remain as bodies that were independent of the state. Lenin spoke against what was termed the "nationalization of the trade unions," and upheld the view that while trade unions should co-operate with the state and even "perform certain of the functions at present discharged by the Soviets" and "aid in the setting up of various state institutions," they should not be transformed into state organs. . . . Trotsky wanted the virtual militarization of the unions and their transformation into units of a state labor corps; and at the other extreme there were those (termed the "workers' opposition") who advocated a kind of syndicalist regime under which the control of industry should be placed entirely in the hands of the trade unions.

. . . The trade unions are democratic bodies, with their officials subject to election from below and not to appointment from above, and charged with the principal duty of acting as representatives of the workers in regard to wages and working conditions. At the same time they were given certain rights of participating in the control of industry, and factory committees, while having no powers to encroach on the management's control over factory administration and discipline, were given substantial rights of joint control over matters of working conditions. Today the position roughly is that the trade unions regard it as equal parts of their function to protect the wages and working conditions of their members and to co-operate with the management in furthering the interests of production; and while they remain independent and democratic organs of the working class, subject to the principle of election, they have assumed certain functions of the state (those concerned with social insurance and factory inspection) that had previously been in the hands of the Commissariat of Labor.

THE ORGANIZATION OF SOVIET AGRICULTURE *

The large area cultivated causes the mass of Soviet production to be enormous. In 1938 the U.S.S.R. produced 25% of the world's wheat, 40% of its rye, 20% of its barley, and 25% of its oats. Even in rice, a semi-tropical crop, Russia was exceeded in Europe only by Italy. Of the principal food of the temperate zones, potatoes, the Soviet Union produced 20% of the world's supply, also 20% of the beet sugar, 70% of the hempseed, and 70% of the flax. Even cotton, large-scale planting of which is fairly recent, came to 14% of the world crop. The U.S.S.R. produced 25% of all the phosphates for the world's agriculture and 14% of the world's milk.

Bearing in mind that the Soviet Union comprises about 9% of the world's population, we may note the items in which her production is less than her population quota (that is, less than 9%). She supplies 6% of the world's butter, 3% of its margarine, 3% of its cheese, 2½% of its tea, 7½% of its tobacco, 8% of its wool. Soviet fisheries produce more than their world quota—12%—but the Soviet meat supply was only 40% of that of the U. S. A., a deficiency that becomes appreciable when one realizes the population difference between the two countries. Forest production, lumber, and paper are extremely important but the relative figures are not certain.

Since the Soviet government began to emphasize the necessity for transforming the country into an industrial power, the excessive proportion of people engaged in agriculture has declined. Whereas in 1926 only 26% of the people lived in towns and cities, by 1939 the town population had risen to 56%. The population of the countryside has actually diminished. Rural areas had been overpopulated in pre-revolutionary Russia because the farms were wretchedly primitive and required great numbers of hand-laborers. As machinery was introduced under Soviet collective farming, the number of men needed was considerably reduced. These men have emigrated to the industrial regions.

Soviet agriculture is organized on a unique cooperative basis. The system is somewhat complex, being neither wholly Socialist nor cooperative in the sense of associations of individual landowners, such as are found in Denmark. About nine-tenths of the Soviet farmers are organized in "collectives,"

* Sumner Welles, *An Intelligent American's Guide to the Peace* (New York: The Dryden Press, 1945), pp. 114–5.

termed *kolkhozes*. The remainder are nearly all in "state farms," which are Socialist enterprises conducted in the same way as Soviet factories. There are a few unassociated farmers left, mostly in primitive communities, but they play almost no part in the over-all productivity of the country.

Agriculture is planned by the Central Planning Institutes of the Soviet Union. Data and suggestions are gathered from meetings of the collectives of farmers, their local needs are then measured against the total food requirements of the country, and a schedule is reached to harmonize these needs. Hence, sowing is determined partly by local and partly by national considerations, and not, as in the U. S. A., by the reflections of consumers' demands as shown by changing market prices.

The collectives allow each farmer to own his own home, vegetable and flower patch and lawn, some poultry, pigs, fruit trees, and berry patches; but the "instruments of production"—that is, farming machines, tractors, fertilizers, and other large equipment—are owned in common, as are the fields and cattle used for general production. No farmer can hire another and pay him wages or in any other way make a profit out of another man's work. His individual property is for him and his family to work; all other work is collective and the financial rewards are assessed by elected representatives. In addition, the central government sends "Agronoms" (or county agents) to advise the collectives on methods of soil conservation and of increasing yields. The "agronom" is paid by the collective if it has a surplus, or by the government if the collective is still in a process of development.

Among the many changes resulting from farm collectivization, at least two must be mentioned because of their long-term effects. In economic planning, there has been a tendency to shift from an excessive dependence on cereal crops to "technical" crops—silk, cotton, and items used as sources of chemical materials. In the personal life of the farm worker, there has been a tendency to convert the collective into a community center of cultural interests, thus counteracting the former rural isolation—and reminding one of the best features of the American "grange."

Collectivizing the farms was a bitter process. The wealthy peasantry resisted with all its strength and the contest with the "kulaks" ("fists," as these rich farmers were called) became a veritable civil war. The "kulaks" slaughtered far too many animals, with a consequent serious loss in livestock, and food shortages reached famine proportions in certain areas. The livestock shortage had been almost completely remedied by 1941 when World War II exposed the country to the Nazi invaders, whose plunder can scarcely be estimated. The struggle for collectivization of the farms is considered a glory by the Russians; but many critics have deplored its cost and suffering. Whatever the cost, the collective farm is permanent in the Soviet Union of today. When the scarcity of animals is remedied, the collective farm should be able to show an increasing yield in every product.

Though the Russian farm economy exceeds the American in *yield per acre* by about 45%, it is well below the American economy in crops *per man-hours worked*. Until this latter ratio equals that of western Europe, let alone that of the U. S. A., the Russian farmer has far to go. However, since 1933, when collectivization was completed, there has been a tendency to higher yields per man-hour, which seems to have continued even during the war.

THE FARMER'S INCOME *

In any discussion of collective farming the term "workday unit" is sure to crop up. Indeed, it is an essential part of the collective farm system. The term is peculiar to collective farm life. The work of a collective farmer is not measured by the time he has spent on a particular job, but by the results of his work in terms of quality and quantity. Those results are assessed in "workday units."

Here is a simple example. Two collective farmers have plowed some collective farm land with horse-drawn plows. Both have worked the same number of days and put in the same number of hours each day. But that does not mean that their earnings, as expressed in workday units, will necessarily be the same. For their earnings are determined not only by the time spent in plowing, but by the area each has plowed. If one, say, has plowed 3.6 hectares, while the other, working the same time, has plowed 4.5 hectares, the latter will be credited with a correspondingly larger number of workday units.

Norms are not, and cannot be, the same on all collective farms. For norms are established in accordance with local conditions, which may vary in different areas. It is one thing, for example, to operate a reaping machine on the level ground of the Volga steppes, and quite another to operate one on the hilly fields of the Valdai Region. It is one thing to mow low grass growing on sun-scorched hillocks, and another to mow lush, moist meadows.

Each collective farm, therefore, sets its own norms, which are discussed and approved at a general meeting of the collective farmers. Sometimes norms vary on one and the same collective farm. For example, of two plots planted to millet, one may be more overgrown with weeds than the other. In this case the collective farm establishes two or even three norms: one for plots with few weeds, another for plots with a normal growth of weeds, and a third for badly overgrown plots.

The leader of each collective farm brigade or team keeps a daily record of the work performed by the members of his brigade, and using a table of norms, translates the amount of work done into workday units. One copy of the record is turned over to the collective farm office, where it is entered on the personal account sheet of the particular collective farmer. The brigade

* Georgi Blok, "How Collective Farm Income Is Divided," Embassy of the U.S.S.R. *Information Bulletin*, June 7, 1945.

leader makes another entry in the workbook with which every collective farmer is supplied. This book enables the collective farmer to check up on his personal account whenever he likes.

At the end of the agricultural year the workday units earned by each member are added up. It may happen that one collective farmer has earned, say, 180 workday units during the year, another 200, another 250 or even 300. Then the workday units earned by individual members of the collective farm are added up, and the grand total shows the number of workday units earned by the entire membership of the collective farm.

At the same time, stock is taken of the harvest for the given year, for each particular crop. From the total are deducted the amounts to be delivered to the State at fixed prices, and the amounts that are to be set aside for the collective farm's seed fund and reserve funds (the latter amounts are determined by the general membership meeting). The remainder represents the net income of the collective farm which is to be distributed among the members. It is not distributed equally, however, but according to the number of workday units earned by each member.

Under the workday unit system of distributing income every collective farmer is directly interested, first, in earning the largest possible number of workday units, and second, in the collective farm's obtaining the largest possible crop.

The system consequently achieves two aims: on the one hand, it insures absolutely equitable distribution of income among the collective farm members in accordance with the amount of work put in by each; on the other hand, it serves as an incentive for more and better work.

The collective farmer who displays special skill in performing his work receives a bonus in addition to the workday units he has earned on the basis of the norm. The bonus, too, is expressed in workday units.

PRIVATE PROPERTY *

The economic system of the Soviet Union is based on Socialist ownership of the means and instruments of production. Socialist property in the U.S.S.R. exists either in the form of State property, or in the form of cooperative and collective-farm property.

The land, its natural deposits, waters, forests, industrial enterprises (mills, factories, mines), rail, water and air transport, banks, postoffices, telegraph and telephones, large State-organized agricultural enterprises (state farms, machine and tractor stations, and the like), as well as municipal enterprises and the bulk of the dwelling houses in the cities, are State property, i.e., belong to the whole people.

The prevailing form of agriculture in the U.S.S.R. is collective economy,

* P. Ognev, "Private Property," Embassy of the U.S.S.R. *Information Bulletins,* October 18, 1945, October 20, 1945, and October 23, 1945.

i.e., collective farming of the land. In a collective farm all the principal instruments and means of production are pooled as public property—all the draft animals, agricultural implements, seed stocks, fodder in quantities necessary for maintaining collective-farm cattle, farm buildings needed for running the collective farm and all installations for processing the produce of the collective farm.

In collective farms and cooperative organizations all the basic means of production as well as all the output, as distinct from State enterprises, are the common property of the members of the collective farm or the cooperative organization who use this property, as indicated by the general meeting of collective farmers or members of the cooperative organization.

The land occupied by collective farms is secured to them for their use free of charge and in perpetuity, by special Government deeds, and cannot be bought, sold or leased.

In a collective farm the members retain for their personal use a small plot of land attached to their dwellings (from one-half to two and a half acres), and as their personal property a dwelling house, livestock, poultry, and agricultural implements needed for farming the plot. Soviet law permits the small private economy of individual farmers and handicraftsmen, based on their personal labor.

The prevailing form of economy in the U.S.S.R. is the Socialist system. A total of 98.7 per cent of the productive capacity of the entire national economy consists of public property, 1.1 per cent is the personal property of collective farmers and only 0.2 per cent is owned by private individuals— farmers and handicraftsmen.

Private property of citizens exists on the basis of the two main forms of public property: State property and cooperative-collective farm property.

In the Soviet Union the income from State enterprises, and the output of publicly-owned enterprises, do not go to private individuals, thus creating an undue accumulation of wealth in their hands, but are put at the disposal of the State and are the property of all the people.

The distribution of all output of State enterprises follows certain main channels. One part is designated for making good the wear and tear of the means of production and for the construction of new mills and factories. Certain sums are allotted to insurance and reserve funds. Allocations are also made for maintaining the Government's administrative machinery and for strengthening the country's defenses.

The rest of the output is earmarked for consumption. It is divided into two main parts. The first is designated to satisfy the requirements of the people—allocations for cultural and public services and for the incapacitated. The second part is for personal consumption.

The distribution of that portion of the public output earmarked for personal consumption among workers, intellectuals and office employees is effected in the U.S.S.R. in the form of wages. Everyone receives in the form of wages that share of the public output which is due him in accordance with the quantity and quality of the labor he has expended.

All commodities produced by State enterprises and destined for consumption by the population, are sold through the State trading machinery. Every citizen may acquire, out of his earnings, any commodities he desires for his personal consumption.

The citizens of the U.S.S.R. are not limited in any way in acquiring personal property if it is not used as a means of exploiting another person's labor. Every citizen, for example, may be the owner of substantial personal savings but he may not lend this money out at interest or practice usury. Every citizen may purchase for his own needs an automobile, a sewing machine, a tractor, a threshing machine, a mowing machine, or any other means of production, but he has no right to use them as a source of unearned income or as means of profiting from the labor of workers hired to operate them.

The right of citizens to acquire out of their own earnings commodities necessary for their personal consumption is insured by law. Article 10 of the Constitution of the U.S.S.R. reads as follows: "The right of citizens to personal ownership of their incomes from work and of their savings, of their dwelling houses and subsidiary household economy, their household furniture and utensils and articles of personal use and convenience, as well as the right of inheritance of personal property of citizens, is protected by law."

The income of working people in the U.S.S.R. is not limited to wages. A large share of the public output is set aside to meet the needs of the country as a whole in the form of schools, public health services, and so on. In the U.S.S.R. all deductions made by the State from a person's private income are returned to him as a member of society either directly or indirectly.

The amount of the public output set aside for personal consumption by the population increases concomitantly with the growth of the public output and the national income. The national income, for example, increased from 48,500 million rubles in 1933 to 105,000 million in 1938. During this same period the annual earnings of workers and office employees rose from 34,953 million rubles to 96,425 million rubles.

The systematic increase of that part of the public output marked for personal consumption stimulates the citizens of the Soviet Union to do everything in their power to promote the growth of the public wealth, to take a most active part in the well-being of the enterprise in which they work, to increase labor productivity and to overfulfill the plans. The improvement of the general welfare of the State leads to an improvement in the welfare of its citizens.

Every citizen of the Soviet Union has the right to acquire as his own private property all he requires for satisfying his personal needs. But every citizen knows that, the richer the State, the more his private property may expand.

The right to private property, as laid down in the Constitution, has no restrictions whatever. The private owner has the unlimited right of ownership, use and disposal of his property. This right is established by Article 58 of the Civil Code of the Russian Socialist Federative Soviet Republic and corresponding articles in the civil codes of other Republics.

The owner has the right to appeal to a court for the return of his property if it has been unlawfully appropriated, or to demand reimbursement of the value of the property, if it has been lost or damaged, and also to demand reimbursement for all the costs involved (Article 59 and following in the Civil Code). This means that neither the State, the public, nor other persons have the right to encroach on the ownership, use or disposal of the private property of citizens. The owner has sole discretion over his personal property.

There is only one reservation—the use of private property must conform to its social-economic purpose, as established by Article 1 of the Civil Code. This can be explained by the following example. Let us suppose that a citizen owns a home. Instead of maintaining this dwelling in suitable condition and repairing it when necessary, the owner allows it to fall into disrepair. In such a case the responsible state authorities warn the owner that he must take better care of his property. If such a warning fails to bring the desired results, the authorities may appeal to the court with a suit to take this dwelling from its owner. In the event that sufficient evidence is provided, the court may grant the claim. Only by decision of the court and by the owner's failure to exercise his right in accordance with the social-economic purpose of the property in question, can the State interfere in the citizen's right to private ownership. The court decides against the owner only if he intentionally and willfully allows his property to fall into disrepair.

The main source of every Soviet citizen's property is his wages, earned by his own labor. No one has the right to interfere in a citizen's disposal of his wages. If necessary, the right may be established by appealing to a court.

Wages are also a source of savings, which the citizen may keep wherever he desires. The State guarantees the inviolability of savings bank deposits, and information on such deposits is given only to court investigators in the event a criminal charge is brought against their owner, and this information is requested by the court (Article 7 of the Statutes of the State Savings Banks of the U.S.S.R.). An established rate of interest is paid on private deposits in savings banks. The owner has the unreserved right to dispose of his deposits and to withdraw them either completely or in part from the bank.

Citizens of the Soviet Union have the right to own dwelling houses and subsidiary establishments connected with them. Each person, however, has the right to own only one home and to own it for a whole family—husband, wife and minor children. But this does not imply that the owner is obliged to reside in his own home. On the contrary, both the owner and his family may, at their discretion, reside in another dwelling—in a summer home for instance. In such a case the owner may rent part or all of his dwelling to another party. Dwellings which are the property of private individuals may be bought, sold, mortgaged, given away or willed, as may all other forms of personal property.

To avoid possible abuses of the right to buy and sell private dwellings, the law provides that each citizen has the right to purchase a dwelling no oftener than once in three years. This precludes the possibility of misusing this right as a means of making profit.

No limits or controls are placed on the right to the personal ownership of utensils and articles of personal use and convenience. Household linen, clothing, furniture, cutlery and china—everything that a person needs, everything that he can use—books, ornaments, musical instruments, articles needed for the practice of sports, trades or professions—in a word, everything conducive to a full cultural, professional, social and domestic life, may become his personal property. This property may be sold, mortgaged, given away or bequeathed by will.

Every citizen of the Soviet Union may acquire the commodities he needs as his own property, either individually, or jointly with other persons. Each party to such jointly-owned property has the right by law to demand the part belonging to him at any time. If the property is indivisible then the owner has the right to sell or turn over his part to other persons, the other parties to the property having the right of first option of purchase. This right of the participants in joint property ownership to acquire shares of a common indivisible property (a dwelling, for instance), is established by Article 65 of the Civil Code of the Russian S.F.S.R. and corresponding articles of the civil codes of the other Union Republics.

Family property also exists in the U.S.S.R. Only husbands and wives are recognized as owners of family property. . . . Articles which belonged to the husband and wife before they contracted their marriage continue to remain the personal property of each individually after marriage. Property acquired during their married life belongs to husband and wife jointly, as established by Article 10 of the Code of Laws on Marriage. This joint ownership of property does not depend on which of the parties to the marriage earns the means by which the property is acquired. It is understood, however, that articles of personal use, such as clothing or occupational materials, are considered the property of the party using them.

On the subsidiary establishment on the plot of land attached to the household of a collective farm family, the articles of private property are the dwelling, the livestock, poultry and agricultural implements. These articles are not the property of separate members of the family but of the household in the aggregate.

The property of the household is jointly owned by its members. Prior to its division or to the allotting of any portion of it, no member has a separate share in this property. Therefore the death of one of the members of the household does not involve the question of the inheritance of his share but simply reduces the number of joint owners of the property.

A distinction must be made between the property of the collective farm family as represented by the property of the household itself (the dwelling, livestock, agricultural implements) and the property belonging to separate members of the family (clothing, books, etc.), which is their personal property.

The collective farmer's main source of income is from the collective farm enterprise. The farming done on the subsidiary plot of the household has only a secondary significance and is a supplementary source of income for the material security of the collective farm members. The main means of agricultural labor are pooled together as the public property of the collective farm. The statutes of the collective farm permit only minor agricultural implements to remain the property of the collective farm household.

The income which a member receives from his part in the general work of the collective farm constitutes his indivisible personal property. Collective farmers usually sell any surplus products on the open market and purchase needed commodities with the money realized from the sale.

The richer a collective farm and the stronger it is economically, the greater is the income of each member for his part in the work of the collective farm and the greater his opportunity to satisfy his cultural requirements.

There also exist in the U.S.S.R. a few small farms run by individuals who are not members of collective farms, and individual handicraftsmen who are not members of cooperative organizations. The Soviet Constitution permits the small private economy of such individuals on condition that the private owner expends only his own labor on his means of production and does not exploit the labor of others.

There remains the question of rights of inheriting private property in the Soviet Union. According to Soviet law property may be inherited by children (including adopted children), wife or husband and incapacitated parents, as well as other incapacitated persons who were dependents of the deceased for not less than one year preceding his death. If any one of the children dies before the will is read his share devolves upon his children (the grandchildren of the deceased), and in the event of the death of the grandchildren, upon their children (the great-grandchildren of the deceased). In the absence of heirs of first precedence or in the event of their refusal to accept the inheritance, the next in line are the able-bodied parents or, in their absence, the brothers and sisters of the deceased.

Every citizen of the Soviet Union may will all his property or part of it to one or several of his legal heirs as well as to state organizations. He cannot, however, deprive his minor children or other dependent heirs of the share due to them by law. In the absence of legal heirs, the property may be willed to any person indicated by the testator.

Finally, if there are no legal heirs and the deceased dies intestate, the property reverts to the State.

Such, in general outline, are the salient features of the laws governing the ownership of private property in the Soviet Union. Soviet law protects the right to own private property against all infringements. Every citizen may appeal to the courts for the protection of his rights. The violation of the rights of private property by others is punishable by law.

Embezzlement, fraud, misappropriation and any other possible infringements of the rights of private property are punishable by severe penalties which may include imprisonment for various terms (Articles 162, a, b, and c, Article 169, Part 1, Article 168 and others of the Penal Code of the R.S.F.S.R. and corresponding laws of the penal codes of other Union Republics).

Every citizen of the Soviet Union is well aware of his right to own private property. He also knows, however, that the welfare of the Soviet State is created by the labor of its citizens, of which his labor is a part. The higher the level of welfare in the State, the higher the level of his own personal welfare. It is for this reason that Article 131 of the Constitution of the U.S.S.R. states: "It is the duty of every citizen of the U.S.S.R. to safeguard and strengthen public, Socialist property as the sacred and inviolable foundation of the Soviet system, as the source of the wealth and might of the country, as the source of the prosperous and cultured life of all the working people. Persons committing offences against public, Socialist property are enemies of the people."

* 5 *

Soviet Science and Medicine

THE ROLE OF SCIENCE IN THE U.S.S.R.*

The first striking character of Soviet science is the scale of its operations. The budget for science in 1934 was a thousand million rubles. We shall not attempt to estimate the purchasing power of this sum, but it represents at least 1 per cent of the national income at the time, a sum relatively three times as great as that spent in the U.S.A. and ten times as great as that spent in Britain.

This constitutes the practical recognition that science is to be taken no longer as a luxury but as an essential part of the social fabric. Science is in fact, in the Soviet Union, linked closely at every stage to the productive processes, but it is linked to them in a way quite different from the connection that it has in other countries. The prime practical object of Soviet science is the satisfaction of human needs, either directly or indirectly, and not the increasing profitability of production. Necessarily a concern for human needs involves the improving of production processes, and in so far as it does so Soviet science will tend to shorten these processes and reduce their effective costliness in terms of human effort. . . .

The other chief difference is that Soviet science is completely integrated. The problems are not faced separately but as an interconnected whole. The development of science is pushed forward according to a plan, and that plan itself forms only a part of the wider plan of material and cultural advance. Naturally the planning of science possesses quite another order of definiteness than does the planning of any kind of production. The field in which science works contains far too many surprises for it to be possible to estimate in advance what is going to be found, or what can or cannot be done. These difficulties are overcome by planning not for the results of science, which cannot be anticipated, but for research surveys of definite fields in which valuable results may reasonably be expected. The plan's main feature is the distribution of the resources available for science between the various branches and institutes for scientific research in a proportion that seems likely to give the best results both from the point of view of immediate improvement of production and from the longer-range view of the development of a more adequate Soviet science. . . .

The organization of Soviet science is somewhat complex and is by no

* J. D. Bernal, *The Social Function of Science* (New York: The Macmillan Company, 1939), pp. 224–9.

means yet fixed. In the early stages many improvisations were made, some of which have been retained and others dropped. The present structure is still to a large extent flexible. The general direction of scientific work throughout the Union is in the hands of the Academy, but the research institutions under the Academy represent only a small proportion of the research carried on throughout the country. The main bulk of research is carried on by the university research laboratories and by the research institutions under the control of the different Commissariats, such as those of Heavy Industry, Light Industry, Food Supply, Health, Agriculture, etc. The Academy, which was originally built on the model of the French and Prussian Academies as an honorific body for distinguished scientists, has expanded its work, not by adding to its members, but by making each member responsible for one or more institutions in his own particular sphere.

The main function of the university and technical schools is, of course, educational, but each has its research laboratories which are linked very closely with those of the Academy. More important still, however, are the research institutions attached to industry, various metal institutions, silicate, fibre, etc. These are not industrial institutions in the narrow sense but are occupied with basic problems connected with the industry and include in them scientists of great distinction. On another level are the innumerable works laboratories and field agricultural stations. The responsibility for the finance of the institutions and works laboratories falls on the Commissariats, and it is their needs that determine the line of research to be undertaken. From the scientific point of view the research institutions in industry and agriculture are closely linked with the Academy, and the separation which exists in Britain between academic and industrial science is largely non-existent.

The idea behind the organization is that there should be a two-way flow of problems and solutions. The problems of industry put in a precise form by works laboratories are passed on to the technical institutes. In so far as their solution falls within the scope of existing technical knowledge, they are solved there. But if some more fundamental ignorance of the working of nature is revealed, this is passed on to the Academy. Thus industry serves to present science with new and original problems. At the same time any fundamental discoveries made in the universities or the Academy are immediately transmitted to the industrial laboratories so that anything which can be turned to useful purposes may be used in practice as soon as possible. A beautiful example of this integrated working is shown by Vavilov's bureau of plant industry. There the economic need for producing varieties of plants to suit the multiple climates and conditions of soil in different parts of the Union has led to a very thorough development of genetic principles, and also, through the investigation of wild varieties of cultivated plants, to the discovery of the centres of domestication and consequently of civilization in distant pre-history, at the same time as providing a number of new plants and crosses of great practical value.

The detailed carrying on of scientific work, apparatus, and laboratories does not differ fundamentally in the Soviet Union from that outside it. There is an interesting development, however, in the production of apparatus, which, instead of being left to individual firms, with the resultant high prices and small turnover, is centered in the institutes themselves, which permits a rationalization of production and a consequent cheapening and multiplying of scientific apparatus so that in nearly every field the Soviet Union has become independent of foreign apparatus, a feat which is all the more remarkable in that there was practically no scientific apparatus made in the country before the Revolution.

In the question of personnel, however, and internal management of scientific research, there are totally different ideas at work. In a few years many changes have taken place, and the present inner organization is the result of the modifications usual in all enterprises in the Soviet Union. In the light of the experience of the peculiar needs of scientific research, it is a combination of individual responsibility and collective consultation. The director of the institute is responsible for the general work of the institute, and its finance and administration, even where these last two functions are vested in a different person. He alone takes ultimate decisions. The main work of the institute is planned out by the discussion among the workers themselves in their own meetings, and these workers include not only the scientific staff but what would count in other countries as mechanics and assistants. At the beginning of the year the general planning of work is discussed; it is then taken by the director or the representatives for modification in the light of plans of other institutes or of the needs of industry or education, and after a series of negotiations a short plan is approved and the budget is fixed. Necessarily the plans are left somewhat vague, particularly in relation to time of fulfilment, but some account of the work done and that still to do is expected at definite intervals. In the author's experience this scheme is capable of working extremely well in general, where the director and the staff are naturally willing to work together, but in other circumstances it may be the cause of friction and inefficiency. Luckily, at the rate at which Soviet science grows, those personal struggles, which seem to be inevitable between scientists of different temperaments or beliefs, need not lead to the same embitterment that they do in other countries, because, owing to the rapid expansion of science, there is always the possibility of the aggrieved or misunderstood junior setting up an institute of his own.

Science in the Soviet Union is, however, by no means only or even mainly a question of research. The Marxists have always conceived of a society thoroughly permeated by science, one in which science becomes a corner-stone of education and culture. Consequently, one of the most noticeable things in the Soviet Union is the place of science in education and even more so in popular interest. Science both in its theoretical and practical aspects is taught from the very beginning in the schools and, though considerable time is left for literary interests, it dominates the higher stages. The teaching of the universities both in science and technics is extremely thorough and effective, while the number of students is of course out of all proportion to that existing before the Revolution, and higher in relation to the population than it is in technically far more advanced countries, such as Britain or Germany. The difficulties of setting up this educational system were immense, as the few teachers that were to be found were also needed for the more immediate tasks of scientific and industrial research. In the earlier stages the need was so great that many of the students were sent out after short courses, very incompletely trained, but this no longer occurs. Actually the training is prolonged on English standards: a five-year university course followed by three years learning research is needed before the final degree. The enormous advantage which Soviet education has over that of other countries, with the partial exception of the U.S.A., is that it is able to draw on the intelligence available in the whole of the population and not only on that of a certain section of it, arbitrarily marked off by wealth. There can be no doubt that once the system has had time to get under way we shall have a body of intelligent scientific workers not to be paralleled elsewhere in the world.

Even more striking, however, than the educational system is the great interest in science shown by the adult population. This is marked, among other ways, by the great sale of scientific books—not only popular books on science, but also practical and serious scientific works and technical handbooks. The main aim of the former is not, as with us, to cause the reader to meditate on the mysteries of the universe, but to show how men can use science to struggle with nature and improve their conditions. Almost every scientific book of any importance, however difficult, is translated into Russian, and has an extensive sale. Thus, the first edition of Dirac's *Quantum Mechanics* sold 3000 copies in Russia in a few months and only 2000 of the English edition in three years. Scientific news of discoveries or the proceedings of congresses are given the same prominence and arouse the same interest as news about royalty, crime, or football matches in England. The recreation parks run scientific side-shows which are always well patronized, and every visitor to the Union notices the insatiable curiosity which the people evince for anything of a technical or scientific nature. . . . The power and interest of science is suddenly opened to a population to whom hitherto it was a closed book, and the effect is the same, though greater than at the other periods of transference of a learned tradition, as between the Egyptians and the Greeks, or the Greeks and the Arabs.

THE ORGANIZATION OF SOVIET SCIENCE *

The organization of science in general and scientific work at the Institute under my charge in particular were problems which greatly interested me when I returned to work in the U.S.S.R. I was quite familiar with the organization of science and scientific work abroad. I had been director of an institute in the very center of English scientific thought—at Cambridge —for a number of years. On the basis of that experience I felt that the organizational forms of scientific work accepted in the West could not be applied in our country as they stood. It occurred to me that we had to seek our own forms of organization of scientific work at the Institute, and, even more so, of the organization of science in general.

This is principally caused by the fact that in our socialist country science occupies a special place. Science is recognized as one of the essential mainstays of the development of culture and is accorded a leading position in the development of our technology and national economy. The organization of science in our country must have a more purposeful character than that to be found in other countries, where it is more accidental and spontaneous. The connection between science and life must be close and more complete in our country. The problems of the organization of science are particularly important to us—workers of the Academy of Sciences of the Soviet Union.

In dealing with the organization of scientific work in our Institute I shall first try to outline a picture of the general principles from which we developed and then speak of what we actually succeeded in accomplishing.

Our Institute is young; it is only 7 or 8 years old. Though I came here as a more or less experienced scientist, still it was difficult to set up an institute without having a school or scientific workers. For this reason the development of the Institute has been much slower than would have been the case if it had branched off from another institute and continued to grow from that basis. The selection of the personnel presented additional difficulties connected with the peculiarities of our work, which belongs to the sphere of strong magnetic fields and low temperatures—a sphere of scientific work which was but little developed in the U.S.S.R. at the time. During the first years we were busy forming and training the scientific personnel and staff of the Institute. It could only begin to grow and expand normally after the working nucleus had been formed. This explains why our Institute is less developed than it will be in time to come.

The question I put before myself from the very outset was what sort of problems must an institute of the Academy of Sciences work up? Of course, in putting this question, I had in mind an institute of physics, or, at any rate, an institute devoted to research in the field of natural science; naturally, the problems of an institute working in other fields of knowl-

* P. L. Kapitsa, "The Organization of Soviet Science," *Voks Bulletin* Nos. 9–10, 1943 (Moscow: U.S.S.R. Society for Cultural Relations with Foreign Countries, 1943).

edge will be different; therefore I wish to stipulate in advance that too broad generalizations of the several theses which I shall develop must not be made.

I emphasize further that I am speaking in particular of the organization of an institute of the Academy of Sciences. What is the Academy of Sciences? In my opinion it is called upon to direct all our science ideologically, from top to bottom, along a sound channel. Each of its separate institutes may pursue the same policy, i.e., aspire to wield a directing influence on science in the field in which it is working, and strive to bring it into the front ranks.

For this reason, the first task which an institute of the Academy of Sciences must set itself is to study a "great" science. "Great" science is the science that studies the essential phenomena necessary for the most profound knowledge of nature. The task of a science is to give the necessary knowledge for transforming nature so that it can serve man in his cultural development. For this reason, the choice of the Institute's thematic material, the choice of fields in which its work is directed, is extraordinarily important. The direction which the work of the Institute takes must correspond to the trend of scientific development which is the most promising at the given moment, and in the given state of science, which may advance most rapidly and fruitfully taking into consideration the methodical possibilities.

In my opinion three such essential trends exist in the field of physics: research in the field of low temperatures, in the field of atomic nucleus, and, finally, in that of solid bodies. I cannot here justify the reasons which lead me to consider these directions the most important, and, perhaps, some of our physicists may not agree with me. Our Institute is working on phenomena occurring at temperatures approaching absolute zero and it must be noted that, in recent years, this has been one of the most rapidly developing trends in physics and many new and fundamental discoveries may be expected in this field.

The scientific work at our Institute is done by a small number of leading research workers. This gives the Institute's work purposeful character and concentrates it around a small number of main subjects. Nothing is so dangerous for the scientific work of an Institute as when it is cluttered up with petty themes which distract attention from the essential problems and aims. The main themes of the Institute are worked out by a small number of its scientific personnel—3 to 4 scientists—and are thus given a unified purpose.

The problem next in importance to that of deciding on the general trend is the selection of scientific workers. Only a person with a profound creative talent and one who treats his work creatively can achieve considerable success in "great" science. For this reason the leading group of the Institute must undoubtedly be formed from a small number of carefully picked scientific workers. This group must devote itself wholeheartedly to scientific work. The Institute must be organized so that the working conditions are such that the scientific workers are able to spend not less than 80 per cent of their time on actual research, with no more than 20 per cent of their time consumed by social and other activities. Only if suitable conditions are created will the scientific workers be able to stay in their laboratories and work themselves. Only when one works in the laboratory oneself, with one's own hands, conducting experiments—even the most routine parts of them—only under these conditions can real results be achieved in science. Good work cannot be done with other people's hands. A person who devotes ten or twenty minutes a day in directing scientific work can never be a great scientist. At least, I never saw or heard of a great scientist who worked in that manner, and I do not think it can be done. I am certain that the very moment even the greatest scientist stops working in the laboratory himself, he not only ceases to develop but, in general, ceases to be a scientist.

It is particularly important to inculcate these principles in scientific beginners. For this purpose I try to put their work into rather rigid organizational frames. For instance, a scientific worker must not be occupied with several subjects at one time, especially if he is at the beginning of his scientific career. When the scientific worker has grown somewhat and becomes more experienced, he may be able to work simultaneously on two or three subjects as a rare exception; but he must always begin with one.

The next point in the organization to ensure successful work is that the scientist must work in the laboratory a limited number of hours. Long spells of work are harmful; it is exhausting and lowers a person's creative powers. In our Institute, for instance, it is a rule that all laboratory work stops at 6:00 P.M. The scientist leaves for home, to ponder on his work, read, study and rest. In exceptional cases, by permission of the Vice-Director, work may be permitted until 8:00 P.M. Night work is sanctioned only by the Director and may be justified by technical requirements, caused by special conditions of the experiment. This is the regime observed by the scientific workers of our Institute.

An institute which, by the quality of its scientific forces and that which it has produced, is capable of becoming a center of major science, may still develop into a closed and isolated unit, not satisfying the requirements we set in the beginning, i.e., actively to influence the science and culture of the whole country.

How can an institute manifest its influence on the development of the leading science of the country? How can it bind itself to the other seats of scientific thought of the country? There are several means of doing so. I shall name the principal ones.

First of all, it must avail itself of the advantages it should have as an Institute of the Academy of Sciences. These advantages consist of rich and modern technical equipment, the possibility of selecting experienced personnel which make it possible to accomplish scientific work inaccessible to other institutions. For instance, in our Institute the possession of a special plant for obtaining quantities of liquid helium gives us exceptional possibilities for conducting experiments in the field of low temperatures, which other institutes lack. Thus, taking advantage of this, our Institute offers the workers of other institutes opportunities to come and do their work in the field of low temperatures, which cannot be done elsewhere. This work is usually not of leading importance and sometimes in no way connected with the essential themes of the Institute.

Such visits of comrades from other institutes are usually arranged as follows: The person who wishes to work at our Institute is invited to our scientific meeting where he reports on the experiment he proposes to conduct. This is discussed and, if the proposal is of scientifically grounded interest and the author is sufficiently qualified, he is given the opportunity to do his work. At our Institute such work is very limited, usually consisting of not more than two or three outsiders at a time so as not to disorganize the main work of the Institute.

So far there have been many more people in the U.S.S.R. who wanted to come to our Institute to work than we were able to accommodate. This is a strong proof that it is an advanced institute, as only in this case would other scientific institutions be interested in the work conducted by an Institute of the Academy and seek to establish connections with it.

The constant presence of workers of other scientific institutions enabled us to establish one of the forms of vital connection with scientific activities outside the Institute. Leaving us at the completion of their work, these guests acquaint their institutes with our other work besides the experience gained by them in the course of their own research at our Institute. Thus our own experience penetrates ever farther into the other scientific institutions of the country. In this manner vital contact is established with other institutions, and we, in our turn, learn what is being done there. The utilization of this vital contact is a good method of influencing the development of science in the country.

In the future similar vital contacts must be established with scientists in other countries. Scientific workers from abroad visited us during the first years of the existence of our Institute. But in recent years the political situation has grown so complicated, that though there were those who wanted to come here, our connections with foreign countries had been severed, so we can only speak of this aspect of our relations with foreign scientists in view of plans for the future. But these relations must, of course, be deemed a normal and sound condition of the work of any academic institute, because science throughout the world comprises one indivisible whole. If an academic institute wishes to claim a leading position, workers not only of its own country but also those from abroad must aspire to come to work in it. This will serve as an objective proof that a leading "great" science is being conducted at the Institute.

The leading academic institutes have one more sphere of influence on our culture and science—that of training scientific workers.

Only the Institute itself can train its future personnel, and it must do so with great diligence, by gradually nurturing them from youth. For this reason, the post-graduate institute which we have set up must be welcomed and supported by every means.

We started developing the method of selection used at our Institute only two or three years before the war so it is as yet difficult to say what results it will yield. It consists of the following. Taking advantage of the fact that we possess greater amounts of liquid helium for experiments at low temperatures than the refrigerating laboratories of the whole world put together, we were in a position to set up a workshop at the Institute, which is attended by every student of the Moscow University School of Physics. Of course, at first this workshop was organized for the best students only, but during the last two years every physics student without exception passed through it, each working on two or three laboratory themes with liquid helium. From the point of view of criogene institutes this is a luxury. For instance, at the Leiden and other laboratories, work with liquid helium is even now considered inaccessible to many scientists, whereas at our Institute every student of the Moscow University had the opportunity to work on such problems as, for example, the properties of super-conductors and magnetic phenomena at temperatures approaching absolute zero.

Naturally, the University welcomed this opportunity and sent their students to us willingly. In the process of the work of the practicum the following system was established: the best students were noted and, if they so desired, were allowed to work on more than the three allotted problems. The scientists supervising the work of the practicum gave them advice; the best students were sent for consultation to me. Thus we were in a position to note our most capable students, establish a closer contact with them from the beginning of their third or fourth university year, and watch them. Later we invited the best of them to do their practical work at our Institute. In this capacity they took part in the research work as junior laboratory assistants, helped our scientific workers in their experiments, kept notes, set up the simpler apparatus, etc. The selection for graduate work was then made from amongst these students, not only on the basis of their answers at the examination, but also by taking into consideration how the candidates had shown up in their work at the Institute. Of course this method of selecting young scientists makes it possible to embrace a larger circle of youths and eliminates the accidental element. At this point our experiment was interrupted by the war but had we been able to continue, it would have developed along the following lines: having completed their graduate work and obtained their Master's degree, these young scientists would have gone to other scientific institutions and spread the scientific experience of our Institute. Further, it is most probable that one out of ten, or one out of fifteen of these students, on completing his graduate work, would have proved sufficiently talented to remain on the main scientific staff of our Institute. Thus, the Institute would have grown.

This method of observing young students from the time they are at the University, the thorough and constant verification of their abilities is, in my opinion, the only correct way of selecting young scientific workers. We must spare no efforts in this work, not only because the young workers represent our future but because they represent our present. As you grow older, it is only young people, only your pupils, who can save you from premature mental staleness. Of course, every pupil must know more about the field in which he is working than his teacher. And who teaches the teacher, but his pupils? Thanks to his experience the teacher supervises the general course of the work, but he is taught by his pupils, who deepen his knowledge and extend his scope. Without pupils the scientist very soon dies as a creative unit and ceases to advance. I have never forgotten the words of my former teacher Rutherford: "Kapitsa," he would say, "do you know, it is only because of my pupils that I, too, feel so young." And as I myself am approaching old age, I feel that intercourse with youth must be the modus vivendi, safeguarding one from withering away and insuring the maintenance of courage and interest in all that is new and advanced in science. Conservatism in science is worse than premature death to a scientist; it acts as a brake on the development of science.

The propaganda of science is not merely a recounting of ideas in simpler language. It is a creative process, because it is not quite so clear and easy to see for oneself and explain to others how any particular scientific achievement is likely to influence the development of science, technology and culture as a whole.

I always try to encourage the most extensive discussion of all scientific work and when disputes arose at our scientific meetings I not only never objected but considered it a good thing to egg on disputants somewhat, to make them argue in earnest. Any, even the most extensive, discussions of scientific work must be welcomed. The more disputes, the greater the contradictions; the keener the disputes, the greater the stimuli for the healthy development of scientific thought.

Many people think that all scientific work must be immediately and directly applied to technology. This approach is naive and leads to harmful simplification. Even the superficial study of the history of science and culture shows that every great science inevitably influences not only technology, but the whole mode of our life as well. It is perfectly clear that such modern weapons of human culture as the dynamo, telephone, etc., were only possible owing to Faraday's fundamental works and discoveries. But it is quite obvious that we cannot insist upon the Faradays themselves building the dynamo and telephone. Faraday did not possess an engineering turn of mind, nor was the industry of his time ready to materialize all his ideas. Bell, Siemens, Edison and other great engineers did it some few decades later. There are many such examples. But the fact that Faraday did not embody his ideas in technology does not in any way belittle his highly gifted discoveries of the laws and properties of electric current. In our country the achievements of science are often judged by their practical results, and it appears that he who plucks the apple does the principal work, whereas, as a matter of fact, it was he who planted the apple tree which produced the apple.

AN AMERICAN SCIENTIST REPORTS *

The invitation to scientists from many nations to attend the 220th anniversary of the founding of the Academy of Sciences of the U.S.S.R. within a month after the end of the war against Germany proves the desire of the Soviet government to cooperate in a constructive way with other nations. It also shows that the Soviet government gives extremely high priority to pure science. The work done in the eighty-seven Institutes of the Academy of Sciences of the U.S.S.R. is mainly of fundamental type. There is every indication that it is based on a very long-range view of the importance of science in a nation which expects a continuous improvement in the standard of living over a long period of years. At the meetings at various Institutes, American scientists were told freely of the work done in the fields of pure science where the Russians have already made contributions of major importance. Nothing was asked in return, except our friendship and good will. The scientific meetings at the Academy were entirely in Russian, but they were of a general nature and were all translated into English and French, so that you could read the English as you went along.

I visited the Institute of Inorganic Chemistry and the Physical Institute of the University of Moscow. The thing that impressed me most was the extent to which they were working on pure science. The Institutes had no connection with industry. They were devoted to problems in pure science. Many of them had a good start toward the inclusion of technical problems. For example, they were working on the chemical reaction of combustion, studying the most detailed reaction of oxygen and hydrogen at high pressures. A new building was going to be put up for the study of explosions. They were doing fundamental research on an important problem which was not only interesting from a scientific point of view, but which would have ultimately important practical application.

The thing which struck me most in the Soviet Union, outside of their

* Irving Langmuir, address reported in *Science in the Soviet Union*, Bulletin of the American-Soviet Science Society, October, 1945, pp. 3-4.

important scientific work, is the great emphasis which the Soviet government places upon providing incentives to bring forth the best abilities of every individual. In our own country the growth of our industries, and the developments which have made possible our high standard of living, have been based on incentives supplied through the profit motive. In the Soviet Union many clever schemes have been devised which provide even stronger incentives. It is taken for granted that a skilled worker or a scientist who is capable of directing important projects should be able to obtain more rationed food and other goods. For instance, he can get a better house, more and better clothing, or an automobile with a chauffeur. The use of a rationing system to provide incentives removes much of the importance which is attached in our country to money. As far as I could observe, this system of incentives seems to be working very effectively in the Soviet Union.

Another thing that impressed us all is that there are no signs of undernourishment and everybody looked very healthy, robust and full of energy. The Soviet Union . . . will advance in science and will go ahead very fast and very effectively. I think there is every chance that they will be the foremost nation in the world, along with America, in the advancement of science.

FREEDOM IN SOVIET SCIENCE *

It is somewhat difficult to get an objective view of the state of science in the Soviet Union. On the one hand, along with genuine records of fine achievements, exaggerated stories of Soviet discovery and invention are put about. Typical communist success stories, did you say? We Europeans are often amused to read newspaper cables from the U.S.A. claiming credit for American discoveries which had actually been made in Europe some years earlier. And no doubt you have your laughs at similar stories from capitalist Europe.

As against this, we are told that science is at a very low ebb in the Soviet Union. No research is encouraged except what is thought to be of immediate value to industry, agriculture, or war. No theory may be published which does not conform with the canons of dialectical materialism. The intellectual liberty which is an essential condition of scientific progress is completely absent. And so on. One of the most important and successful lines of German propaganda in preparation for the war was the spreading of such views as the above, with the object of preventing any co-operation of the British and French ruling classes and the Soviet Union, which could have prevented the outbreak of the war.

As a matter of fact some branches of science are highly developed in the

* J. B. S. Haldane, "Soviet Science," *Soviet Russia Today,* December, 1940, Vol. IX, No. 8, pp. 9, 11, and 32.

USSR, and others rather poorly. Thus physical chemistry is making great strides. Semenov's work on gas reactions is of the first importance. On the other hand, research along the lines of classical organic chemistry is unimportant, in spite of the good work of pre-revolutionary Russian chemists such as Reformatsky. In mathematics very little is being done on such favorite American topics as group theory, but in the study of probability the Soviet Union seems to be ahead of America. It is easy, for propaganda purposes on either side, to pick on the bright or dark patches. In a general way Russian science resembles American science forty years ago. Many of the leaders are training students in a number of different subjects rather than concentrating on one line of research. So many new institutions are being opened that a larger number of second-rate men and women are obtaining posts than in England before the war, or America today, where expansion is or was much less rapid. We may look for a gigantic flowering of Soviet science in another generation, corresponding to that of America in the last fifteen years, but on a considerably larger scale, since the opportunities for education are more widespread.

Nevertheless even today the Soviet Union is leading the world in certain branches of science. In geography the Soviet Arctic explorers have taken the lead which was held by such men as Peary and Amundsen. In cryology (the study of cold) Soviet scientists are ahead of the rest of the world in methods of separating gases from mixtures by liquefaction and fractional evaporation. Their work on soils and their transformation is superior to that of other countries, though here it must be admitted that Glinku laid the foundations before the revolution, and so in many other branches. In the rest of this article I shall deal with Soviet genetics, my own branch of science, of which I naturally know most.

Let us begin with the criticisms which have been made. Two first-rate Russian geneticists have refused to return to their country and are occupying positions elsewhere.

In the Soviet Union some have lost their posts. And Lysenko, who is admitted to be a first-rate plant physiologist, has attacked the basic theories of genetics.

Now let us look at the credit side. Under the guidance of Vavilov an immense mass of data on the genetics of cultivated plants has been accumulated. His school has also studied the related wild plants not only in the Soviet Union, but as far away as Abyssinia and Peru. This work has led to some very important results. Vavilov was the first to formulate the law of homologous variation in related species, now confirmed and extended by Sturtevant and other workers in America. He determined the places of origin of our more important cultivated plants. This was done under the direct stimulus of Marxist theory, according to which the domestication of these plants was a far more important historical (or rather prehistorical) event than the wars and other political happenings with which written history is mainly concerned. Special attention was paid to the evolution of weeds. These may evolve into cultivated plants. Thus rye is a weed in the wheat crop in warm climates, forms a mixed crop with wheat in primitive agriculture at intermediate temperatures, and replaces wheat in the north or on mountains.

A vast amount of detailed observation of plant chromosomes was done by Levitsky, Navashin, and others. This was necessary for Vavilov's work, and has put the whole question of crop plant hybridization on a more scientific basis. A number of very remarkable hybrids, for example between wheat and couch grass, are now being tested out.

In the field of fruit genetics we may notice Rybin's synthesis of the plum from the hybridization of the wild cherry-plum and sloe. There can be little doubt that our cultivated plums originated in this way. On the other hand Soviet geneticists have done little or nothing on the genetics of ornamental plants such as the sweet pea, the poppy, and the various *Primulas,* which have led to important theoretical results elsewhere. They have concentrated on economically important plants, though their studies of them have been very thorough, and have included problems of no immediate economic importance.

In animal genetics, Soviet workers on poultry such as Serebrovsky have covered much the same field as those of other lands, but as regards sheep, cattle, camels, and other larger animals, they are in a class by themselves. For example Vassin is now mapping the genes on sheep chromosomes. The large scale of Soviet animal husbandry makes artificial insemination on a vast scale possible. A single ram or bull may have several thousand children available for study. A particularly interesting line is the study of the biochemical differences between and within breeds. For example the blood chemistry of race-horses and cart-horses is compared, and also that of efficient and inefficient members of the two breeds. Nothing of this kind is being done elsewhere.

"Formal genetics," as it is called in Russia, received a great impetus from the visits of C. B. Bridges and H. J. Muller, two leading American geneticists, who introduced *Drosophila* to the Soviet Union. This little fly gets through 30 or more generations a year, and you can grow 400 in a milk bottle, so it is uniquely suited for the study of inheritance. Russian workers took it up enthusiastically, but much of their work was inspired by Muller, and was of the same general character as similar work done in the U.S.A. However one group took up the genetical analysis of populations, which had been started by Soviet poultry geneticists, and applied it to *Drosophila* populations. It turns out that although the flies look alike, large numbers of them carry concealed recessive genes. So when their offspring are inbred, a great variety of abnormal insects is produced. This line of work was started by Tsetverikov, but carried on, on a vast scale, by Dubinin and others. It has been confirmed on a smaller scale in the U.S.A. and Britain, and has led to new perspectives, both of evolution and of human congenital disease.

Let us now look at the criticisms against this background of solid and often brilliant achievement. Dobzhansky and Timofeev-Ressovsky got good jobs abroad, as dozens of British scientists have done in the last twenty years without any suggestion that British science is persecuted. Of three dismissed workers two had not done work of great originality. But several good British geneticists have recently lost their posts, one for marrying a Chinese wife, another for trying to expose corruption in an institute, and a third for disproving one of his professor's pet theories. Similar events have occurred in America.

Lysenko's attack on genetics is much more interesting. The public in the Soviet Union is intensely interested in biological problems, and Lysenko's attacks were widely reported in the daily newspapers. Now such attacks are not uncommon. Professor Jeffrey of Harvard has attacked genetical science much less temperately and on much flimsier evidence than Lysenko. So has Professor MacBride in London. But such attacks are not hot news in New York or London, because the publics of those cities are much less interested in genetics than is that of Moscow. Some of Lysenko's points are, I think, valid against genetics as often taught, rather than against the theories held by competent geneticists. He was quite right in saying that so-called pure lines of plants are generally mixtures, and that an exact three to one ratio in accordance with Mendel's law is very rarely obtained. He also stated that in tomatoes and related plants a number of characters described as hereditary can be propagated by grafting. In just the same way Little, Bittner, and other workers at Bar Harbor, Maine, found that the tendency to breast cancer in mice, formerly regarded as hereditary, was largely transmitted through the mother's milk. Lysenko further pointed out that a great deal of successful animal and plant breeding is carried out without any reference to the results of genetical research in the last forty years, and that geneticists have made exaggerated claims for the economic value of their science. In both cases he was right, though the economic value of genetics is greater than he thinks.

I am convinced that he went much too far both in his attack on the chromosome theory, and in his claims concerning the possibility of transferring characters by grafting. But what has been the result of his attacks? Vavilov was their chief target. Vavilov still directs research on a vast scale. So far from having been muzzled for his alleged anti-Darwinian views he communicated seventeen papers on genetical topics to the Moscow Academy of Sciences between January 1st and April 10th of 1940. Lysenko attacked "formal genetics," that is to say genetics which is concerned with such questions as locating genes in chromosomes, rather than in finding out how they act in the development of an individual, or arise and spread during the evolution of a species. It may be that under the stimulus of so brilliant a teacher as Muller, an unduly large fraction of the younger Soviet geneticists had occupied themselves with formal genetics. However that may be, formal genetics goes on in the Soviet Union, and the output of work in this field is a good deal larger than in England, even before the war.

In the controversy between Vavilov and Lysenko, I would personally give Vavilov best on most points. Nevertheless I welcome the controversy, and wish that similar debates elsewhere were given equal publicity. I have little doubt that when I taught genetics (owing to the war I no longer do so) I made a number of misleading statements. I should be a better teacher if these were pointed out in a public debate to which I could reply. But in England things are done differently. Five years ago there were two professors of genetics in England. Now there is none. These chairs were not suppressed as the consequence of a public debate, but in all probability as a result of some old gentlemen talking the matter over privately after a good dinner. If my science must be attacked, I prefer the democratic Soviet method.

I think the position of genetics is fairly typical of that of Soviet science in general. Large-scale work, so far as possible, is concentrated on organisms, substances, or processes, which may be of economic importance; but a great deal of latitude is allowed. Any knowledge about cows, coal, gas explosions, or arctic ice, may be of value some day. So there is no restriction on what is investigated. If basic principles can only be worked out on economically unimportant objects such as *Drosophila,* then these are used. In all research the historical angle is stressed so far as possible, whether it be a question of human history as in the case of Vavilov's work on crops, or of changes in insect populations, as in Dubinin's. This latter tendency, along with a distrust of over-mechanical theories, is no doubt an effect of dialectical materialism, and to my mind a desirable one.

But as dialectical materialism is a method of thought and action, not a dogma, it is hard to see how it could influence decisions on such controversies as this, even were every Soviet scientist compelled to adhere to this philosophy (which is of course not the case), except indeed by suggesting that certain possibilities should be explored. Anyone who studies the record of the genetical controversy, and particularly of the discussion, will certainly realize that thought on scientific topics is pretty free in Moscow.

PHYSICS IN THE SOVIET UNION *

Within the next few years Soviet physicists intend to concentrate on the basic problems of science brought forth by new developments, the solution of which will open up new perspectives in the study and utilization of nature.

* A. Joffe, "The Main Problems of Physics in the U.S.S.R.," *Scientific Monthly,* August, 1945, Vol. LXI, pp. 154–6. Translated and condensed by the American Russian Institute from *Izvestia,* November 25, 1944.

The research work of the last decade proved the existence of two types of cosmic rays: light electrons and mesotrons two hundred times heavier. Academicians A. I. Alikhanov and A. I. Alikhanian discovered in the composition of cosmic rays a new, third component. The study of the physical nature of these particles will comprise the most important problem of the expedition of 1945.

Long before the war, the French physicist Auger had already discovered at great heights showers of particles, covering an area of dozens of square meters. The total energy of all the particles of such a shower is so great that we do not know any one source in nature which could create it. The largest known concentration of energy is the heavy atom of uranium, where there is a concentration up to 0.3 ergs. Auger observed showers of thousands of ergs, and A. I. Alikhanov and A. I. Alikhanian, during this year's expedition, observed showers of hundreds of thousands of ergs. We are faced with a riddle, the solution of which may change our views on the structure of the universe.

Academician O. U. Schmidt brought forward a new theory of the origin of the earth and other planets through the accumulation of universal dust, which adhered to the planets while they were revolving around the sun, and through the participation of the entire solar system in the revolving of our galaxy. He has already provided a number of convincing proofs of his contentions. Their mathematical development is our next problem and Soviet scientists are going to work on it now.

Questions pertaining to the history of the earth are connected with the properties of the earth's crust, with the origin of earthquakes, with the composition of the upper strata and the finding of valuable minerals in them (especially in the Soviet Union). All means at the disposal of physics will be used for the solution of this problem: seismic waves, created by explosions; radio waves; and electric, magnetic, and thermal prospecting. The expeditions which were conducted by the Academy of Sciences in the Second Baku, in Bukhara, and especially, the expedition this year on the Apsheron Peninsula and on the Caspian Sea, assure the success of the work scheduled for next year. Next year we expect to be able to publish conclusions on the research work conducted during the past few years on the process of the movement of air-layers and their intermingling in the atmosphere; on the nature of fogs and mists.

The work connected with the complete solar eclipse of 1945 is of special importance. Many properties of the solar atmosphere, concealed from us by the bright light of the sun, can be studied only during an eclipse. Sixteen scientific institutions will participate in the study of the eclipse of 1945.

At all times, the most important problem of physicists and chemists has consisted of the study of the properties of substances, for the purpose of mastering them and developing technological materials with the necessary properties. Soviet physicists succeeded in solving a number of such problems. They are responsible for establishing the basic laws and physical theories which explain the mechanical and electrical properties of crystals and glasses, polymers (rubber materials, plastics), electric insulators and semiconductors.

During the past few years Soviet physicists developed new, valuable, and easily obtainable materials: frost-resisting rubber, heat-resisting "escapon" (a product of synthetic rubber) which is at the same time a wonderful insulator in radio and many other fields. Somewhat earlier Soviet physicists introduced polysterole and titanium dioxide, which later became widespread in the electrotechnical field. All of these products are being manufactured successfully by our factories and aid in solving many difficult technological problems.

The new semiconducting materials have—in the hands of Soviet physicists—increased tenfold the current in solid rectifiers of alternating current, in solid photoelements and thermoelements. The work, which has been interrupted by the war, will be resumed next year. In addition to the solution of practical problems, our theoretical understanding of the properties of semiconductors has become richer and more profound. And this opens up new, still unused means for improving the quality of products and their properties.

The phenomenon of luminescence by way of irradiation with an electron beam, as well as by using some chemical and physiological agents, has been known for some time. But only of late have they acquired an extensive practical significance in war work, in the technique of illumination. The fluorescent lamps, which convert the invisible ultraviolet rays into visible light, made it possible to use the light of the gas discharge instead of the heated steel wire. This makes for a great economy of electric energy and makes it possible to create light of any tint. Soviet scientists succeeded in creating conditions under which one may accumulate in phosphors large deposits of lighting energy and with a good coefficient of efficiency utilize this accumulated supply. The study of such phenomena, projected for next year, will clarify their mechanism and bring us to still more perfect kinds of phosphors.

This utilization of spectral analysis in our metal industry, in the fuel and chemical industries is being widely developed.

The most important discovery of Soviet physicists during the past few years is the superfluidity of liquid helium when it nears absolute zero. Academician P. L. Kapitsa found and proved that under such conditions the viscosity of helium, even if it exists, is billions of times lower than in all other known liquids. That is where all the amazing phenomena come from: for instance, helium in a tube at one and the same time flows in two opposite directions; sounds of two different velocities spread simultaneously, etc.

Here, near absolute zero, new quantum properties are opening up—properties which have created a revolution in physics of the twentieth century. Further research on superfluidity has great fundamental significance.

Thirty years have already gone by since the discovery of another analogous phenomenon, which is still not understood—the phenomenon of the super-conductivity of certain metals near absolute zero. And here, too, Soviet physicists theoretically predicted and proved in practice that there is no inter-mediate state: in the transition from superconductivity to the usual proper-ties the metal breaks up into a number of layers which alternate from one state to another. This discovery creates a new approach to the phenomenon of superconductivity.

Soviet physicists have set themselves large and difficult problems. We are certain of their successful solution. The enthusiasm for work which em-braces our entire country has created among scientists the desire to give all of their strength and knowledge for attaining new heights in science.

SOVIET RESEARCH ON ATOMIC ENERGY *

Worldwide public attention has in recent months been centered on atomic power, a subject once reserved for restricted academic discussion. Today vast economic and social significance is generally attributed to the discovery that certain heavy elements, notably Uranium 235, undergo fission or split-ting on bombardment with slow neutrons, a process which releases such reserves of energy per unit weight that serious consideration of this new energy source for industrial utilization is warranted. Two official reports have admirably summarized the accomplishments of the United States and Great Britain in atomic energy. No such report has been released about Soviet progress in atomic research; there has been considerable dark specu-lation but little light on the subject. How far such a technologically ad-vanced nation as the USSR has progressed in atomic power is a question of wide interest, to laymen as well as to scientists. This brief review of Soviet achievements in the field of nuclear energy attempts to give the answer insofar as it can be ascertained from Russian scientific literature.

It should be remembered that advances in this field are dependent on advances in the whole field of nuclear physics and in allied fields, especially electrical research and physical chemistry.

Nuclear physics research in the Soviet Union received a great impetus with the discovery in 1932 of the neutron by the English scientist Chadwick. However there were some Soviet accomplishments before 1932 which are of great importance. Notable was the use by D. V. Skobeltzn in 1925 of a strong magnetic field in a cloud chamber. This enabled him to study the charge and energy of particles, particularly those induced by cosmic rays. In fact, Skobeltzn demonstrated that associated with cosmic rays are charged

* Gerald Oster, "Research on Atomic Energy in the USSR," *American Review on the Soviet Union,* February, 1946, Vol. VII, pp. 47–50.

particles possessing tremendous energies of the order of several million volts. Another early Soviet discovery was that by L. V. Myssovsky, who in 1927 observed the tracks made by nuclear charged particles in thick photographic emulsions. This technique has been utilized to study the tracks of the fission products of uranium under neutron bombardment.

By 1932, three major Soviet institutes were carrying on extensive nuclear research—the State Radium Institute and the Physico-Technical Institute, both in Leningrad, and the Ukrainian Physico-Technical Institute in Kharkov. Prior to this date there were only fifteen scientists working in this field in the USSR. These institutes have received generous financial support from the Government, in addition to a gift to each institute of one gram of radium.

In 1934, soon after Lawrence's development of the cyclotron in America, the State Radium Institute started construction of a cyclotron. A few cyclotrons have since been built and construction of very large cyclotrons has been continued during the war. A huge 4.5 million volt van de Graaff electrostatic generator was completed in 1937 by the Ukrainian Physico-Technical Institute. Soviet developments of compact electrostatic generators and large ion sources are particularly important in this connection.

Construction of very powerful betatrons is now under consideration in the USSR. Of particular interest is the possibility of utilizing in a betatron Kapitsa's impulse dynamo with which he obtained the highest magnetic field strength ever produced. As an example of coincidence in scientific effort, it is interesting to note that a Soviet paper on the theory and some of the details necessary for the successful operation of the betatron appeared independently of Kerst's development of the betatron in the United States. The construction of betatrons for accelerating electrons with voltages higher than 100 million volts is particularly important in the light of observations on the splitting of nuclei by cosmic rays, a field of investigation in which Soviet scientists have made outstanding contributions. In 1944, a State commission headed by the Armenian physicist A. I. Alichanian was set up to conduct extensive research in cosmic rays and to construct permanent cosmic ray laboratories on high mountain peaks.

Soviet theoretical physicists have made important contributions to the theory of the atomic nucleus. Ivanenko in 1932 was the first to propose on well-founded theoretical grounds the present picture of the nucleus as composed of protons and neutrons. Statistical models of heavy nuclei have helped explain a number of properties of atomic nuclei. Another example of coincidence in scientific effort is the very important paper by J. Frenkel in 1939 on an explanation of nuclear fission worked out independently by Bohr and Wheeler, who proposed a similar explanation at the same time.

There is abundant evidence in Soviet scientific literature of their knowledge of the energies associated with nuclear fission. Studies by Soviet nuclear physicists on the nuclear fission process include studies on the behavior of uranium under bombardment, the spontaneous fission of uranium, and the pair formation in uranium fission.

Chemists have collaborated with nuclear physicists in the identification of fission products, in proposing laws of conservation in nuclear "chemical" reactions, in studying the conditions for explosive nuclear reactions and in the separation of isotopes.

Studies on the separation of isotopes have been carried on for the past ten years in the USSR. In 1937, the Soviet Government established a commission to intensify research on isotope separations. A. E. Brodsky, a member of the commission, has conducted research on the separation of heavy water, an important material in atomic energy production, and on Uranium 235. In a paper in 1939, Brodsky presents complete details of a pilot plant for the separation of heavy hydrogen and oxygen by thermal diffusion. A theory of thermal diffusion for cascade processes is also given. In a review paper in 1940, Brodsky discusses the various methods of preparing heavy water including a successive stage electrolysis method. In 1942 he separated Uranium 235 by thermal diffusion of the hexafluoride of uranium and concluded that the power consumed in the separation process renders this method of obtaining atomic power impractical except where very high concentrations of power are needed. Theoretical studies of the thermal diffusion method have also appeared.

It is important to note that Brodsky's experimental work was carried on at Dnepropetrovsk, site of the gigantic Dneprostroi power project. During the war it was necessary to move this laboratory, like others in Leningrad and Kharkov, to Siberia.

There has not been considered in this short review the important Soviet discoveries in cosmic ray research, in investigations of B-ray spectra, in nuclear scattering of neutrons and in metastable energy states of nuclei. However, sufficient references have been given to indicate the Soviet contributions to nuclear research.

Certain characteristics of the nuclear research of Soviet scientists are immediately apparent to anyone studying their technical papers. Among these are the rapid increase in the quality and quantity of their output, the freedom to publish and discuss their work, and the large Government support of pure research. It is of interest to note that most of the extensive cosmic ray studies carried on in the Soviet Union during the war did not have a direct bearing on the war effort but may ultimately be of considerable importance for the whole world in the production of cheap atomic power.

THE ORGANIZATION OF SOVIET MEDICINE *

On July 11, 1943, the Soviet Union celebrated the twenty-fifth anniversary of the foundation of its first People's Commissariat of Public Health. At the time of the October Revolution emergency conditions prevailed, but the Military-Revolutionary Committee in Petrograd already had its medical division. In February, 1918, a Medical Council was established and then, on July 11, upon Lenin's personal initiative the People's Commissariat of Public Health was founded with N. A. Semashko as its first commissar. This was an event of world significance because it created a totally new type of administrative health agency, one which to the present day has not been paralleled in any other country.

The first years from 1918 to 1922 were extremely difficult. The country was completely disorganized, was torn by civil war, blockade, foreign intervention, famine, and epidemics. The commissariat had to concentrate its efforts on providing medical services to the Red Army and on fighting epidemics, particularly typhus, a more formidable enemy than White Guards and foreign troops combined. But in 1922 the battle was won, and the work of reconstruction along socialist lines began.

The Soviet Union was founded on December 30, 1922 as a federation of Soviet socialist republics. The Constitution ratified in 1923 established People's Commissariats of Public Health in every constituent republic. Decentralization seemed advisable considering the vastness of the territory and the uneven development of the various regions. The central government, however, had the power to establish health policies and the Health Commissar of the Russian Federation of Soviet Socialist Republics was chief sanitary inspector of the Union.

Once the major epidemics were overcome, the chief task was to provide medical facilities and services to the working population in town and country. This was relatively easy in the cities where existing facilities could be used and new ones could be erected without too much difficulty. Where new industries were created, medical centers were established at the same time, and both grew and developed together.

The difficulties were infinitely greater in rural districts. Russia had since 1864 a system of public medical services in rural districts, commonly known as Zemstvo medicine, but facilities were far too inadequate, particularly among the national minorities where they were almost non-existent. Some definite progress already had been achieved in the 1920's, but rural medicine could not be developed fully before the collectivization of agriculture that took place during the period of the First Five-Year Plan.

In tsarist days, the number of physicians and medical institutions had

* Henry E. Sigerist, "Twenty-Five Years of Health Work in the Soviet Union," *American Review of Soviet Medicine,* October, 1943, Vol. I, pp. 67–78.

been shockingly inadequate. And now there was a crying need for more doctors, nurses, hospital beds, sanatoria, dispensaries, for more of everything. This was at a time when all other fields of Soviet activity were also demanding more personnel and equipment. The new industries needed tens of thousands of engineers. The overcoming of illiteracy called for legions of school teachers. The 13 medical schools of tsarist days, all located in the European section of the country, could obviously not satisfy the demand. New medical schools had to be founded over the entire Union and particularly among the national minorities where instruction would be given in the native languages. New schools, however, required new scientific teaching personnel that had to be trained first.

We can easily realize what a superhuman task the Commissariats of Health were facing. It was so big also because the Soviets were always thinking in terms of the whole country. They always refused to develop one section at the expense of another and, on the contrary, concentrated their efforts on the backward regions.

In spite of all difficulties, in 1928, only seven years after the Civil War, the number of physicians had been increased from 19,785 in 1913 to 63,162; the number of general hospital beds from 142,310 to 217,744; of maternity beds from 6,824 to 27,338; of rural health stations from 4,367 to 7,531; of women's and children's consultation bureaus from 9 to 2,151. In 1913 free nursery facilities were available for 550 children while in 1928 the country possessed permanent nursery facilities for 62,054 and seasonal ones for close to 200,000 children.

During the First Five-Year Plan, fulfilled in four years, from 1929 to 1932, all medical facilities were increased. The health budget jumped from 660.8 million rubles in 1928 to 2,549 million in 1933. But industry came first, particularly the heavy industries. They had first claim on manpower and materials. It would have been impossible to increase the number of physicians substantially if women had not enrolled in the medical schools in increasingly large numbers. There was a time when close to 75 per cent of all medical students were women, and today women are playing a very distinguished part and are holding leading positions in every medical field.

During the years of the Second Five-Year Plan, from 1933 to 1937, the Soviet people began to reap the fruits of their labors. The new plants produced large amounts of consumers' goods. Agriculture had been collectivized and food was plentiful. While industries continued to be developed very rapidly and a formidable, highly mechanized Red Army was being built, more funds, more people, and more equipment were available for health work and for cultural purposes. When the war clouds were darkening on the horizon, the army budget had to be increased tremendously, but it is noteworthy that this never led to a curtailment of public health funds. The health budget grew from 2,540 million rubles in 1933 to 9,433 million in 1938 and was 11,960 million in 1941.

The development of health facilities during those years was stupendous. The number of hospital beds was almost doubled, the number of maternity beds trebled. Many lavishly equipped sanatoria were built in the health resorts of the country. New research institutions were founded and the existing ones were enlarged considerably. The number of physicians increased from 76,027 in 1932 to 112,405 in 1938. The progress was not only one in quantity but also in quality. Standards were raised throughout. Medical education was reorganized, producing not only more but better trained physicians. The new hospitals, dispensaries, and rural health centers had much higher standards than in the past. The chief impression of the visitor in 1938 was that there was not only more of everything but everything there was was greatly improved.

These developments continued unabated until the country was engulfed in the war, and since figures speak the most eloquent and at the same time the most objective language, the total growth of health facilities from 1913 to 1941 is best illustrated by the table on page 119.

The constitution of the Soviet Union which was adopted in 1936 created a new health agency, the All-Union People's Commissariat of Public Health. It is the central, federal health agency and the All-Union Commissar of Health is a member of the cabinet, of the Council of People's Commissars.

The People's Commissariat of Public Health of the U.S.S.R. is the apex of the administrative pyramid. It establishes health policies, directs and coordinates the work of the health commissariats of the constituent republics, and attends to health problems that concern the Union as a whole. It is an institution that has no parallel in any other country. No ministry of health anywhere has such great responsibility or such vast power. The commissariat, indeed, is responsible for the health and well-being of 170 million people and controls all health activities, preventive, diagnostic, and curative. But more than this: it also produces the personnel, equipment, and knowledge required for its work.

Like the health departments of other countries, the commissariat is in charge of sanitation and the control of epidemic diseases, and sanitary inspection is one of its important functions. Since all health services are public services, the commissariats—federal and state—are in charge of hospitals, dispensaries, rural health stations, nurseries, sanatoria, health resorts, pharmacies, etc., and of the services they render. The standardization of health institutions has greatly accelerated developments, and the setting of standards [for health services] is one of the important functions of the all-Union commissariat.

The commissariats, furthermore, produce the medical personnel they need. In other words, they are in charge of educational institutions. Requirements and curricula are uniform throughout the country. The U.S.S.R. has today 51 medical, 12 dental and 9 pharmaceutical schools training at the moment 120,000 students. Medical students have a five-year course which is supplemented by a period of three years spent in rural practice. All rural physicians have regular post-graduate courses of several months' duration every three years.

At the outbreak of the war, the medical course was accelerated, very much as it is with us; but in 1942 the accelerated program was abandoned because it was found that a competent physician cannot be trained in less than the normal time.

The Soviet Union has furthermore 985 schools for the training of so-called middle medical personnel, that is, feldshers (medical assistants), midwives, nurses, dental and pharmaceutical assistants.

The commissariat is also responsible for the equipment required for the health work of the nation. In other words, it controls the medical industries, the pharmaceutical industry, and the industries that produce instruments, apparatuses, appliances, and other medical commodities. This also was a very revolutionary step. Patent medicines and swindle drugs, which in every country cause the waste of millions of dollars quite apart from the harm they often inflict, are inconceivable in the U.S.S.R.

Attached to the health commissariat of the U.S.S.R. are 26 All-Union Scientific Research Institutes devoted to the various fields of medicine. They are large, well-equipped and well-staffed research centers combining laboratory and clinical divisions. Foremost among them is the All-Union Institute of Experimental Medicine, commonly called VIEM in its abbreviated form, one of the world's great medical research centers. From these institutes the commissariat draws inspiration, advice, methods, and to them it refers its scientific problems. The heads of these institutes together with other outstanding researchers constitute the Scientific Council of the commissariat. [At the end of 1944, the Academy of Medical Sciences of the U.S.S.R. was established to advance scientific research in medicine.]

Other medical research institutes are attached to the commissariats of the constituent republics, to municipal health departments or similar agencies, and the medical schools obviously all take a very active part in the scientific life of the country. In 1941 the Soviet Union had 223 medical research institutes staffed with 19,550 scientists.

Thus the commissariats of health have great responsibilities and great power. The administration of health, however, is not carried out in a dictatorial way but, on the contrary, most democratically. Special committees of the Medical Workers' Union are in constant touch with the commissariats and no decision concerning medical workers is taken without consultation. Every commissariat has a special bureau for the examination of complaints. Whoever thinks that he did not receive the services to which he is entitled or was not satisfied with the service is free to complain and every case is investigated very carefully.

Every factory, every farm has its health committee that cooperates very closely with the health agencies. Soviet medicine was born with the slogan that the people's health is the concern of the people themselves. It was recognized from the very start that health cannot be forced upon the people, that it cannot be dispensed to the people, that they must want it, and that the best measures are in vain unless they are carried out under broadest participation of the population.

The health program of every civilized nation consists of four major tasks: (1) the promotion of health; (2) the prevention of disease; (3) treatment of the sick; and (4) the rehabilitation of the former patient. Let us discuss briefly how the Soviet Union is handling these problems.

From the first day on, for twenty-five years, the Soviet Union has been carrying on a vigorous campaign of health education. Beginning with the nursery, through kindergarten and school, sound health habits are developed in the children. In youth organizations, in factory and farm, wherever people work, no opportunity is lost to teach health. Hundreds of thousands of men and women are members of health committees in their working places, take an active part in improving the health conditions of their immediate environment and in preparing the health plans of the nation. This is in itself a great educational measure. Mass-feeding in factory kitchens provided an unusual opportunity for improving dietary habits. The radical change in the mode of living effected among backward national minorities had great hygienic consequences.

The development of physical culture on a mass scale was another measure to promote health. The movement has reached millions of people, students, factory and office workers, and farmers alike. Systematic training under medical supervision has greatly contributed to developing a healthy and sturdy generation of men and women "ready for labor and defense."

The energy spent in labor must be restored, and the provision of facilities for rest and recreation is therefore an extremely important public health function. Annual vacations of from two to six weeks, according to occupation, with full pay are good but not enough. Facilities must be created so that the worker can spend his vacation in a way that will give him maximum benefit. In the early days of the revolution, abandoned palaces of the nobility were turned into rest-homes. Since then an endless number of vacation camps, rest-homes, and resorts have been built in the country, at the seaside, and in the mountains. Every Soviet rest-home has physicians and medical facilities attached to it so that minor ailments can be treated before serious illness develops. This is undoubtedly a sound program of human conservation.

The traditional barrier between preventive and curative medicine has been broken down. There are, of course, physicians who are working as public health officers and surgeons who are primarily therapists, but a new attitude has been created in training and practice. Prevention is emphasized all along the line of medical activities, and every clinical case is a reminder that prevention has broken down somewhere. The fact that preventive and curative services are controlled by the same agencies has, of course, greatly contributed to overcoming age-old barriers.

The prevention of infectious diseases is carried out through general epidemiological measures, through sanitation and immunization. The task was gigantic in a country of such magnitude covering vast territories of the Asiatic continent. Tsarist Russia was very backward in sanitation and even Petrograd, the capital, did not possess an adequate water supply in all sections of the city. Smallpox vaccination was far from general in spite of Zemstvo physicians. Thus, in many sections of the country, work had to start from scratch. If we wish to realize how much progress has been achieved in the short period of twenty-five years, we must compare conditions not with those of a small country like England but rather with those of the British Empire, including the Asiatic and African possessions.

Special preventive measures have been developed for the protection of those individuals who physiologically or socially are particularly threatened. Great attention was paid to the protection of motherhood, infancy, and childhood. Not only was every form of discrimination against married women abolished, but special protection was extended by law to pregnant and nursing women, who enjoy many privileges. The country today has 5,803 Women's and Children's Consultation Bureaus where women can get advice for themselves and their children in all their physiological and pathological problems.

The protection of labor, the creation of the best possible working conditions is the responsibility of the trade unions, that is of the workers themselves, a task in which they cooperate very closely with the health authorities. In the U.S.S.R. the All-Union Council of Trade Unions takes the place of our Department of Labor, in other words labor is administered by the workers themselves. They collect and spend the vast social insurance funds amounting to about ten billion rubles a year. One of their tasks is the protection of workers against accidents and disease. Labor inspection is very strict and is carried out by sanitary inspectors and specially trained labor inspectors. They are aided in their task by workers' delegates who in every plant and every shop are elected by their fellow-workers. Every case of occupational disease must be reported and is investigated by specialists. The unions support over 40 research institutes for the protection of labor, many of which have budgets of several million rubles and are equipped with laboratories and clinical divisions.

Periodic examinations of workers take place regularly and their frequency is prescribed by law. In harmful industries, workers must be examined once every six months, in some even once every four months.

Periodic examinations are undoubtedly a very important preventive measure, but it is even more important for a nation to have a system of medical care that encourages people to seek medical advice at the slightest symptom before serious illness has broken out. The Soviet Union has

GROWTH OF MEDICAL FACILITIES IN THE U.S.S.R., 1913–1941

	UNITS	1913	1928	1932	1938	1941
Hospital Facilities (Non-Psychiatric)	Beds City	93,223	158,514	256,158	450,694	491,543
	" Village	49,087	59,230	116,075	153,129	169,888
	" Total	142,310	217,744	372,233	603,823	661,431
Psychiatric Facilities	" City	36,240	30,016	39,945	66,265	73,992
Maternity Hospitals	" City	5,192	18,241	26,984	74,480	75,612
	" Village	1,632	9,097	16,673	60,323	66,261
	" Total	6,824	27,338	43,657	134,803	141,873
Sanatoria and Health Resorts	Institutions	2,000	36,100	63,300	102,000	132,000
Urban Medical Centers	"	1,230	5,673	7,340	12,645	13,461
Rural Medical Centers	"	4,367	7,531	9,883	11,594*	13,512
Tuberculosis Dispensaries and Stations	"	43	498	498	925	1,048
Venereal Disease Dispensaries and Stations	"	12	800	683	1,351	1,498
Women's and Children's Consultation Centers	" City	9	1,383	2,126	3,103	3,499
	" Village	—	768	1,162	1,765	2,304
	" Total	9	2,151	3,288	4,868	5,803
Permanent Nurseries	Capacity City	550	53,748	257,659	460,911	554,448
	" Village	—	8,306	342,519	280,568	299,598
	" Total	550	62,054	600,178	741,479	854,046
Seasonal Nurseries	Capacity Village (in Thousands)	10.6	195	3,929.1	3,242.3	4,045.6
Physicians	Total	19,785	63,162	76,027	112,405	130,348
Health Budget	(In Millions of Rubles)		660.8	2,540.0†	9433.0	11,960.0

* On January 1, 1938.   † For 1933.

realized this by establishing a wide network of what we call medical centers, what they call ambulatoria or polyclinics. This leads us now to a discussion of the treatment of disease, although the distinction is purely artificial since medical centers serve preventive, diagnostic, and therapeutic purposes.

Group medicine practiced through medical centers makes the best possible use of the present advanced technology of medicine and is therefore best adapted to it because of coordination between the services of the general practitioner and those of a wide range of specialists. The Soviet Union from the very start adopted the plan of medical care through medical centers and developed it on a nation-wide scale. Large factories or state farms have their own medical centers, staffed sometimes with more than a hundred doctors representing all specialties. Plants that are too small to justify a fully organized medical center share one with other small plants. Since industries usually develop in the same sections of a city, a large medical center can very well handle the workers of several small factories. In addition to the medical center all factories, whether large or small, obviously have first-aid stations staffed with nurses and a few doctors. Other medical centers serve residential districts. In the cities every district has its complete medical center. The organization of medical care is never rigid but is adapted to local needs.

All doctors are appointed on salaries and the salary is determined by three factors: experience, responsibility, and hazard. They have four weeks' vacation with full pay and frequent post-graduate courses. They see patients at the office and in the homes. In addition to the regular staff, the medical centers have consultants, usually professors of the medical school, who are called for special cases. Private practice has never been forbidden, but the better the public services became, the less demand there was for private physicians so that the private practice of medicine has practically died out.

Some medical centers are directly connected with hospitals, others are not. A rural medical center will usually have its own general hospital and maternity beds, while in the city this may not be advisable. The center should be as easy of access as ever possible, therefore as close to the working place as possible. The factory grounds, however, are usually not the ideal location for a hospital. Patients are therefore hospitalized in institutions of the neighborhood. Large factories often have their own wards in definite hospitals and maternity homes of the city just as they have their own rest-homes and sanatoria.

Rural medical centers are obviously simpler. The medical station of a collective farm with a population of about 800–1000 may have one doctor, one dentist, a few nurses, a couple of midwives, and a dozen beds. This is ample for general medical care and minor surgery. Specialized services are provided by the district hospital, and all health institutions of such a rural district are under the constant supervision of the district health department. The health officer in charge is responsible for all health activities of his district.

By 1941 the Soviet Union had created 13,461 fully organized medical centers in cities and 13,512 medical stations in rural communities giving free medical services to the people, using all means of medical science to protect and restore the people's health. This truly is a great achievement, the greater when we consider the difficulties that had to be overcome and the shortness of time.

From 1918 to 1941 the number of hospital beds was increased almost five times and standards of hospital construction were revised every year. In addition to general hospitals, the country is now well equipped with special hospitals for children, for the treatment. of infectious diseases, chronic diseases, mental diseases, and tuberculosis. And treatments are continued in convalescent homes and sanatoria. No country has ever made such wide use of its natural curative forces, of mineral springs and climatic stations, and the results achieved in the treatment of chronic diseases have been very remarkable. The Soviet Union is today the leading country in the field of balneology and balneotherapy with a central research institute in Moscow and a number of other research institutions in various health resorts.

Physical restoration is not the final goal of the physician's activities. No patient can be considered cured before he has been restored socially, and in this field, the Soviet Union has done pioneer work also. This was to be expected since the rehabilitation of the patient serves the individual's welfare as well as that of society. Every effort is made to reintegrate the former patient into society and to prevent the skilled worker from dropping into the ranks of unskilled labor as the result of physical disability.

In every factory one can find highly handicapped workers, blind men, cripples, former tuberculosis patients performing skilled labor, and many factories have special workshops for them where the conveyer belt moves more slowly. Most factories have diet kitchens, and the costs involved by such special provisions are met from social insurance funds. Disabled craftsmen join cooperatives where they can continue their work with government aid. And when a man's disability does not permit him to resume his former occupation, he is trained for the work for which he is best fitted at government expense.

In war time, every country does a great deal of rehabilitation work, and the U.S.S.R. probably more than any other country. But in the Soviet Union, rehabilitation is carried out in peace as in war. It is considered one, and not the least important, aspect of the general health program.

Thus from 1919 to 1941 . . . the country stubbornly and planfully built up its health system, built it along new lines as a public service to which the people, all the people, are entitled. It created the social organization that the modern technology of medicine required if medical progress was not to be wasted. . . . Plans had been made that foresaw more of everything, more personnel and more equipment and still higher standards. . . . And then, suddenly on June 22, 1941 the Nazi hordes invaded the country and the Soviet people found themselves plunged into the turmoil of the war.

. . . Over night the entire health system was geared to war. Military medicine had always been a subject of instruction in medical schools, and all physicians, men and women, were prepared to take their place without delay in the armed forces, in war industries, or wherever their services were needed most urgently. Medical centers had always been an integral part of industrial plants. When industries had to be moved to other sections of the country, the medical centers were moved with them, and where new industries developed medical facilities were created at the same time.

Medical research had always been carried on in a coordinated and planful way, and the Scientific Council could therefore without delay concentrate on problems of war medicine and mobilize all research institutions of the country for the purpose. The government took a very wise step in appointing the chairman of the Scientific Council, N. N. Burdenko, surgeon general of the Red Army.

Even so, the difficulties that had to be overcome were gigantic. The loss of territory deprived the country of essential resources and the systematic destruction carried out by the Nazis exceeds all imagination. The Soviet Union is facing a tremendous task of reconstruction.

★ 6 ★

Soviet Art, Music, and Literature

CREATIVE ARTS IN THE U.S.S.R.*

Maxim Gorki coined a singing phrase to describe the function of the creative artist. He is, Gorki said, "the engineer of the human soul." That phrase fits very well the attitude of the contemporary Russian writer, or composer, or artist of any sort, towards himself. It is, by our lights, a self-conscious attitude. And yet it is one which connotes a great sense of responsibility—to fellow men, to fellow artists, to art itself, to posterity.

The first thing that needs to be said about these earnest engineers, is that they work terrifically, amazingly hard. They are absolute slaves to their various arts. Early this year I asked Aram Khachaturian, who after Shostakovich and Prokofiev is generally regarded as the third-ranking Soviet composer, what he was doing at the time. "Oh," he said in a most apologetic way, "I am doing very little just now. I am writing a song cycle, which I will call *Three Airs,* with orchestra; finishing up the music for the film *Girl Number 217;* working on an *Overture for 1944;* staging my ballet *Gayane;* and writing a concerto for 'cello. I am very lazy." This year in Moscow four works by Prokofiev, and incidentally four large and important ones, any one of which would have satisfied most composers for a pair of seasons, were heard in a single season. They were his Fifth Symphony, the musical score for Sergei Eisenstein's monumental moving picture *Ivan the Terrible,* an opera based on Tolstoi's *War and Peace,* and the music for an evening-long ballet, *Cinderella.* He wrote the film score in between the first draft and orchestration of his Fifth Symphony; during rehearsals of *War and Peace* worked on a violin sonata; and three days before the premiere of his Fifth he told me about plans for his Sixth Symphony. This extraordinary output is also characteristic of Russian writers. Konstantine Simonov, whose novel about Stalingrad, *Days and Nights,* was published in this country, . . . is famous in Russia as a poet, a novelist, a playwright, a journalist, a pamphleteer, and a writer of film scenarios—and at thirty he has a large body of works in each capacity. During the war he has worked, literally, as hard as six men. And in his desk at home he has

* John Hersey, "Creative Arts in the U.S.S.R.," Address at *New York Herald Tribune* Forum, October 30, 1945.

two hundred notebooks full of jottings about the war. He intends to spend the next year going through them, and then he wants to write a large work —to which, as he puts it, *Days and Nights* will be "no more than a preface."

The second important thing about Russian creative artists is the closeness with which they work together. Each of the arts has a "Union," which is not a trade union in our sense of the word, but rather a guild dedicated to the greatest possible, and best possible, productivity on the part of each member.

A third notable thing . . . is the self-criticism and group criticism in which Russian artists indulge. In all the arts, frequent sittings are held for the purpose of mutual criticism. No important work in music or literature or painting or the theater or ballet is presented to the public before the work is thoroughly criticized in such a sitting. By chance I got, one evening, some first-hand insight into the workings of this group criticism. I had heard a lot about sittings of the Writers' Union, and had expressed a wish to see one. I was delighted finally to be invited to a sitting—delighted, that is, until I discovered that the meeting was going to discuss a novel I had written. That night a group of about twenty-five Russian writers, critics and editors gathered around a long, oval, felt-covered table. At each place there was a tea cup and a wine glass, and there were plates of chocolates and cookies scattered along the table. There were also business-like pads and pencils at each place. I was invited to say a few words. Then, one by one, the writers spoke about the book. Their remarks were perfectly frank. They seemed not at all inhibited by the fact that I was a foreigner. They were brutal but tactful: there were many literary allusions during the evening, but not one of them was to the work of a Russian writer—every one was to some American or English writer. The speakers catalogued the things they liked very specifically, exactly and, I may say, briefly. Then, at greater length, they spared no words in attacking the things they did not like. . . The surprising thing to me was the amount of study and thought they had put into the evening. Each person present had read the book. Several had read it in English. Each man knew exactly what he was going to say; some had extensive notes. I must confess that no single American professional writer has ever paid me the compliment of putting so much effort and consideration into lambasting anything I have put on paper.

The literary allusions to American and English writers that evening suggest a fourth point of interest about Russian artists. This is the care with which they study all the work which is done abroad in their various fields of endeavor. While I was in Moscow there was a sitting of the Composers Union at which the composers spent a whole evening listening to newly arrived recordings of Roy Harris's *Third Symphony* and Barber's *Adagio for Strings,* and they discussed the music as passionately and critically as if it had been their own work. In *Days and Nights,* the Simonov novel, . . there is a passage in which the author has some soldiers, sitting in a dismal dugout in Stalingrad, discussing moving pictures. They do not talk about Russian actors, of which there are plenty of good ones. They talk about Charlie Chaplin and Buster Keaton. Russian writers keep extraordinarily current on American literature. Most American writers have studied fairly carefully, I imagine, the writings of Tolstoi, Dostoievski and Chekhov. I doubt, though, whether they have put in much time on other great Russian writers like Gogol, Gorki and Pushkin, much less on our contemporaries, Simonov, Sobolev, Leonov, and that giant, Sholokhov—although work by all of them is available in English. I know I certainly haven't put as much time in on those Russian contemporaries as they have on American writers.

The fifth point I would like to make is that Russian creative artists are among the most wealthy, influential and honored people in the Soviet Union. This fact both rewards them for their hard work and constantly reminds them of their responsibilities as engineers. The best paid people in Russia today, aside from the highest ranking officers of state and army, are writers, composers, actors, movie stars, musicians, architects, directors, painters, sculptors and dancers. Last year Dmitri Shostakovich earned about 250,000 rubles —at the standard rate of exchange, $50,000. Taxes are figured on separate items of income in Russia, and are not as steeply cumulative as they are here. Furthermore, because he was awarded the Order of the Red Banner early in the war, Shostakovich is excused income taxes on the first $14,000 of his income, and all his taxes put together did not amount to more than $5,000. Shostakovich has twice won the Stalin prize of $20,000, which is wholly tax free, and having been a Stalin prize winner entitles him for the rest of his life to a 35% reduction on everything he buys in so-called "commercial stores" in Russia. Like all wealthy Soviet citizens, he has given away large chunks of his income to various relatives, and to war and relief enterprises. He has also contributed generously to the "war loan," which corresponds roughly to our war bonds. He still has enough left over to live very well indeed. There are some things, however, which no amount of rubles have been able to buy in wartime Russia. Most of these things the government gives to creative artists like Shostakovich. His large and light four-room apartment in Moscow was given him by the Moscow Soviet. Shostakovich, who was born in Leningrad and is a fiery patriot of that city, also has had an apartment awarded him there. The government has given Shostakovich a car. The composer gets special privileges in food and clothing rations. He is given a summer place on the composers' country estate at Ivanovo to which Russia's best composers retire each summer to write and rest. Shostakovich has four pianos—two Steinways in his Moscow apartment and two Bluthners in Leningrad; one of the latter he considers the best piano in the Soviet Union. Besides rubles and chattels, Shostakovich enjoys considerable position. He has been awarded by the Supreme Soviet the title of "Merited Art Worker," which, along with the words "Professor" and "Laureate of the Stalin Prize," appears beside his name on all programs and in all newspapers.

He is a deputy of the Leningrad Soviet. He wears on his civilian lapel, beside the ribbon for the Order of the Red Banner, a ribbon for the medal for the defense of Leningrad. As consultant of the Committee of Art of the Praesidium of the Supreme Soviet, he has a finger in final decisions on artistic rewards, censorship and general policy. As a member of the organizational committee of the Composers' Union, he helps form all specific music policy and helps dispose of the important musicians' fund. Shostakovich and his fellow artists have as well a social standing comparable to that enjoyed in America in the nineties by the Astors, Vanderbilts and Harrimans. At great state receptions like those on Red Army Day or the anniversary of the October Revolution, the crowd of honored guests consists of government officials like Molotov and Mikoyan, military men like Marshal Voroshilov and Admiral Kuznetsov—and then, exclusively, composers, writers, singers, actors and the rest of the aristocracy of talent, men and women like Shostakovich and his wife. Shostakovich and his colleagues, quite understandably, approve of all this.

One final observation. Russian creative artists these days seem to know exactly what they are doing and what they want to do. They plan far ahead. One night in Moscow a group of us heard a most revealing program set forth by Vishnevsky, a distinguished playwright who during the war has been a naval officer and has written mostly about the Baltic Sea and the defense of Leningrad. Speaking specifically for the magazine, *Znamya*, of which he is an editor, but inferentially for all Russian writers, he said that Russia's postwar literature would, first, gather from partisans, soldiers, sailors, officers and workers the whole truth about the war; second, glorify Russia's heroic traditions; third, promote "Slavism," and see to it that the German enemy, which has twice fought Russia, would never divide the Slavic peoples again; fourth, memorialize German bestiality as it was revealed at Lidice and Maidanek; fifth, explore human honor, conscience and soul; sixth, call on Russians for a new effort of creativeness and rouse them to transfer the heroism they have shown in war to achievements in peace; and seventh, Vishnevsky said, learn more about England and America, whose aid in the war would not be forgotten. "We shall talk," he said, "plainly, clearly and with polemical incisiveness, and we shall expect our British and American colleagues to speak to us in the same language and in the same spirit." I think we owe it to our Russian colleagues, and to ourselves, to speak to them in that way, but before we do, we must gather our facts, clean our pens, and arrange our thoughts. There is much creative work, and some great creative work, being done in Russia these days. It is a challenge, I think, to that spirit of enterprise and competition which we like to think of as typically American.

THE POPULARITY OF THE ARTS *

Shortly before my departure from Moscow, in the course of a visit to a girl's high school, I attended a senior class in literature. The subject under discussion was Chekov's plays. Girl after girl, appraising the character of Chekov's heroes and heroines, spoke of them as "these dear and kindly noblemen," "these tender and helpless noblewomen."

This was new language for high-school seniors in Soviet schools. It had none of the flagrant class bias and class bitterness which surcharged the study of every subject, and particularly literature, in the '20s and early '30s. All the more impressive was the language of these girls because they lived in a factory district and were overwhelmingly daughters of factory workers, than whom there are no more class-minded folk in Russia.

Yet so far removed were they intellectually from former generations of high-school seniors that their language throbbed with tenderness and compassion for the pre-Soviet "lost generation" of Russians, as Chekov portrayed them. To these girls, the gentlemen and ladies of "The Cherry Orchard," "The Three Sisters," "The Sea Gull" or "Uncle Vanya" were no class enemies but human beings who could never fulfill themselves and whose nobility of character and beauty of soul were corroded by idleness and maladjustment, by words and dreams, which never came true, never could come true, because it was not within their power to change the conditions of life which made them what they were. The discussion of Chekov by this class of seniors was one of the most startling experiences of my year and a half in Russia.

This human approach to literary characters in both Russian and foreign classics is only one aspect of the new intellectual ferment that is shaking out of the Russian mentality a host of ideas and preconceptions which once were deemed unchallengeable and infallible. The new attitude toward history and the study of history is equally astounding. I doubt if any people in the world are more history-minded than are the Russians of today. Again and again in the last three tragic and decisive years history has been invoked as guide and comforter. No effort is spared to unravel and emphasize, not the evil but the good which gleams out of the evil in Russia's own very old, yet very young, history.

Pre-war history textbooks in schools are frowned upon. As soon as new textbooks are printed, the old ones will be scrapped. The teacher of history in one of the Suvorov military schools, which have already attained high academic ranking, told me that none of the pre-war textbooks answers the needs of the Russia which is emerging out of this war. His own school, he said, was already at work on a new textbook in Russian history.

* Maurice Hindus, "Russia on the Eve of Big Changes," *New York Herald Tribune,* February 27, 1945.

In the new textbooks the approach will be undeviatingly Marxist. But the role of the individual in the making of history will be high-lighted. "What would have become of Russia in this war," this teacher asked, "had it not been for our Stalin?" Instead of being weighted with theoretical discussion and political dialectics the new textbooks will be livened by the dynamics of human personality, of leaders and peoples.

The new approach to the study of literature and history only dramatizes the increasing importance Russian education attaches to the humanities. Once the step-children in the Russian curriculum, they are now pushing abreast of subjects formerly considered more necessary. Logic, sociology and other kindred subjects are back in the curriculum. At the end of the war the humanities are destined to receive a fresh impetus in schools and colleges including trade and vocational schools for both children and adults.

Russia has become not only history-minded but world-minded. . . . Curiosity about the English-speaking lands has grown until it is now an intellectual hunger. "My pupils," said a geography teacher in a village high school, "devour every book we can find on your country and on England." Nor is this school an exception. The obtuseness of so many bureaucrats with whom foreigners in Russia are obliged to deal should not obscure the overwhelming eagerness of Russians, in villages as well as in cities, to know the English-speaking peoples, to study their history, to read their literature, to appraise and appreciate them as nations and as friends. So popular has the study of English become that it is impossible to buy an English-Russian dictionary or grammar book anywhere in Russia.

TRENDS IN SOVIET LITERATURE*

Soviet literature does not merely pose the questions as to the fate and path of man: "What to do?" and "Who is to blame?" as classical literature did. It answers these questions, answers with the courage which it overheard in the din of the people's construction. It loves to show the moral transformation of man as he comes into contact with a society which is founded on justice.

The typical hero of Soviet literature is a man of ideas and actions, revealing himself through the historic deed of his people. The deed is so great that often the hero is lost in the contours of the construction, and the real hero turns out to be the factory, the city, the dam, and the mine. The hero of Soviet literature, unlike classical heroes, has little inner conflict or self-analysis. He is a pioneer in a new land, his sleeves are rolled up, he has a gruff voice, he is a man of few words, he knows where he has to go and what he has to do. The humanism of classical Russian literature is on a different principle from the humanism of Soviet literature. In classical liter-

* Alexei Tolstoi, "Trends in Soviet Literature," *Science and Society,* Summer, 1943, Vol. VII, pp. 235–48.

ature there is pity, sorrow for man, and a sharing of his suffering; in Soviet literature, a real actual struggle to build the conditions for human happiness. In the former, there is psychological humaneness, in the latter, historical humaneness, defined by the very content of the people's ideals and strivings. Man in classical literature is an object of psychological vivisection; in Soviet literature, there is historical man.

It is no accident that in Soviet literature there has been such a wide development of the historical novel, which did not exist in classical literature. Then they spoke of the Messianism of the Russian people, and often harsh feudalism and reaction were disguised under these cloudy ideas. The Soviet writer saw in living actuality, the real character of the Russian people, historically conditioned, which in our days has flowered in unheard-of, selfless, creative movements, and in the bloody struggle against fascism. . . .

All the experience of the literature of the previous century did not give us the artistic experience, the tradition and the style to express an optimistic, life-asserting force, assertive of life and approaching life in order to transform it.

Having no antecedent experience, Soviet literature is seeking a form and a style for a life-asserting realism. In it there is still much that is inept and unripe. Style and form develop most favorably in periods of lull, of certain stability. We have no lulls. Our twenty-five years have been an ardent movement forward, in bitter struggle, in perpetual overcoming. Hence the still immature hand of many of our writers, and their rectilinear quality, often attained at the expense of many-sidedness and richness.

The first basic achievement of our literature was the articulation of socialist ideas. The second achievement was that of belonging to the people. Soviet literature, as a whole, did not win all at once, this greatest of all vistas open to the writer—to speak to the people and be understood by the people. In this respect, some phases of the history of the literature of the last quarter of a century are instructive. Basically the development of literature went through two stages, corresponding to the two great stages in the recent development of our country. The first stage was from the October Revolution to that year which Stalin named "the year of the great transition." The second was from the beginning of the thirties to the War for defense of the Fatherland. In our day, a new stage of Soviet literature has begun.

From the October Revolution to the year of the great transition, the question had not yet been settled of "Who will beat whom?" Within society there went on the struggle of socialist and capitalist elements, a war for the direction and for the content of the revolutionary process. All this found its expression in the ideas, themes, subjects and style of literature.

With the thirties the new classless society began to take form. The land was intensely building the five-year plans. Literature endeavored to express these new social processes. The struggles of groups and directions which characterized the previous period came to an end, yielding to a new solidarity which sometimes took the undesirable character of a general leveling. The choice of themes, the manner of their elaboration, the relation to the object and to man—everything that we call style—was subordinated to the surge of construction going forward in the land. Literature was colored by the feeling of the time and strove for knowledge and expression of actuality. The sketch flourished, and often realism came dangerously close to naturalism.

There was much in the literature of the twenties that it had to pass through, as through a disease, and various writers did not easily achieve what is called "remodeling," that is, they did not adjust their ideas to the needs of the period of the great transition. There was factionalism, blindness to ideas, inability and sometimes an arrogant unwillingness to see and express the historically conditioned reality. The printings of books were limited to five or ten thousand copies. Within ten years the printing of a book like *And Quiet Flows the Don* totalled 2,500,000 copies.

At the beginning of the thirties, under the influence of the decisive victories of Socialism, a profound change of ideas took place within the ranks of the writing intellectuals. Literature drew closer to the basic, vitally necessary aims and objectives of the party and the Soviet power.

The literature of the second period is characterized above all by the unity of its conceptual trends. And this was a step on the path to a people's literature. In these years a many-millioned reader rose up to face the writer, namely the builder-people, set in motion in the cultural revolution. All this taken together gave new character to our literary life and deepened our awareness of the responsibility of literature to the people.

This growing contact between literature and the reader is generalized by the deepening of the economic, political and cultural bonds of the Russian people with the brother peoples of the Soviet Union. The process of fusing literature with the reader is activated by the people's work in the fulfillment of the five-year plans. Day and night in all the land, through the teeth of steam-shovels' crunch, and by means of the pneumatic hammers' stutter, the walls of cities and factories arose. In the villages plans are made for transition from the individual strips to the massive areas of a collective economy.

All this invited and called forth a literature which eagerly served as the artistic chronicler of the economic transformation, or, in the words of Hertzen, which "follows in the traces of the great army of the movement of history."

Thus there arise industrial and *kolkhoz* novels, tales, and plays, about socialist construction and its people. Among the multitude of works of these years many are notably significant in that they introduce into literature materials never before treated. Such for instance are Gladkov's novel *Cement,* Ehrenburg's *Second Day,* Leonov's *Hundred,* Kataev's *Time, Forward,* Ilin's *The Great Conveyor,* Sholokhov's *Virgin Soil,* Panferov's *Rails,*

Shaginian's *Central Hydrostation,* Tvardovsky's notable poem *Muravia Land,* Krymov's *Tanker "Derbent,"* and many another. At the same time a new generation of writers established itself in literature, such men as Sobolev, Korneichuk, Pavlenko, Simonov, and others.

From the romantic approach of the recent past, literature went over to historic concreteness. A new literary hero appeared: no longer the mass-man, not the abstract romantic personage of the civil war, but the man of today. He is the builder, but he is still rather generalized than typical; he is depicted by external signs rather than by internal characterization; he is still the representative of his occupation rather than a living personality; he has a dangerous tendency to flash across the pages of a story, also a tendency to appear as a mere product of conditions; as the "leather jacket" or rubber stamp.

The last years before the war were notable for the literary war for the elimination of characters depicted as mere products of conditions. Literature was fighting for the re-establishment of the ties which lead from the contemporary man to the historical past; in the first stage these threads were broken. . . . In the search for its great historical inheritance, literature has been turning to the historical novel, which has taken the lead over other genres.

The war has opened a new stage, a new period. It might have been thought that the thunder of war would drown out the voice of the poet, would coarsen and simplify literature, confine it to the narrow limits of the trench. But the embattled people, finding in itself ever greater moral strength for the bloody and merciless war, where there is only victory or death, ever more firmly demanded a superior literature. And Soviet literature in time of war became really a people's art, the voice of the heroic spirit of the people.

The third cornerstone of our literature, laid by the October Revolution, is the multi-national character of the Soviet literature movement. The history of the world's literature has never known such concord of a many-voiced and mutually fructifying literary chorus, as in the Soviet Union. Taras Shevchenko says with proud irony in his poem *Caucasus,* that in tsarist Russia all the nations from "the Moldavian to the Finn, in all tongues, all (were) silent." The forcible Russification carried out by the Russian empire is all too well known; the suppression (by tsarist censorship) of the national development of the peoples, as if it were possible to make them forget their native tongue, their historic past, to suppress in them the sacred urge toward freedom. But for the October Revolution with its straightforward and honest Stalinist national policy, Russia without doubt would have shared the fate of every patchwork government. . . .

It would be unfair to assert that the Russian intelligentsia participated in the stupid and short-sighted process of tsarist Russification. The advanced Russian intelligentsia always maintained a different viewpoint, the one which was realized by the October Revolution. Russian literature had a progressive influence on the formation of social self-consciousness among the national intelligentsia of the peoples of tsarist Russia. If we turn to the biographies of the most prominent national leaders of the middle and end of the last century, it is obvious that they got their leading ideas, knowledge of life and history from our classic literature.

Where the map of the Russian Empire had blank spaces of silence and illiteracy, the map of the U.S.S.R. blooms and flourishes with national literatures. The October Revolution and the Stalinist national policy called all to cultured life, even the "little-known and unknown peoples" seemingly forgotten by history. Stalin says in his book *Marxism and the National-Colonial Question* that it is the nature of the revolution not to diminish but to increase the number of languages, and therefore of literatures. Over the period of a quarter of a century, dozens of peoples of the Soviet Union have for the first time in their history established their written language. On the eve of the War in defense of the Fatherland, we printed books in 90 languages, some of which were previously all but unknown: Saam, Mansii, Abazin, Vep, and others.

Naturally, not every people and tribe has always succeeded in founding its own fine literature. Soviet literature is not only many-nationed and many-languaged, but many-staged—all stages, or degrees of development, coexist in it, from the naive song of the Ashug, or the first rhythmic effort in the language which has just received its written form, to the stories, novels, poems and dramas which are translated into all the languages of the world.

It may be estimated that we have, besides the Russian, 35 or 36 literatures already formed, and if we add to this the literatures of the Baltic peoples, the number totals 40 in all.

We possess literatures of peoples which have travelled the road of industrial capitalism and have their developed literary traditions; these are the Ukrainian, Bielo-Russian, Jewish, and Baltic peoples. Close to them are the literatures of the Transcaucasian peoples with their thousand-year old culture: the Georgian, Armenian and Azerbaijan. The peoples of Central Asia have ancient and deep literary traditions. This refers in particular to Uzbekistan. But the conditions of feudal relations and colonial oppression were especially onerous there; with the exception of oral folk song, literature, with all the marks of an outworn world, served the feudal aristocracy almost exclusively. The people were totally illiterate. On that account, the Soviet literary movement was, for the peoples of Central Asia, a renaissance, a rebirth of national cultures, after centuries of almost total silence. The Uzbek and Kazakh literatures were enriched in the years just before the war by the tale, the novel and the drama, in addition to their native poetic genre. The same can be said of the literature of the Tajiks, the Turkmens, the Kirghiz, the Kara-Kalpaks, and the peoples of Dagestan.

The literatures of the "little peoples," which count their age in two or three decades, were entirely founded by the October Revolution; these literatures are those of Bashkiria, Chuvashia, Komia, Maria, Iakutiia, Mordoviia, Kabarino-Balkariia, Cherkessia, Ingushetiia, Abkhaziia, Adygeia, Oirotiia, of the Buriats, the Kalmyks, the Lazgins, the Avartzy, the Udmurti, the Chechentzi, and other nationalities and tribes.

Two factors must be distinguished in the development of our national literatures. First, the rebirth and extraordinary blossoming of oral folk creativeness; and, secondly, as remarked above, the development of new forms, hitherto little or not at all known to them—the novel, short story, drama, film scenario. In the development of these forms the Russian language has played an enormous role, since it was the second native tongue for the literary intelligentsia of the peoples of the Soviet Union.

HOW THE SOVIET PRESS FUNCTIONS *

Pravda, Izvestia and the other big Soviet dailies do not entertain—they inform. They are austere newspapers, any one of which could win the Ayer award for typographical excellence, and their columns are filled with industrial and agricultural intelligence, with production figures, with foreign dispatches and signed and unsigned editorials on foreign affairs, with party and government business, with sarcastic feuilletons and sardonic cartoons.

They are alert, too, on the cultural front. It surprises no one to pick up *Pravda* and read an article on Soviet music by a reviewer named Dmitri Shostakovitch, or the latest installment of the great new novel by Mikhail Sholokhov, *They Fought for Their Country,* a work which is still in progress. We first read chapters from Simonov's stirring novel *Days and Nights* in *Red Star.*

Russia has just celebrated the 28th anniversary of the Soviet revolution. On the eve of that revolution there were 859 newspapers in the Czar's entire realm, with a total circulation of 2,700,000. Today there are 9000 separate newspapers, printed in 80 languages, with a circulation of 40,000,-000, a figure which in no way meets the demand. In addition, there are thousands of weekly and monthly periodicals with tremendous circulation. Thus, the 400 magazines devoted to politics and economics had a total circulation of 150,000,000 before the war, a large part duplicated, no doubt, but impressive nevertheless. The 800 agricultural, industrial, technical and transport magazines had 50,000,000 readers; the 350 scientific, mathematical and medical journals had 7,000,000; the 175 literary and art magazines had 50,000,000; and the 100 pedagogical journals had 15,000,000.

* Alexander Kendrick, "The Soviet Press," Address at American-Soviet Cultural Conference, under the auspices of the National Council on American-Soviet Friendship, New York, November 18, 1945.

Before the revolution the 859 Russian newspapers were owned by bankers, industrialists, manufacturers, and landlords . . . and the Russo-Asiatic Bank dictated much of their policy. Today the 9000 Soviet newspapers are published by trade unions; local, district and national government councils; various committees of the Communist Party; government commissariats and trusts; sports groups and the like. Policy is dictated by the interests of these organizations and of Soviet society as a whole.

The best-known of the Soviet newspapers is of course *Pravda.* Every morning in Moscow, except Tuesdays, 2,000,000 copies of it are sold in the time that it takes to stoop over and tie your shoelace. Simultaneously in Leningrad and Kharkov, 500,000 more copies, printed locally from plates flown in, are distributed. *Pravda,* the Soviet "Thunderer," is the organ of the Central Committee of the Communist Party and as such the very conscience of the socialist revolution. Its chief editor and foreign affairs specialist is David Zaslavsky, a bearded, sprightly man in his sixties, who also uses the name Konstantin Demidov, and who is equally vitriolic in either identity against policies and personalities in other lands deemed to be in need of criticism. Zaslavsky likewise writes many of the unsigned Pravda editorials, which are so frequently quoted in the Moscow dispatches as straws in the wind of Soviet policy-making. *Pravda,* printed in a super-modern plant on Pravda Street, is a far cry from the clandestine newspaper born in a St. Petersburg cellar on May 5, 1912, under Lenin's direction from abroad and under the editorship of a modest man named Molotov.

Pravda's principal competitor, at least in the spirit of socialist competition, is the organ of the Supreme Soviet, *Izvestia.* As the spokesman of the government *Izvestia,* which also has 2,000,000 circulation, is concerned with such matters as education, collective farms, drought, the training of local government leaders, and the activities and achievements of the various nationalities and republics of the Soviet Union. It is less polemic than *Pravda,* and I am fond of its editorials, which bear such titles as "Make an Auspicious Start of the Harvesting Season," "Assiduously Work to Fulfill the Third Quarterly Plan," and "In Preparation for the 28th Anniversary of Great October Let Us Try Socialist Emulation."

Pravda means truth in Russian and Izvestia means news, and there used to be a Moscow saying that "there's no news in *Pravda* and no truth in *Izvestia.*" This cannot be said today. Both papers are models of careful editorship, and the conciseness of their news, the straightforwardness of their self-criticism, and the restraint of their editorial opinion are wholly refreshing.

Moscow has at least six other dailies and a host of tri-weekly, semi-weekly and weekly newspapers. During the war *Red Star* and *Red Fleet,* the organs of the Army and Navy, were outstanding for their front dispatches, the work of such correspondents as Konstantin Simonov, Eugene Krieger, Eugene Petrov, Ilya Ehrenburg, Valentin Kataev, Leonid Sobolev and

Vsevolod Vishnevsky. Many of the *Red Star* and *Red Fleet* correspondents were killed in action. One of them was killed ten feet away from me when the Germans bombed out the American shuttle base in the Ukraine last year.

Trud, or *Labor,* the organ of the Central Council of Soviet Trade Unions, is perhaps the best-written newspaper in Moscow. In addition to labor news, it carries trenchant political articles, such as on the American presidential campaigns and on the differences between the A.F.L. and C.I.O. The *Moscow Bolshevik,* organ of the City and District Soviet, is chiefly interested in local affairs; *Komsomolskaya Pravda,* the central organ of the Communist Youth, has its own obvious special interests and also is the only Soviet newspaper to carry crossword puzzles. The *Evening Moscow,* the capital's only afternoon newspaper, resembles an American newspaper more closely than any of the others. For one thing, it carries help-wanted ads inserted by government trusts and agencies. I have even seen an ad for movie actors, and another urging Soviet citizens to make money in their spare time by selling insurance for the state.

Evening Moscow carries divorce notices, now compulsory under the new laws; news of the local movies and theaters; what's new at the public library; articles about the weather and how Kuznetsky Most and other streets got their names; and many pictures of the city. It also devotes a good deal of its space to sports, such as football, tennis, chess and, believe it or not, yachting.

In the non-daily field the Soviet press includes notable newspapers like the English-language *Moscow News,* edited by the picturesque Borodin; *Literaturnaya Gazeta,* the literary and publishing newspaper; *Ogonyk,* or *Little Flame,* the Soviet *Colliers; Krokodil,* the satiric weekly; the literary monthly *Znamya* or *Banner;* and the political monthly *Bolshevik.* I will not discuss the wall newspapers, factory newspapers, traveling newspapers and others of the so-called second-level press, printed by the hundreds of thousands.

A few minutes ago I spoke of the self-criticism of the Soviet press. This is one of its principal characteristics. It strikes out unmercifully at improprieties and mistakes in every phase of government administration, ranging from the lack of motor transport stations in Kazakhstan to the dirty floors and delayed curtains of some Moscow theaters. It assails bureaucracy, stupidity and ignorance wherever it finds them. . . . I know of *Pravda* and *Izvestia* reporters who spent months tracking down stories of mal- or misadministration, and when their exposés appeared they would usually be followed in a day or two by a brief notice announcing that Comrade So-and-So had been relieved of his duties. One of the typical weapons used in Soviet press crusades is the sarcastic feuilleton, such as the one I remember in *Pravda* about the "fireproof matches" made by a Baikal match factory.

The crusading strain is very apparent in the Soviet press. With it goes something I have never seen anywhere else—direct and continuing contact between the individual newspaper and its readers. . . . In the Soviet Union letters to the editor pour in by the thousand, but in addition newspaper staffs hold regular meetings with readers to discuss matters in which the readers are interested, and most newspapers hold an annual readers' conference at which they actually give an account of their stewardship to the public. Some of the more technical newspapers, by direct contact with engineers and Stakhanovites, serve as disseminators of information about, and veritable instructors in, the latest industrial techniques.

Lenin once declared that the Soviet press must be propagandist, agitator and organizer, and in this triple capacity it has played an overwhelming role in popularizing the Stakhanovite movement, aiding the Five Year Plans, stimulating industrial production, explaining local and district elections, and maintaining wartime morale and vigilance against Nazi spies and saboteurs.

Another of the major strains in the Soviet press is that of objectivity. I have never seen news presented so strictly as news anywhere else, so de-emphasized of sensationalism, speculation, idle rumor, and that cloying, wholly manufactured "human interest" we seem to be so proud of here. Of course, much of the personal war reporting of the past few years has not been very objective, nor could it have been, but I am not thinking of this type of news so much as of the everyday reporting of everyday events.

So we come to the burning question of freedom of the press, about which I don't propose to say much except that freedom of the press in the Soviet Union gives to those who never had newspapers before the actual means of owning and printing them. Working people and their organizations are literally guaranteed printing presses and stocks of paper by the Soviet Constitution. The Soviet press is a controlled press, but it is controlled for the best interests of a majority of the Soviet people by their own organizations.

HOW SOVIET COMPOSERS LIVE AND WORK *

During the recent war Soviet music took on a special and dramatic significance for us and we were all stirred by certain works—especially the songs of the Red Army, and Shostakovich's Seventh Symphony, written during the siege of Leningrad—which revealed how closely Soviet musicians were bound up with the life and struggles of their people. When the war broke out, composers, instrumentalists and performers of all kinds immediately took to making music for the war. And the Soviet government,

* Elie Siegmeister, Address at American-Soviet Cultural Conference, under the auspices of the National Council on American-Soviet Friendship, New York City, November 18, 1945.

realizing how powerful a voice music was in rallying the people, never forgot—even in the darkest hours—to protect its musicians, and enable them to continue their work. All through the war, although half the nation was devastated, millions homeless and starving and the national finances sorely strained, the government continued to appropriate large sums every year to commission the writing of new symphonies, operas and concertos, and to ensure the performance of classic and modern music—even though the orchestras and opera companies had to go to Central Asia to do it.

There is something awe-inspiring about a nation whose people are suffering untold misery and destruction, that yet continues to give badly needed funds so that artists may be protected and continue their work. And incidentally, the government refused to permit any composers to enter the armed forces—feeling they were too precious to be exposed to danger—although many volunteered for the Red Army.

During the war we began to learn a little of how the Soviet composer lives and works. *Life* magazine carried pictures of Shostakovich, Gliere, Khatchaturian and other composers on the Composers Farm where they go each summer to raise pigs and write symphonies. We heard that Soviet composers live in a specially constructed house in Moscow, that they have written tremendous amounts of music for the war and other things.

Yet, by and large, Americans have but a vague idea of how the Soviet composer lives and works from day to day. How does he make a living? Who employs him? Does the music he writes remain his property, or does it belong to the State? Is he told what kind of music to write? Does a commissar peek over Prokofieff's shoulder every morning to see that he's toeing the "line"? Is there an official kind of music that he must write? Is one composer free to get up and speak his mind about the works of another? What about expressing your own individuality in music? These are questions which I believe are not too clear in the minds of many people.

First, I would like to say that ten years ago I visited and spent two months in the Soviet Union, much of it in the company of Soviet composers. I found them personally and in temperament not much different from many American composers I know. They were eager to hear about the latest music from other countries, and would argue for hours about various performers and conductors and the music of their colleagues. But in one way they did seem different—not one of them complained that he did not have enough time to write music. In most countries, due to economic reasons, serious composers spend a large part of their time trying to earn a living, as teachers, music critics, arrangers, concert performers or what not—and they write music in their spare time. The Soviet government, almost from the time it was first founded, decided that the job of a composer is to devote all his time to writing music, and it was the duty of the State to see that he had complete economic freedom to do so.

Soviet music is organized under a sub-section of the All-Union Committee of Art, which is almost like a department of the government in our country. Each year the Music Section of this Committee of Art receives a certain sum of money from the national Treasury, which it allots among its various departments: orchestras, opera houses, music publication, composers, and so forth. The composers work through what they call the Union of Soviet Composers—which is not a trade union in our sense, but a sort of combination of professional guild, commissioning body, an agency to secure performances and publications, a copying bureau, and a fraternal mutual aid society, all rolled into one.

The Union consists of some 900 professional composers, both serious and popular composers. To become a member, you write a letter to Gliere, who is president of the Union, stating your qualifications and enclosing a few sample scores. If there is any doubt as to a young musician's eligibility, he is invited to appear in person before a committee on admissions and perform his own works. The Committee then decides; and if you don't get in one time, you can always apply again. The Union is not without standards, and the mere fact that your work is popular and widely performed does not automatically qualify you for admission. Peter Zburski wrote a song which became a tremendous hit during the war, called "The Blue Handkerchief." It was sung from one end of the country to the other. But he was not admitted to the Union of Composers.

When a recognized composer wishes to write a work, he submits a project to the Union committee in charge of such things, with an estimate of the length of time it will take. Usually the plan is accepted without much discussion and the composer goes ahead to write his work. Sometimes, however, a composer gets too one-sided for a time, and then the Union committee will suggest that he develop another side of his talent for a time. If a man has been writing too many chamber or theatrical works, they may suggest that he write a symphony. Thus in the spring of 1944, the Union of Soviet Composers commissioned Prokofieff, who had not written a symphony since 1929, to write his Fifth Symphony.

The Union has a huge fund—the Musfund—at its disposal for commissioning new works. Last year it was 6 million roubles ($1,200,000 at the official rate of exchange). When a composer's project is accepted, he is allotted a stipend for his support during the time he is writing the new work. The deadline for a symphony is usually six months, and the stipend between 8,000 and 16,000 roubles ($1600–$3200). Sometimes it is more. Khatchaturian was given 18,000 roubles ($3600) for his Second Symphony and completed it in three months. In addition, if the work turns out to be particularly good, the Union awards an additional 50% bonus after its first performance. This is an outright payment, not an advance, and has nothing to do with other fees that may be earned by the composer from this particular work.

After the Union has passed on the work (in a manner which I will describe presently) the composer then signs two separate contracts: first, with a music publishing house, for its publication. A vast number of compositions written by Soviet composers is published—even lengthy orchestral and opera scores for which there is practically no market, as the motive here is musical interest, not commercial profit. The publication contract gives the composer a lump sum for his work. Khatchaturian, who received $3600 from the Union for writing his Second Symphony, got $4000 more for the publication rights, so that he had an outright $7600 as a result of three months' work. Not bad for what would be called in this country a "long-haired composer."

The second contract a composer signs is with the Radio Committee and with each orchestra or opera house giving them the right to play his music. For each performance he receives a minimum of $40 to $100. When you realize that there are 70 orchestras in various cities of the USSR which regularly perform the works of living Soviet composers, you begin to see how Soviet composers are among the richest men in the Soviet Union— far more wealthy, for example, than the director of an automobile factory or the president of a railroad. Even when I was in the Soviet Union, I earned enough money in one day to live on for six weeks. I did it by signing a publication contract for the Russian rights to two short pieces. And I wasn't even a member of the Composers' Union.

Other services that the Union performs for its members include finding them apartments to live in, furnishing them with pianos or other musical instruments, sending them piano-tuners and piano-movers when needed. The Union maintains a copying bureau, where a composer may have his scores copied and instrumental parts extracted at no charge. This relieves the composer of a major headache. In addition, the Union maintains special stores for composers only where they may buy clothing, shoes, food at or below prevailing prices; and a special medical clinic, where they are given free medical care—and this includes their wives and children too, if any. And incidentally, a composer retains perpetual copyright to his music, during his lifetime, and his heirs for fifteen years after his death.

No wonder with all these conditions, composers—and creative artists in general—enjoy a very fortunate and secure place in the Soviet Union. You might wonder, does not all this security lead to a kind of spiritual softening in Soviet composers? When I was in Russia, I too, remembering the old idea that you must starve to be able to write good music, got kind of worried. I met Reinhold Gliere, who was then in his 60's. Before the Revolution he was a struggling composer who had written much of his music in a cold garret—and now with his *Red Poppy* ballet playing regularly to audiences of 10,000 at the Bolshoi Theatre in Moscow and in about 20 other opera houses throughout the nation, he was one of the wealthiest men in the country.

"Mr. Gliere," I said with an anxious look, "doesn't all that money affect you in some way? Haven't you changed your way of life?"

"Well, yes," he told me, "I used to live in one room, and now I've gotten a three room apartment—two for my family and one for myself. I have a Bechstein piano, which I've always wanted, I contributed an airplane to the Red Army, and I now have a Fedora hat."

Recently Khatchaturian was awarded a Stalin Prize of 100,000 roubles. He returned the money to Stalin and asked that it be used to build a tank. Various composers have endowed hospitals, rest homes, have bought machine guns or musical instruments for a regiment and established music schools in small towns, with their royalties.

Composers are among the most honored men in the Soviet Union—the names of Gliere, Miaskovsky, Kabalevsky, Prokofieff, Khatchaturian and Shostakovich are known not only to music lovers but to tens of millions who play and sing their music in amateur music groups which are scattered through the land. Yet if anyone thinks that a good economic and social position has a bad influence on an artist, let him just look at the sheer quantity of work these men turn out each year . . . [for example, Prokofieff (see page 123)].

Prokofieff's music is the product of a rich and fertile genius—which does not seem to be hampered, but rather immensely helped by favorable conditions of work. Nor does his genius seem to have suffered but rather blossomed forth since he has returned to the Soviet Union and worked as one of the 900 members of the Union of Soviet Composers.

And here I would like to say something about the system of mutual aid and criticism which is the characteristic feature of the work of the Union of Soviet Composers. Soviet composers define it as the responsibility of all for the work of each; and the aim, to get each composer to turn out the finest and most music of which he is capable. This operates by a technique of creative criticism by various composers of each other's work, and constant challenging and suggestions, which—I am afraid—would be very hard for us Americans to take.

When a man has finished a new work, he brings it to a closed meeting, or "sitting" of the Union, to which performers and critics are also invited. The composer plays his work, and his colleagues listen and then one by one take the floor and discuss it. Sometimes the criticism is sharp and sweeping; sometimes it is specific and technical. Often the comments are mutually contradictory and the composer waits silently while two other men argue heatedly about a certain passage in his work.

It is hard to understand the nature of such a "sitting" until you have taken part in it. I do not speak on this point without passion, for when I was in Moscow, I was asked to play a series of my own compositions before an invited audience of Soviet composers. I played for about three-quarters of an hour; and what I did not expect was what happened during the next two hours. There were about fourteen composers in the room (it was in the summer time and all the rest were in the Caucasus or some other country place—otherwise, I was told, there would have been two hundred). When I stopped playing the fireworks began; one after another the composers got up and said exactly what they thought about each composition I played; listing in detailed technical language first all the things they liked and then all the things they did not like very frankly and very fully. The fact that I was a foreigner did not seem to disturb them at all; and the only thing that smoothed my feelings was that I did not understand a word of what was being said as the speakers were saying it, and I am sure the man who translated for me always used the politest English equivalents he could find for the strong language that was obviously sometimes being used!

Now I survived that session, and so, apparently, do the Soviet composers, who each and every one must submit every new composition to this kind of "sitting." Often of course there are conflicts of personalities at such meetings, but the amazing thing is the fact that by and large the criticisms are given and accepted in a spirit of friendship, confidence and sincerity. Composers often make changes in their music, as a result of these discussions—and this includes even top men such as Prokofieff and Shostakovich. Prokofieff made changes in his opera *War and Peace* after hearing the criticisms of some of his colleagues, and he himself was very clear in his criticism of Shostakovich's Eighth Symphony.

This criticism is so frank and honest, and so characteristic of the manner in which Soviet composers discuss each other's work, that I would like to quote from it, if you will permit me. Speaking at a meeting, Prokofieff said of his younger colleague's symphony:

"One of Shostakovich's chief merits, it seems to me, is that he is a thinking composer, reflective and ingenious not in the pedantic sense but in the best, creative sense. . . . As far as the form of the Symphony is concerned, it seems to me that in a work of such length the composer should exert himself to retain the attention of the listeners. After the second half-hour the listener begins to demand something more effective in order to combat his fatigue. And it is just at this point that the slow Fourth Movement begins. It is written in the form of a *passacaglia* where first the theme is presented and then recedes into the mass while the counterpoint appears in the upper register. . . . This is an excellent form but Shostakovich was unable to find a sufficiently vivid counterpoint . . . If the *Eighth Symphony* did not have this Fourth Movement but went directly into the final movement with its superb Coda, if it did not have its Second Movement which is not new but is rather crude, but instead had only the First, Third and Fifth Movements, I am sure there would be much less argument about it."

American composers would doubtless find it difficult to work under a set-up in which they were obliged to listen to such frank and unadorned public estimates of their work by their respected and distinguished colleagues. Soviet musicians, however, not only endure, but seem to thrive on it. About nine years ago there was much discussion here of the manner in which Shostakovich's music was criticised and debated in his own country. Yet, it is generally admitted now that Shostakovich has grown immeasurably in the past nine years since those criticisms were made of his work.

Not all works are met with analyses and criticisms at the "sittings" of the Composers' Union. Sometimes a superior work is met with enthusiastic applause and statements of appreciation. When Prokofieff played his Fifth Symphony there was nothing but applause and statements of extravagant praise from Miaskovsky and Kabalevsky, both distinguished composers and leading members of the Union.

One other question might worry an American who studied the workings of the Soviet Union: does not this group spirit stifle a composer's individuality, and originality; does it not create a uniformity in Soviet music? I think those who are familiar with Soviet music can answer this question for themselves. Of course, there are always those who imitate a few top men, and this happens in any country. But beyond this there is a striking variety of styles, forms and techniques in the works of Soviet composers. Each one follows his individual interest and taste. There are conservatives and modernists, those who write simply and those who write in a more complex style. The influence of the older Russian composers such as Tchaikovsky and Rimsky-Korsakov is strong in the works of men like Gliere, Miaskovsky and Steinberg. Goedicke is what we would call in this country an academician. Krein and Weprik write on Jewish themes, and their music is more like that of certain American composers than it is like Miaskovsky, Gliere or Shostakovich. Feinberg and Oborin have written largely for piano, in a style reminiscent of Scriabin. Nothing could be further from this than the straightforward, foursquare opera music of Dzherzhinski (who wrote *Quiet Flows the Don*), or the oratorios of Koval, Biely, or Shaporin which are in a hard-hitting but harmonically conventional idiom. Dunayevsky, who has been called the Irving Berlin of Russia, and who has written some of the most stirring Red Army songs, is certainly a composer whose gifts are quite different from those of Kabalevsky, Shostakovich or Prokofieff—and each of these is a distinct personality in his own right.

During the war a great wave of patriotic feeling swept all the people of the Soviet Union and it was not surprising that composers too should have felt it. Perhaps this has brought about certain changes in Soviet music —a certain new warmth and human sympathy, and at the same time a new sense of the heroic that is perhaps without parallel in the contemporary music of any other nation. The feeling of unity and brotherhood among the Soviet peoples has led the composer to come even closer to the folk music of these peoples, and this has been a striking influence, even in a country where composers have long drawn upon the music of the people for their themes.

The one thing that all Soviet composers seem to agree on is an opposition to what they call formalism—or the kind of music that only the composer himself, and a few of his friends, pretend they enjoy. The composer Shebalin defined formalism as "music which is devoid of content, of idea, of emotion. . . . it is a search for tricks and an expression of extreme subjectivity. It is like a man who is empty in soul and puts on fancy clothes, hoping they will make people think he has a very fine soul."

I think most of us can agree that the best Soviet music of today has plenty of what the Russians call "soul."

SOVIET ART *

Tradition and innovation, internationalism and patriotism are forces that have always been present in Soviet art and thought. The relative emphasis on one or the other has shifted with circumstances. The heritage from the past was considered by Lenin to be indispensable for the creation of a Soviet culture, which was best defined by Stalin as national in form and socialist in content. The Soviet writer Shklovsky has aptly said that the Soviet man is the end-product of all Russian history.

The October Revolution found most artists unprepared. While many waited and hesitated the "Futurists" boldly assumed leadership. With the help of the government they transformed radically the art institutions of the country. Before the Revolution the Futurists had sought the source for their art somewhat inconsistently in the icon, the popular print, and the shop sign. To emphasize their nationalism and to differentiate themselves from the Italians, they coined a Slavonic word "Budietlanie" (literally "will-be-ers") for Futurism. After the Revolution their attention became focussed on the struggle for the consolidation of the Soviet State. Some of their members (Mayakovsky, Lebedev, Lavinsky) made hundreds of posters in the bold style of the popular prints, which were widely distributed and helped to rally the people against foreign intervention and in support of Soviet reconstruction.

Other artists (Tatlin, Bodchenko, Medunetsky, Popova, Gabo) evolved "Constructivism," which was industrial in origin, logical in method, utilitarian in aim, and defined by them as "a transfer station between art and life." These "constructions" were designed presumably to be the equivalent in art of the social ideal embodied in the Soviet State and were intended to mold social consciousness conformable with that ideal. The school exercised considerable influence on architecture, on the theatre, on the films, and even on poetry.

* By Louis Lozowick. This article was written especially for this book.

Another pre-revolutionary movement whose influence was still more far-reaching was represented by the "Travellers" (Riepin, Perov, Kramskoy, Pukirev). Organized in the seventies of the last century, these artists possessed an apostolic faith in the Russian masses, particularly in the peasantry, and were imbued with the ideal of "going to the people." They were highly critical of the shams of western capitalism and its artists who maintained what they regarded as "delicate silence" about social wrongs. The "Travellers" on their part were very outspoken about the social and economic evils of the Tsarist regime. By the time of the Bolshevik Revolution, however, their former idealism had become hopelessly outdated. At their 17th exhibition in 1922 they passed their torch on to a new organization called "AKHRR" (Artists' Association of Revolutionary Russia).

The slogan of AKHRR (the artists Kustodiev, Brodsky, Kassatkin, Yuon, and Petrov-Vodkin) was "Heroic Realism." By this phrase the artists meant the true delineation of the heroic epoch through which they were living, to serve as a record to posterity and a stimulus to the masses. Their themes were: revolution, intervention, civil war, the life of the Red Army, the national minorities, and workers in the factories.

As the civil war subsided and life began to return to normal, there arose a great demand on the part of the people for an art that would speak about the present in comprehensible language. Consequently, new groupings sprang up in addition to AKHRR, such as "The Four Arts" and "The Society of Easel Painters." Despite their stylistic variety, all these schools agreed on the social function of art and the social responsibility of the artist. Hence in 1932 all groupings were organized into a Federation of Soviet Artists. The character of the audience and the art consumers, that is, the trade unions, the Red Army, the collective farms, and scientific bodies explains the popularity of certain pictures of the period, such as "Defense of Leningrad" by Deyneka; "Whites Cross-Examine a Bolshevik" by Yoganson; "Death of a Commissar" by Petrov-Vodkin; battle scenes from the civil war by Grekov, Savitsky, and Samokish; portraits of political and scientific personalities by Korin, Gerassimov, Nesterov, and Brodsky (whose "Second Congress of the Comintern" contained about three hundred portraits); landscapes by Baksheyev and Grabar; and still lifes by Konchalovsky and Mashkov. Young artists such as Pimenov, Plastov, and Yefanov came forward to depict the new man and the new epoch. The national minorities also made significant additions to Soviet art.

Sculpture evolved in a similar manner from the "constructions" of Altman and Tatlin to the heroic figures of Merkurov, the Leniniana (figures and busts) by Andreyev, and the statues and monuments by Mukhina, Lebedeva, Chaikov, Manizer, and Sabsai.

During this period the term *socialist realism* came to be widely applied, not so much to a school in a technical sense as to a broad social esthetic, the aim of creating a true image of Soviet reality in motion, from the standpoint of one who is an active builder of it.

When the Nazi armies invaded the Soviet Union the artists rallied to the support of their country immediately. Sokolov-Skalya, Kukryniksi, Cheremnykh, Sakrisyan, Shmarinov, Toidze, Deni, and many others prepared war posters, postcards, illustrations, and caricatures. Hundreds of artists worked with the Soviet armies on the Leningrad, Ukrainian, and other fronts and with the navies on the Baltic and Black Seas, recording battles and painting portraits of individual participants. Each national republic and its territorial subdivisions commissioned its sculptors, painters, and graphic artists to depict its own contributions to the patriotic war. Thousands of titles were represented in all-Union exhibitions of art portraying "The Great Patriotic War," "The Heroic Front and Rear," and "The Red Army in the Fight against German Aggression." The trend toward the treatment of historic themes which had begun earlier, became more pronounced during the war, as illustrated by "Alexander Nevsky" by Korin, "The Battle of Lake Peipus" by Serov, "The Uprising of Bolotnikov" by Gorelov, and "Stepan Razin" by Svarog. Events depicted were chosen for their progressive significance in the growth, unification, and development of the country.

The end of the war, as its beginning, found Soviet artists prepared. Immediately after the cessation of hostilities, the Federation of Soviet Artists and its affiliated branches held conferences to plan for the reconversion of art to peaceful tasks, and they approached this problem with the same zeal that they had exhibited in applying their skills to war needs.

THE SOVIET FILM *

On August 27, 1919, Lenin signed the decree nationalizing all private Russian film firms and transferring the entire film industry to the People's Commissariat of Education On March 15, 1946, the Supreme Soviet changed the status of all commissariats to that of ministries. Some of the former commissariats were split into separate ministries, but one entirely new office appeared on the list—a ministry of cinematography.

Between these two dates—the date of economic changes and the date of elevated social and national responsibility—lies all that has become familiar to us as the Soviet film: the great artists who overturned and reorganized our concept of the film medium, the great titles of films created as revolutionary or analytical though now regarded as classic, and the great ideas. These twenty-seven years contained not only the emergence of a national film culture whose prerevolutionary existence had meant nothing to the rest of the world, but also fresh national film cultures that had no pre-

* By Jay Leyda. This article was written especially for this book.

revolutionary existence of any sort. (Although Soviet films are often called "Russian," one of the greatest Soviet film-artists, Alexander Dovzhenko, is an Ukrainian whose entire film career, with the exception of one film, has been spent in Ukrainian film studios, and the Georgian film studio has given us at least two important and original talents, Kalatozov and Chiaureli.) It has always been impossible for even the most non-materialistic critics to avoid the obvious conclusion that these achievements derive from a particular social point of view, and that this is not a point of view counter to or apart from the main social and political currents of the country (as in the best film work of our own country, for example) but that this is a point of view identified with the basic ideas and needs toward which the whole country aims its efforts.

Sergei Eisenstein has repeatedly defined the nature of cinema as a synthesis of all other arts. This analysis can be extended to find, in the Soviet film, a synthesis of all aspects of Soviet life and art. In Eisenstein's own historical sketch of Soviet film art ("The New Soviet Cinema: Entering the Fourth Period," *New Theatre,* January, 1935), one can see, in each of his five-year periods, a clear reflection of the main ideological trends during those years: "the first five-year period of our cinematography can be defined as essentially a stage of economic stabilization, organizational shaping and the cultivation of the first shoots of a budding Soviet cinema" —*Polikushka* (1920), *Little Red Devils* (1923); the second "sometimes in detriment to thematic depth, was able to capture the spectator's attention by its revolutionary thematics, by its poetic means and skill of presentation" —Eisenstein's *Potemkin* (1925) and *October* (1927), Pudovkin's *Mother* (1926) and *The End of St. Petersburg* (1927), Dovzhenko's *Arsenal* (1928) and *Earth* (1930), Kozintzev and Trauberg's *New Babylon* (1929), Ermler's *Fragment of an Empire* (1929); the third "prosiac" period "is characterized by a decisive abandonment of all elements of cinematic expressiveness that were peculiar to the previous period . . . ," demonstrating "a demand for deeper penetration into the inner problems of the individual, a psychological treatment of the human material, and an integrated plot. . . "—*The Road to Life* (Ekk, 1931), *Counter-plan* (Ermler and Yutkevich, 1932, *The Patriots* (Barnet, 1932), *Deserter* (Pudovkin, 1933); the fourth period "must necessarily become a stage of synthesis, permeated with the best elements of the two preceding stages," announced by *Chapayev* (Georg and Sergei Vasiliev, 1934), and followed up to the war years by the *Maxim* trilogy (Kozintzev and Trauberg, 1935–37–39), *Peasants* (Ermler, 1935), *Baltic Deputy* (Zarkhi and Heifetz, 1936), *The Last Night* (Reisman, 1936), *Lenin in October* (Romm, 1937), *Great Citizen* (Ermler, 1938–40), *Shchors* (Dovzhenko, 1939), *New Teacher* Gerasimov, 1940), *Wings of Victory* (Kalatozov, 1941).

It was always characteristic of the Soviet film's relation to its audience that just as active "civil" functions were undertaken by film-makers, so were active film functions assumed by "civilians." This harmonious inter-dependence was at its most conspicuous during the war. If the Soviet film industry had accomplished nothing before June 22, 1941, it would still have earned its ministry for war-time services "beyond the line of duty." Its material situation had not been as bad since the Civil War but, in spite of bombed studios and the dislocation associated with total evacuation beyond the Urals, it can boast a fuller record of serving its people at war than can the film industry of any other warring nation. Its informational job was surperb; from those first painful months of retreat up to the last shot in the capture of Berlin, a well-mobilized and disciplined army of news-reel cameramen, many at the price of their lives, kept the reality of war before all Soviet audiences. The artists went to work, too, adapting them-selves to more urgent schedules for more urgent themes, and inventing at least one admirably useful new form, the "almanac." Some outstanding directors, such as Dovzhenko and Reisman, worked on newsreel and docu-mentary films. On the part of the "laymen"—now inclusive of both work-ers and guerilla-fighters—they increased not only their advice but also their nonprofessional film-writing to such an extent during the war that the film industry was obliged in 1943 to establish a "scenario workshop," with one of its main tasks being the training and assistance of such "amateur" writers.

The general direction to be taken by the film industry in its new status can be plotted. We know that during this first year of the ministry fifty films are scheduled for production and release, and that the previous year's budget of two hundred million rubles for all production (with each studio film costing from half a million to two million rubles) will cer-tainly be increased. We know that these films will be produced in the twenty studios of twelve different cities (Moscow, Leningrad, Kiev, Tbilisi, Yerevan, Minsk, Tashkent, Sverdlovsk, Alma-Ata, Baku, Ashkha-bad, Riga. In addition to these studios, there are 14 documentary studios, 19 studios for scientific films, one studio in Moscow devoted exclusively to the production of children's films, and a studio for stereoptic films.). We know also the work of most of the artists into whose hands the final creative responsibility of these fifty films will be placed. We also have the minister's statement of policy. Three months before his appointment as minister of cinematography, Ivan Bolshakov, then Chairman of the All-Union Cinema Committee, published this statement in the first post-war issue of the journal *Iskusstvo Kino* (Art of the Cinema). Here it is, in summary:

In achieving victory, Soviet film workers played a vital role. Their films of the past four years showed us the best qualities of our fighting people at the front and behind the front. The truth and reality of these films were weapons in our fight against fascism. Now, with the rest of the country, our film art is confronted by new and greater historical tasks. "The first and most urgent task of Soviet film art is to show with dignity in their new artistic film productions the heroism in the Great Patriotic War of the Soviet people. . . ."

The transition to peace is not merely a return to a peaceful life that war interrupted. Films must reveal the dynamics and dialectic of this new period. Our people were injured more than materially; of "the millions of our Soviet people who were destroyed and mutilated, there are many who have suffered profound spiritual *trauma* and they need warm human relationships." Work on the healing of these wounds, as well as on the restoration of our ruined communities and industrial centers, will provide a major portion of our film themes.

Our films have the added responsibility of speaking to foreign audiences as well as to Soviet spectators. The audiences of countries recently freed from fascism look to Soviet films for information and inspiration, and we cannot fail them. [Mr. Bolshakov cites comments on Soviet films from newspapers and magazines of Prague, Bucharest and Paris.]

"The enormous attraction of our youth towards learning, towards science, compels our film workers to consider this question seriously." These are duties that cannot be delegated to instructional and scientific film studios. American films such as *Edison the Man, The Story of Louis Pasteur,* and others, have proven this excellent material for artistic purposes. "We are also behind in our development of films of adventure, scientific fantasy and sport, which our spectators, particularly our younger ones, expect from us."

We must also continue work on historical films, though, unfortunately, our national studios place more stress on historical themes than on modern subjects. "We must also produce new films on the unity of the fraternal Slav nations, on their united, heroic struggle against the German-fascist invaders."

Questions regarding our comedy and musical films require more thought now than we have ever before given these genres, that need not be tied to cheap *clichés*—more courageous experiment is demanded of us. Both full-hearted gaiety and sharp satire await our attention.

One cannot speak of ideas and artistics tasks without considering the organizational-creative questions, on which the physical structure of our cinema stands. Before the war we released from 40 to 45 films a year. This was cut down during the war to from 25 to 30 titles. With a not too distant perspective of 80 to 100 releases annually, we start towards this goal during the coming year.

In connection with the expansion of our directorial and acting staffs we can point to an increasing number of directors drawn during the war from the ranks of experienced film actors (Babochkin, Zharov, Dmokhovsky), and to the formation [in September 1944] of a special Theatre for Film-Actors, "which will act as a regularly active experimental-creative laboratory for the daily heightening of the actor's craft within Soviet film art." Studios and directors must be encouraged to draw more on the large number of young actors who have qualified for film work.

"Our directors must definitely get away from over-simplified, declarative, frontal resolutions of their themes. . . . Our film-writers and directors must strive for films with subjects that give the actor a chance for sharp, expressive acting, for the revelation and formation of profound characters. Bold and persistent search in artistic form, in order to embody the ideas of our time with maximum acuteness, is necessary for all the linked, creative elements in our cinema. . . ."

"It is no small part in the progress of Soviet cinema that must be played by the film studios of our fraternal national republics, each of which possesses large numbers of highly talented masters of art and literature," who have not yet been drawn into film work. And the majority of these studios are still working with inadequate physical equipment, far below the level of their productive and creative potentialities. This can be corrected both locally and centrally.

Among a large number of such organizational problems are: the expanded construction of "Mosfilm," which can easily, within the next few years, increase its output to 40 features annually; an increase in efficiency and speed in the actual filming process; a reorganization of all technological departments (new laboratories and equipment factories are an important part of the broad reconstruction program now in work. The bombed film industry is collecting reparations, from the Agfa and Zeiss factories in the Russian zone of occupied Germany), a stepping-up from experimental work to a full production schedule on the part of the newly organized studio, "Stereokino," for Semyon Ivanov's stereoscopic invention.

"The creative-production plan of the Soviet cinema . . . is, in comparison with former years, far more interesting and varied both in themes and genres. . . . The masters of Soviet cinema must direct all their creative strength and knowledge to be worthy of those tasks placed by the government and the great leader of the Soviet people—Comrade Stalin—before our victorious land."

The authority and comprehension of Mr. Bolshakov's statement justifies this extended summary, but the worth even of a cinema minister is no more than the worth of the people who actually make the films. He can advise them, inspire them, correct them, nurse them, fight with them— but it is still they who produce both the industry and the art. From the viewpoint of a foreign reader, Mr. Bolshakov's statement lacks an important item: how, exactly, do they work together?

The machinery of this collaboration was worked out at the end of 1944, and continues to function within the ministry. An Art Council of 22 members was appointed to plan all productions and, with duties and powers rather like those of a supreme court, to handle all questions (except purely industrial or technological ones) that could not be settled within the lower art councils at the studios. The composition of the Council is formidable: 6 directors—Eisenstien, Pudovkin, Romm, Alexandrov, Chiaureli, Savchenko; a cameraman—Moskvin; 4 writers—including Konstantin Simonov; 5 actors—including Babochkin, Cherkasov, Okhlopkov; 4 composers —including Shostakovich; and 2 military consultants. The powers of this Council are genuine, and its agenda is always crowded. At its weekly sessions it examines current production plans and hears all cases for the week (troubles and problems of all degrees), and attends the screening of a newly completed film or an unfinished problem film. Everyone concerned in each case appears at the following discussion, and the entire crew and cast of the new film take part in the Council's deliberation on it. After a balloting on each point at issue (for example, is this change required or only recommended?), the Council's findings are turned over directly to the film's director. Mr. Bolshakov endorses this judgment, intervening only in an equal division of votes. If any member holds out against the majority decision, not only may he file his minority opinion, but he may also have the entire question reviewed at the following week's meeting. This whole democratic procedure may well be unique in administrator-artist relations of the world's film industries.

Another unique aspect of the Soviet film industry is the thorough training given the next generation of directors, actors, cameramen and writers, film research workers and economists. Not even war and evacuation interrupted the work of the State Institute of Cinematography (in continuous activity since 1919), which has now returned to Moscow with an increased annual state allotment of six million rubles. The Institute guarantees Soviet film progress.

Social Life in the U.S.S.R.

THE SOVIET FAMILY *

Our attitude toward Soviet family life will depend a very great deal on our own understanding and demands of family life. If we regard family life as a milieu in which the male can express his authority over the female, and in which both can express their authority over their offspring, then we shall disapprove of Soviet family life. If we regard family life as a means of obtaining domestic comforts for the man and economic security for the woman, we shall equally disapprove of Soviet family life. But if we regard a family as a group of people in which the man and woman have joined their lives, not only because of the sex impulse, but because they desire permanent companionship and children, and in which the children are regarded as personalities to be helped to develop according to their inclinations, and not as property, then we shall approve of Soviet family life.

Family life has undergone considerable change in the short existence of the Soviet regime. The early stages of a revolution give opportunity to all those people whose idea of being revolutionary is to shed all restraint and self-control, for whom being advanced means being undisciplined, and who apply these ideas particularly to sex. They have a great influence on the youth of a country which has had no experience of life and which is eager to respond to so-called freedom. If to this are added the material difficulties of the early years of the revolution, the scarcity of housing as of other commodities, the constant change of employment, it will be realized that it was inevitable that the first period of the revolution should be a period of experiment in marital and family relations as in other spheres. The legalization of abortion and the ease with which it could be obtained contributed to the light relations that existed among masses of the young people.

But this was never approved by the leaders. In 1920 Lenin, writing to Clara Zetkin on the subject of sex relations, expresses the views of the genuine Communist. It is worth quoting in some detail:

"With us in Russia, too, a great part of youth is vehemently striving to 'revise' the 'bourgeois' point of view of morality in the matter of sex."

He goes on to describe how a revolution dissolves old values; they lose their binding power before the new values have had time to crystallize.

* Beatrice King, "The Soviet Family," *New Masses*, August 26, 1941, pp. 8–11.

"It is obvious that youth is particularly occupied with the intricate series of questions [relating to sex]. Young people suffer especially under the defective sexual conditions of today, and they rebel against them with impetuousness."

Discussing the so-called "revolutionary" and "new sexual life" of youth, Lenin goes on to say:

The revolution will not tolerate an orgiastic state of affairs such as is normal for d'Annunzio's decadent heroes and heroines. Licentiousness in sexual life is . . . a symptom of degeneracy. The proletariat is an ascending class. It needs intoxication neither as narcotic nor as stimulus. Self-control, self-discipline is no more slavery in love than in anything else.

This . . . represents the Communist attitude toward sex and family relations. With the development of the country, with an increase in knowledge and experience, Soviet youth's attitude toward sex and family changed considerably. The effort of a group of so-called advanced revolutionaries about 1920 to have all children sent to State homes failed, chiefly because parents refused to part with their children, but also because it was opposed to Communism.

Russians have an immense affection for children, and they express this affection through a respect for the children, through an infinite patience, through an eagerness to learn to do the best for them, and through a desire for their presence. Boarding schools exist only for orphans or homeless. It is only under very special circumstances that parents will agree to send their children away to school. . . . They are horrified at corporal punishment in a civilized community. And today the development of their country permits Soviet citizens to indulge their love for children.

There are certain essential conditions without which there can be no satisfactory family life, which have been realized by the Soviet government. One of these is the complete equality, economic as well as political, between men and women, so that the woman shall seek marriage only because of love and the desire to live with the loved one, while the man, seeking marriage for similar reasons, no longer has the proprietary attitude toward the woman, no longer feels he is being sought for ulterior motives, but meets the woman as an equal. This economic equality creates a new and very happy relationship between man and woman unknown elsewhere.

Equally important is economic security for both, so that marriage does not have to be postponed for years and years, and, in order to preserve the health and satisfy the natural needs, temporary substitute relations indulged in. It is now common knowledge that there is more work than workers in the USSR, that university students obtain posts six months before taking their final examinations. There is therefore no obstacle to marriage, provided the legal age is attained. The possibility of early marriage and the economic freedom of women have had a shattering effect on prostitution. As a social phenomenon it has entirely disappeared. That is

Students at work in a microbiological laboratory

Workers attending a lecture at a
machine-building institute

trations courtesy Sovfoto, New York City

Harvesting rye on a collective farm

A recreation and education building of an automobile plant in Moscow for employes and their families

probably a unique achievement, and has contributed considerably to a clean and happy family life. . . .

Another essential for a happy family life is adequate housing conditions. This problem has naturally taken much longer to solve than some of the others. While the conditions are rapidly improving—the object aimed at is one room per person—there is still much overcrowding. This is mitigated, however, by the communal amenities offered by the State. There is first the crèche and nursery-infant school, where the baby or older child can be left under qualified supervision in completely suitable surroundings. This does more than relieve the mother while she is at work. It frees her from the perpetual contact, from the unending demands which small children make on the adult, and which is such a factor in ageing working class mothers, and in making nervous wrecks of many mothers. The crèches and the nursery-infant school do much more efficiently, more satisfactorily, for the children of the workers, what the private nurse does for the children of the well-to-do in capitalist countries. Incidentally the crèche and nursery-infan' school act as incentives to parents' education. Parents are however entirel· free to keep their babies at home if they wish, and many do.

The second social amenity in the USSR is the club. Again the worker has, on a much higher cultural level, those communal facilities available only to the rich in other countries. In the adult clubs there are sections for children, so that if it wishes the family can be in the same building, but sensibly enough not engaged in the same activities.

Since the USSR was only recently created out of oppression and backwardness, it is necessary to have laws for the safeguarding of the children, for the regulation of relations between the man and woman. The marriage laws are very simple. As the Soviet government is concerned with realities and not with forms, cohabitation for six months is regarded as marriage, with all the consequent duties and liabilities to each other and to children. Registration of marriage is encouraged, but is not compulsory, while registration of children is compulsory. Religious marriages are freely permitted, but have no legal status. Marriage entails the support by either partner of the one who may be incapacitated. This obligation continues six months after separation.

Divorce, too, is simple. Application is made by one party, both have to appear at the registry, and, when the registrar is convinced that the difficulties cannot be overcome, a divorce is given on payment (of 100 rubles, in 1944) by the one applying for it. The custody of the children is if possible given to the mother. The man who is divorced has to contribute a quarter of his income to maintain one child, a third for two children, and so on. It is the business of the court to see that the maintenance is paid.

Contrary to expectations, neither the easy divorce nor the recognition of non-registered marriage makes for instable marriage relations. Soviet authorities consider that monogamy is the best form of marriage and insist on a monogamous relationship. Bigamy is an offense punishable by law. The validity of non-registered marriage makes it difficult for the man to practice bigamy, since the woman in such a marriage has exactly the same claims on the man as the woman in a registered marriage. One other blot on civilization has been wiped out by the Soviet authorities, the blot of illegitimacy which makes the children suffer for the actions of the parents. But it is the organization of society more than the laws which makes for stable marital relations and satisfactory family life.

The sane and healthy environment, characterized by an absence of sex exploitation and exhibitionism, in which youth is growing up, contributes more and more to the right choice of partners. Boys and girls growing up, working and playing together, tend to become much surer in their choice of the right person. Community of interest and common ideals as the foundation for sex attraction are a strong binding force to married life. If we add to this the absence of the irritations, the nerve-fraying caused by economic worry, we find as nearly ideal conditions for successful marriage and family life as it is possible to have. But not only because there still remain sections of the population brought up under the old regime, but because personal difficulties do arise and will probably arise under any regime for some people, it is necessary to enable these people to solve their difficulties in the only honorable way, by freeing each of the obligations undertaken in marriage.

This material and moral environment which the Soviet government is creating in cooperation with all the citizens, has all the prerequisites for the highest type of family life. The family has ceased to be an economic unit, and has become a biological and a spiritual unit, kept together not by economic compulsion, but by spiritual and physical attraction. Because each member of the family feels himself free, and is respected by the others, he makes a spontaneous contribution to the happiness of the family. Because each member allows the others the freedom to develop their own personality, he is not irked by the logical restrictions which living in a group demands.

Most of my time in the USSR was spent living with families. I have lived with all kinds of families, under the difficult conditions of 1932 and under the happy conditions of 1938. I found that the parents were concerned with many of the same kind of problems as parents in other countries, though the problems of Soviet parents were much easier to solve. There was the question of the choice of a profession. Sometimes the children did not agree with the parents. In those cases the children won. Generally they were right, but when they were wrong it was a simple matter to train for another profession. There was for some parents the problem of making their seventeen-year-olds work harder at school. Here the help of the school and Komsomol, the Communist youth organization, was sought. There was the problem of how much time and attention parents can demand from their children. I never met anger, and only in one case resentment, when a mother tried to make her daughter dance for me to music which was unsuitable. I found parents and children very intimate, children particularly hiding little from their parents.

It is not to be imagined that all difficulties have completely disappeared. There are still many parents who have much to learn about the upbringing of a family. There is much help for such parents. The schools arrange lectures, classes, and discussions on child problems to which mothers and fathers come eagerly. There is an excellent series of cheap, simple booklets on bringing up children, and the radio has regular talks on the subject. In one district a Parents' University has been organized as a result of local initiative.

Youth, too, is by no means perfect. The conditions in the early years of the Revolution when the attention paid to children was so great, when the sacrifices made for them by adults were so heavy, when the freedom given them was unlimited, and their importance in the new life was so over-whelming, these conditions did not produce altogether desirable results in all cases. There was a tendency to too great self-importance, a tendency to de-mand too much and give too little in many cases. These tendencies have not entirely disappeared and educationists are concerning themselves very much with problems of children's behavior. It is held that if children have rights they also have duties, that parents, too, have rights; that their free-dom must also postulate responsibility.

Children are expected to learn how to behave in the family, and *Pi-onerskaya Pravda,* one of the children's newspapers, devotes much space to the duties of children.

There may still be changes in the organization of family life, but the family, as the social unit on which the community is based, is firmly fixed in the USSR, at any rate for centuries. Further than that it would be fool-ish to prophesy.

THE PLACE OF WOMEN IN THE SOVIET UNION *

The position of women in town and country before the Revolution was peculiarly arduous and humiliating. The influences of Byzantium preserved by the Orthodox Church encouraged an attitude toward women which owed more to the practices of the East than to the egalitarianism of the West. While the rest of Europe in its renaissance was freeing and glorifying the spirit of woman, Russia kept to its customs—special apartments where women were secluded. In the villages women became "citadels of dark-ness," to use Tolstoy's striking phrase, and in the middle period of the nine-teenth century Englehardt was writing: "Peasants marry their girls in the Autumn rather than in Spring for the same reason that they sell a cow in

* Ralph Parker, "Women Workers of the Russian Miracle," *New York Times Maga-zine,* February 14, 1943, pp. 18, 34.

Autumn—to save Winter keep," and for millions of Russian women life was drearily confined to family affairs.

They developed character, of course—these humiliated Russian peasant women. In the patriarchal structure of the family they were as much queens in certain departments as their husbands were kings. Theirs was control of the pigs, the poultry, the disposal of milk and Spring wool, and of the crop of flax in the late Fall. But they stood meekly with bowed heads and crossed hands while their menfolk ate, and their power was limited to the space between the stove and the threshold.

Their sufferings through ill-treatment produced a peculiar form of hysteria and a bitter, crossed nature that was a cause of much of the brutal tragedies of Russian peasant life. The broodings of these Russian women are expressed by a Russian poet of the nineteenth-century peasantry, Nikolai Nekrasoff:

> *The keys to the welfare*
> *And freedom of women*
> *Have long been mislaid.*
> *God Himself has mislaid them.*
> *And which fish has swallowed*
> *These treasures so priceless;*
> *In which sea it swims,*
> *God Himself has forgotten.*

Russian women protested. Russian literature and history are rich in examples of their dissatisfaction—Princess Trubetskaya following her Decembrist husband to Siberia, Katharina of Ostrovsky's famous play *Storm*. They organized. Many followed the lead of Sophia Pyerovskaya and Vera Figur into secret societies and public manifestation. They fought, like Nadyezhda Constantinovna Krupskaya, Lenin's wife; Kivra Zetkin, Helen Stassova, Emelia Koblonta, Rosalia Zemlyachka Satoelova and other Communist women, politically; or, like Darissa Reissner and Maria Copova, were fighters in the Red Army during the civil war. And they won freedom—for the underpaid women of the Don Basin, the veiled women of Central Asia and the Caucasus—freedom from the tyranny of menfolk and the mental scourge of superstition, from disease, ill health and ignorance.

The part these emancipated women played in the constructive work of the U.S.S.R. during the twenty-five years of its existence is well known. During the two five-year plans the number of women wage-earners increased by millions. Moreover, the kind of work done by women radically changed. According to the Russian census of 1897, over half of the employed women worked as servants in the houses of the well-to-do, a quarter were farmhands on large estates, 4 per cent were workers in educational and public health institutions, 13 per cent were in industry and the building trades. Seven years ago four out of ten of all women employees in the U.S.S.R. were workers in large-scale industry and building trades, two out of ten were doctors or teachers, and in the column of the remaining 40 per cent well over half were workers in branches of industry, science or arts, and but 2 per cent were domestic workers.

The 20,000,000 women on collective or State farms are no longer Gorky's "dumb tools." Each knows exactly how much she brings into the family earnings. The popularity of collectivization of the land is in no small measure due to the support women gave it. Indeed, the coincidence of collectivization with the flow of male labor from the country to the city during the first five-year plan completely transformed the situation in Russia's wide-open spaces.

It was the women who took charge, and many a man returning from a construction job with full pockets had to fight hard for his dignity. A story is told of a famous woman chairman of a collective farm who came to Moscow to receive a high order and buy a bicycle for her husband, the village messenger boy.

The experience in management that women gained during that period in the early Nineteen Thirties has stood the State in good stead now. Many farms, practically deprived of male labor by mobilization, are now being run by women. . . .

Women's contribution to the war is twofold—in the replacement of male labor and in auxiliary services of the Red Army and civil defense.

Between 70 and 80 per cent of workers in the Soviet Union's factories and collective farms today are women and girls, according to figures provided by the Anti-Fascist Women's Committee. Just before the war female labor accounted for only little over a third. As the industrial and agricultural capacity of the unoccupied Soviet Union is greater today than before the war, this remarkable change in proportion cannot be explained solely by the withdrawal of men, though on the farms this is the major factor. Millions of women have been drafted into industry or have turned over the care of their children to crèches and nurseries and the running of their houses to the aged and have taken up work.

During last Winter, while the earth lay snowbound and the evacuated industry was painstakingly being reconstructed, technical training courses were crowded with women. The number of those who in Siberia were learning to drive tractors were scores of thousands. The far-sighted project of the third five-year plan to train over 8,000,000 skilled workers came in highly useful during this period, many women being already fairly advanced in mastering machines.

Today in Moscow it is the rarest thing to see a man driving a street car or trolley bus. Before the war it was as rare to see a woman so driving. There are women on point duty, and you never find a man working in the Moscow subway except occasionally as a motorman.

I remember my first visit to a collective farm. We drove through the stiff mud of the Volga steppe on a cold and gusty mid-November day last year to where two prim lines of wooden cottages, a gaunt well lever and a collection of low-roofed outbuildings indicated a small collective farm. I think that we only met two male officials that day, all the rest were women. The chairman of the local Soviet was a shy little sloe-eyed Tartar girl, the responsible official bookkeeper was a sturdy young Ukrainian, and it was a gnarled old Babushka who did us the honor of the farms in a sweet-smelling, well-scrubbed room hung with ikons and family photographs. When we crossed the stubble to where the thresher was rattling, it was a group of red-faced women who were feeding it with sheaves, tying up sacks and carrying them away to barns.

TENANTS AND HOME OWNERS *

Most of the dwellings in the Soviet Union belong to the State, to co-operatives, or to public organizations. But many individuals own their houses.

Vacant living accommodations in buildings belonging to the local Soviets are allocated on instructions issued by the housing departments of the Soviets. Homes owned by individuals are entirely at their disposal. The right of the citizen to occupy certain premises is laid down in the lease or contract drawn up between the lessee as tenant and the lessor. The tenant has the option of renewing the lease when it expires. Eviction takes place only as a result of a court action brought by the interested person or organization. Legal grounds for the eviction of a tenant without the provision of alternative accommodation may be: the lessee's departure to another permanent place of residence without returning to the lessor the premises formerly occupied, persistent, wanton damage caused to the premises by the lessee or his family and non-payment of rent over a period of some months. In all other cases where the law permits eviction, the tenant must be provided with suitable alternative accommodation.

Special arrangements are made to insure that men called up for military service, or mobilized during wartime, do not lose their homes. In the case of a man living alone, the premises he occupied before being called up are retained in his name, as lessee, throughout the whole period of his military service and for six months after his discharge, if for any reason he does not return at once to his old home. In the case of a man living with his family before his call-up, the premises remain at the disposal of the family during his absence, and are returned to him on his discharge.

Tenants have the right to exchange premises with other lessees of living quarters, all rights and obligations being transferred to the new tenant.

* S. Yerikhonov, "Tenants and Home Owners," Embassy of the U.S.S.R. *Information Bulletin*, September 22, 1945, pp. 6–7.

The provision by organs of the State of housing accommodation for those living in towns and factory settlements makes it possible to guarantee these rights.

Rents in the USSR are extremely low, charged not for profit but to recover the cost of building and maintaining the house. They are calculated according to the type of housing, the lessee's salary and the number of his dependents. The maximum rent payable by factory and office workers is one ruble 32 kopeks per square meter per month. This maximum rent is paid only by people earning a minimum of 420 rubles per month. But an increase in salary over this amount does not lead to an increase in rent. In calculating rent only actual living space is counted. Kitchens, corridors, bathrooms, cupboards and storerooms are not counted. Soldiers in service are charged a special reduced rent of 80 kopeks per square meter.

In a checkup of the budgets of eighty families living in a block of flats in Moscow it was found that the rent charged amounted to no more than two to five per cent of the tenants' total income. Rent is paid monthly in arrears.

The occupation of premises and the uses to which they are put are governed by special legislation in each of the constituent Republics of the Soviet Union. This applies particularly to the minimum amount of floor space to be provided per person. The local authorities have the right to raise this standard, but not to reduce it. Certain categories of tenants have the right to favored treatment in this respect. Special standards have been introduced for artists, scientists and writers so as to insure living conditions that will enable them to work productively. Tenants who have to work at home—industrial and economic leaders, doctors, and lawyers— also enjoy the higher standard.

Some tenants receive housing as a reward for special services rendered (Heroes of the Soviet Union, Heroes of Socialist Labor, state pensioners, etc.). Invalids have special rights, too.

The Soviet Government spends substantial sums on residences. In the Russian SFSR alone, 1,700,000,000 rubles were allocated for the 1945 housing program. In addition, every effort is made to encourage private building. A person who wishes to build is granted the right to do so by contract with the local Soviet. This includes the right not only to obtain a vacant lot in or near a city, but also to occupy a lot containing unfinished or damaged buildings. Leases of land are granted for 65 years in the case of brick buildings, and for 50 years in the case of wooden buildings.

In the Soviet Union private builders are granted credits by the State bank and are guaranteed the necessary materials. Persons who obtain loans are under an obligation to invest not less than 30 per cent of the total cost in the building. This sum, incidentally, may be contributed partly by a man's own labor in building the house. Loans are given for five years at an interest of two per cent. Building rights are transferable.

All Soviet housing laws aim at protecting the rights of the working people and at insuring the provision of good and cheap living accommodations.

RELIGION IN THE U.S.S.R. TODAY *

In 1943 Marshal Stalin invited a committee of three Orthodox bishops to the Kremlin to sit down with him and with Foreign Commissar Molotov to discuss the relationship between the Orthodox Church and the government. Out of this conference . . . came the official announcement that approval was being given to the Orthodox Church to hold a Congress of Bishops for the establishment of a Holy Synod, the election of a Patriarch, and the acceptance by the church of a plan to open a state bureau on church affairs. In addition, it was stated that permission was being given for the opening of theological institutes and pastors' schools, and for the publication of a monthly magazine, *The Journal of the Moscow Patriarchate*.

The Congress of Bishops met in Moscow in September, 1943, and elected the Patriarchal Incumbent, Metropolitan Sergei, as the Patriarch of Moscow and All Russia. . . . Among his first official acts was to receive a delegation from the Church of England, headed by the Archbishop of York, Dr. Cyril Forster Garbett, who returned to England to declare that "the Russian Church is enjoying a freedom such as it has not possessed for centuries."

The leaders in the Kremlin are not religious men. They are Marxists and accept the principles of historical materialism, but as Marxists they are respectful students of history. In recent years they have been paying increasing attention to the roots of Russian culture. The results of their studies have been evidenced in the more recent dramas, the keen interest in all phases of national art and music, text-books introduced into the public schools, and the production of historical moving pictures on great patriotic themes. In the course of this research the Russian Church has been studied as a creative source and vehicle of developing Russian culture. Consideration has been given to its art, architecture, music and cultural influence.

In the earlier period of its life, in theory if not always in practice, the Orthodox Church was an independent institution with a purely religious function existing within and alongside of the state whose secular authority was vested in the Prince and later the Tsar. This co-existence of a church headed by a Patriarch and a government headed by a Tsar made for a certain healthy and creative tension between the two in what is sometimes called a "symphonic relationship." This was destroyed when in 1721 Tsar Peter the Great abolished the independent Patriarchate and created in its place a Holy Synod whose members were appointed by himself and subject to removal by the Crown. Modeling the church organization on the pattern

* William Howard Melish, *Religion Today in the U.S.S.R.* (New York: The National Council of American-Soviet Friendship, 1945), pp. 17–26.

of the State Lutheran Churches in Sweden and Prussia, Peter the Great made the Orthodox Church virtually a department of the civil service.

As a result, the church was secularized, its bishops and higher clergy were salaried on the civil lists, its monasteries and seminaries received state grants, church business was handled by a State Department of Religious Affairs, and the Chief Procurator of the Holy Synod held the rank of a cabinet minister in the Tsar's government. It was this absorption of the ancient independent patriarchal church into the Tsarist state that paved the way for the tragedy which we have witnessed within our lifetime. When the Tsar's government went down, the Church went down with it.

What the Soviet government and the Orthodox authorities were doing in September, 1943, was to turn the clock back to the period prior to 1721 and to revive in a modernized fashion that "symphonic relationship" of the historic Patriarchate and the civil government on the basis of an absolute separation of church and state.

Existence in a socialist economy presents a problem of maintenance that is utterly new in the experience of Christian church, Jewish synagogue and Moslem mosque alike. History provides no previous pattern for it. That is undoubtedly one reason why religious leadership generally feared the socialist revolution in Russia, and certainly a major reason why the Russian hierarchy almost to a man fought the Communists under the White Banner in the vicious Civil War that followed.

In the Soviet economy all capital investments, buildings, land, and subsurface rights are owned by the state or by various collective enterprises in trust for the people. It is no longer possible in the Soviet Union for an individual or for a private institution such as a church or a synagogue to live off unearned income from property or investments or accumulated endowments. The individual must earn his own livelihood. The private institution such as the church, synagogue, or mosque must live off current voluntary offerings, contributions, fees for services, and income from the sale of candles or religious articles; and a congregation's prosperity will be in direct proportion to the size and the prosperity of its membership and the generosity of their support. It owns no property in its own name but by registering its existence in conformity with the religious laws is given the right to lease premises from the government. These are now tax exempt but the parish council must contract to maintain them in good condition.

Furthermore, in the Soviet economy all production and distribution are under the control of the state and are determined in accordance with an over-all plan. Material for church maintenance and repair, equipment, material for vestments, ikons and art objects, printing presses and paper stocks, electricity, water—all such things involve the state in some fashion, and, in view of the many thousands of churches, some provision for religious needs must be included in the current state budget or they cannot be met. Prior to 1943 there had existed no machinery for handling of such details. Procedures had varied in different cities and provinces with a consequent confusion that was as troublesome to the churches as it was to government officials. Some more efficient and uniform procedure was long overdue. Marshal Stalin's invitation to church leaders had the obvious purpose of clearing up this unsatisfactory chaos. Both sides were eager to introduce some elementary business efficiency into an area in which things had been developing without direction. The result of this consultation in the Kremlin, after the approval of the Congress of Bishops had been obtained, was the establishment in the Council of People's Commissars of a new *Bureau on Affairs of the Greek Orthodox Church* headed by Mr. Georgi Gregorievich Karpov. The central office is in Moscow but there are a number of branch offices in other parts of the country and thirty field representatives, a number to be increased up to one hundred as the need of the Orthodox churches appears to require.

From this it will be seen that the new Bureau . . . is simply a clearing-house for matters peculiar to the Soviet economy. The Bureau in all its operations is based on a clear-cut assumption of the complete separation of church and state implied in the Soviet Constitution.

That the government was not especially favoring or promoting the Orthodox Church became apparent in the ensuing few months. Similar negotiations were carried on with other religious bodies. In each case the procedure was roughly the same: a meeting with responsible authorities, the establishment of a recognized institutional structure, the election of a head, and the affiliation of the legal body with a *Bureau on Affairs of Religious Cults* under the direction of Mr. Ivan Vassilievich Poliansky, also with its branch offices and field representatives. Thus the Moslems met in Baku, set up the Central Board of the Transcaucasus and named as their president Sheik Ahund Aga Alizade of Baku. One after another the various religious groups of the Soviet Union went through this organizational process.

Today Mr. Poliansky's bureau handles affairs for the following bodies: the Armenian-Gregorian Church, the Old Believers (a schismatic sect of Orthodox), Roman Catholics, Greek Catholics, Lutherans, Baptists, Seventh Day Adventists, Jews, Moslems, Buddhists, Shamanists and others. It is the law of the land that religious groups shall be given equal treatment. The Orthodox Church has its own bureau simply because the number of its adherents is considerably greater than the total of all adherents of the other religious groups. The opening of these two bureaus has caused great satisfaction among these bodies; it puts an end to what must have been endless haggling between local congregations and local officials over the simplest matters.

The existence of bureaus which can publish official policy has led to a number of interviews in which newsmen have put important questions to

Mr. Karpov and Mr. Poliansky. Among these questions of supreme interest to the outside world is the matter of the religious education of children and the circulation of educational and propagandistic materials of a religious character. A representative of *Religious News Service* received this answer from Mr. Karpov:

The only rule the Soviet government insists upon is that religious instruction must not violate the basic principle of separation of church and state. Under our laws each person may or may not teach his children religion. However, religion may not be taught in the schools. Parents may educate children in the privacy of their homes or may send their children to the homes of priests for such education. Children of any number of parents may also gather or be gathered in groups to receive religious instruction.

He said that no ban exists against the printing and distribution of religious literature and the Orthodox Church may print whatever it wishes.

We have given explicit permission for the church to order any quantity of Testaments, prayer books and liturgical books and are ready to facilitate this step in every way, even to the extent of making representations to the paper rationing authorities. As to distribution of such materials, there is no objection and no restrictions.

In a later interview he stated that Orthodox priests are free to carry on proselytizing work both in churches and outside:

Priests may go to their parishioners and may engage in proselytizing work without any restriction except those placed upon every orderly citizen of the U.S.S.R. They may go about church business wherever they wish. They may officiate in private homes if they so desire, may perform baptismal, marriage and funeral services in or outside churches.

Mr. Karpov was speaking for the Orthodox Church which his bureau serves but when the same questions were also put to Mr. Poliansky substantially the same answers were given, with insistence upon the equality of treatment of all groups, Orthodox and non-Orthodox alike. It is especially interesting, in view of the common opinion in the United States as to religious restrictions in the Soviet Union, to find Margaret Bourke-White in her book, *Shooting The Russian War,* stating that she personally witnessed street-corner preaching by Evangelicals during her tour of Russia. A Russian version of the Bible is now available for distribution. Ikons, which recent travelers state are increasingly in evidence in private homes and even in some public offices, have been manufactured in State Art Workshops since 1939, and it is reported that the Orthodox Church now operates a small cooperative factory for the manufacture of the candles used in its worship. Also, last year the first group of Mohammedans were enabled to make the pilgrimage from their Soviet homes to

Mecca to visit the Ka'aba. These facts indicate that religious bodies do possess freedom of education, movement and utterance, and are able to obtain the basic materials for the conduct of their worship, religious art objects for the adornment of their people's homes, and essential literature for missionary endeavor.

As to the education of the clergy, there is the recent report of Metropolitan Benjamin, the Patriarchal Exarch to the United States, who visited Moscow in January, 1945, that he gave three lectures in the new Theological Institute recently opened in Moscow's Novodevichi Convent. He found the old cells converted into student's cubicles and the larger apartments made into a refectory, class rooms and a library. Twenty students were in residence, ranging from twenty to fifty years of age, the majority being younger men between twenty and twenty-five. These students spend three years in theological study and may then, if they so desire, be ordained to the priesthood. The law provides that young men drafted into the Red Army who wish to study for Holy Orders may apply for a release, and a number of the younger men in residence had done so. These candidates for the priesthood came from various parts of the Soviet Union and were supported by scholarships provided by the Moscow Patriarchate. There was a current waiting list of 108 candidates. . . .

For the training of rank and file clergy, there is in process of establishment a series of Pastor's Schools. The first is in operation with thirty students and the plan calls for the opening of many such schools in different parts of the Soviet Union. The Patriarchate is compelled to move slowly because of the shortage of teachers and the limited library facilities. Promises of assistance in obtaining books have come to the Patriarchate from various Anglican groups in England and America. Since these will be in English, it is interesting to note that the Theological Institute is including an English Language Course in its curriculum.

No similar descriptions are as yet available of schools established by other religious groups for the training of their leadership. It is defiintely known, however, that the Armenian-Gregorian Church has opened a seminary at Erivan in Armenia, and that the Mohammedans have opened a school in Uzbekistan for the training of mullahs. It is reported that the Baptist and Evangelical Unions have an educational center, as well as the Union of Orthodox Rabbis.

Metropolitan Benjamin reported that the Soviet government was encouraging the opening of churches where the local inhabitants wanted them and was demonstrating great generosity in the matter of providing materials for repairs and easing the contract terms of maintenance where the congregations were financially hard-pressed. While, in line with the policy of separation of church and state, there is no financial aid or support ever given, many small things are done to help. "The government," he said, "has gone much more than half-way to meet the people's requests."

THE SOVIETS AS SPORTSMEN *

The announced intention of the Soviets to "import" American-style baseball to the playing fields of Russia is not as unlikely as it seems, even though others in the past have tried to transplant America's national game and succeeded only in confounding the natives. Soviet Russia is one of the most sports-minded nations in the world. Eighty-seven trade union benevolent sporting clubs form the central core of the Soviet Union's sports and physical culture organization. According to official records there are 50,000 "cells" or branches of these clubs in plants and offices throughout Russia which follow directives from a central headquarters established in Moscow. Sports and physical culture are a state function in Russia, whose purpose is to seek not records but the harmonious physical development of the country's men and women, and for this reason they are organized, supervised and controlled by a state committee through six nation-wide bodies.

Two of the country's biggest sporting clubs, however, are entirely independent of these supervisory groups. They are the Dynamo Club, having affiliations the length and breadth of the Soviet Union, and the Spartacus, formed and operated by the craftsmen associations. Dynamo and Spartacus are the principal soccer rivals in the country and control the biggest stadiums.

Each member of a trade union sporting society cell pays a nominal monthly fee of one or two rubles and in return the cells are supposed to provide playgrounds and equipment. The national sports equipment includes some 600 stadiums, 14,000 playgrounds, 6,000 ski stations, 45,000 volley ball and basketball courts and 500 pools or beaches for water sports.

The Dynamo Club owns a stadium in Moscow with a seating capacity of 60,000 spectators. It also owns a big water station for water sports at Khimky, near the capital. Other big stadiums are operated by the Red Army and Navy.

Soccer is the most popular sport in Soviet Russia. Officials say that approximately 256,000 men take part in inter-club games. Clubs are divided into leagues and major leaguers play in final cup matches. Football (American style), rugby and cricket are unknown in the Soviet Union. Tennis is not as widely played as in the West. Skiing, track and gymnastics have big followings. Each of these sports, according to official claims, is practiced by approximately 600,000 to 800,000 persons. Next in order of popularity come hunting, swimming, cycling and skating.

The clubs of the principal industrial unions and their affiliates participate in two of the most popular Soviet annual sports events—the winter

* Ivan Parov, "The Soviets Are Sportsmen, Too," *New York Times Magazine,* October 14, 1945, p. 22.

cross-country ski match and the summer cross-country run. Both are designed to test endurance and skill. About 8,000,000 to 9,000,000 people take part in these two matches alone, according to official figures.

The emphasis in Soviet sports is on mass training and a system of examinations has been in force for the past ten years. Each club member must pass tests in steeplechase (cross-country runs), sprints, swimming, skiing and shooting. The successful candidate receives a badge of the first degree. Candidates for second-degree badges must pass tests in swimming fully clothed, parachute jumping and running 3,000 meters in 12 minutes. According to official reports, some 10,000,000 men have passed these tests.

No attempts have been made to set records in these tests. Nevertheless, Soviet athletes do claim several records, including the following:

High jump, 1 meter 95 centimeters (1 meter = 39.37 inches); pole vault, 4 meters 30 centimeters; 100 meter dash, $10\frac{3}{5}$ seconds; 10,000 meters, 30 minutes 35 seconds; 20,000 meters, 1 hour 3 minutes 51 seconds; 100 meter breast stroke, 1 minute $5\frac{2}{5}$ seconds; 200 meter breast stroke, 2 minutes $29\frac{4}{5}$ seconds; weight lifting with two hands, $132\frac{1}{2}$ kilograms (1 kilogram = 2.204 lbs.); ice skating, 500 meters, 42 seconds.

THE RED ARMY *

Up to September, 1939, the law governing Soviet military service provided that each citizen, upon reaching the age of 19, after acceptance by the draft board, spend five years on active service, part in the army and the rest on "long furlough," the length of these periods varying according to the branch of the service. The great majority, the infantry, served two years and were on furlough three. Service and furlough years were three and two for the coast defense and coast guard, and four and one for the navy.

At the age of 24 the man in service was transferred to the so-called first-term reserve. At the age of 34 he was transferred to the second-term reserve. At the age of 40 he was discharged from further military obligations to his country.

A new military law was promulgated in September, 1939. By its terms the period of active service is fixed at two years for all ground troops, three for air force and border guard, four for the coast defense and coast guard, and five for the navy. The citizen is then transferred to the Reserve of the First Category which is divided into three age terms: to 35, to 45, and to 50. For officers the terms are longer. Active duty for a captain, for instance, continues till he is 40; he remains in first-term reserve till 50, in second-term reserve till 55, and in third-term reserve till the age of 60.

Those not accepted, either because the quota is filled or because of

* Sergei N. Kournakoff, *Russia's Fighting Forces* (New York: International Publishers, 1942), pp. 84–9, 99–106.

family circumstances or physical unfitness, are enrolled in the Reserve of the Second Category, which is divided into three age terms similarly to the Reserve of the First Category. The Reserve of the Second Category can be called to active duty during the first five years.

Men of the First Category Reserve, during the first age term, are called up for training for not more than a total of six periods of two months each, or a total of a year's training spread over fifteen years. . . . Reservists are "refreshed" by frequent training periods. Even the Second Category reservists undergo training totalling twenty-four months or two years of the thirty-one years of their enrollment in the reserve. In the fifteen years between the reorganization of the Red Army, 1925–26 and 1940, some 11,000,000 men had received full military training and another 11,000,000 partial training.

This does not take into account those receiving military "pre-army" training from army instructors in the schools and in clubs and circles. In all educational institutions for youth, two hours are set aside weekly for elementary and preparatory military training for students of 13 and over. It may be said that pretty close to the entire population within the 15–45 age brackets has received some sort of military training. This provides over 75,000,000 people (men and women) useful in some form of warfare if not for active service.

According to the law, women with medical, veterinary, or special technical training may be registered and enrolled in the army and navy and called up during the training periods. In wartime they may be called for service in the army and navy for auxiliary and special duty. Women receive regular army officers' ranks. Formerly they also served in the fighting forces, but three years ago an order of Marshal Voroshilov declared this practice undesirable and limited women officers to technical, medical, and training tasks, although there are exceptions.

Great care is being taken to keep the reserve of the air force up to scratch in the latest technical developments. The air-force reserve "may, by order of the Commissar of Defense, be called up for flying-technical training in addition to the time prescribed by this paragraph, but not oftener than three times during one month." The prescribed time is six two-month calls during the first term.

During training all reservists receive from their respective factories, institutions, or collective farms half their regular earnings. Their jobs are held for them.

Where there are class distinctions in a social system they are reflected in the structure of its army, in the cleavage between the officer corps and the rank and file. While there may be in every army officers of obscure origin, while privates may come from the upper classes, these are the rule-proving exceptions. That rule is that the officers normally belong to the higher social ranks and the privates to the lower.

Such a cleavage does not exist in the Red Army. There, from the top ranking marshals down to the last private, men belong to one class. They are all workers, whether industrial, agricultural, or intellectual.

No obstacles, political or economic, stand in the way of a young man who wants to embrace a military career and become an officer or, according to Soviet terminology, a commander. To get there he does not have to rely on pull or hope for a lucky break in being appointed to a military school. All that is necessary is that he show interest, ability and the necessary moral stamina.

The corps of commanders of the Red Army is recruited as follows: a private showing ability and the desire to devote his life to a military career, goes through the regimental school which trains non-commissioned officers during the first year of his military service. If he makes a good record, he is appointed to a military officers' school, the approximate equivalent of West Point. After several years of study there he is graduated as a second lieutenant. Thus, one important source of officer material for the Red Army is the army itself.

Another source is the Soviet school system. Because of the military training given in all schools special aptitudes and predilections for the military career reveal themselves and can be given fulfillment. Any high-school graduate who has shown such aptitudes may be appointed directly to these military officers' training schools, without passing through the ranks of the army. His record must show high marks and good behavior, and he must have recommendations from the teaching staff.

Since 1938, reacting to the increased prospects of European war that set in with the encouragement to aggression given at Munich, a number of special high schools have been designated as preparatory schools for future artillery officers and flyers. Only top-flight students are accepted in these schools, which they enter at the age of 15, graduating at 18 into an artillery or flying school.

The corps of commanders of the Red Army is very large, and they come from a large network of officers' training schools. There were, for example, sixty-three officers' schools for the land forces in peacetime, and thirty-two for the air force. In addition, there are schools for the navy and the coast guard and for the other services.

Commanders who qualify for higher posts must go through so-called military academies which are equivalent to colleges, somewhat like the United States War College. There are sixteen such special academies, one for every branch of the service, general staff, artillery, mechanized troops, navy, and so on, and six special military faculties in civilian colleges. There are always more than 20,000 student officers studying in these institutions.

The educational level is high for the whole army. It may be gauged by the example of an infantry company of the Moscow military district, drawing its men from the neighboring countryside, not the city itself. In this company of 150 men, thirteen have had a college education, thirty-nine have received full high-school education, and seventy-five men have completed junior high school. The draft of September, 1940, showed 30.5 per cent with high-school and college education, 55.3 per cent with junior high-school education, and only 9.2 per cent with lower educational standards.

The defense budget in 1939 called for an expenditure on culture and education of 230 rubles a year per man. This compares with 72 rubles spent in 1934. These enormous sums maintain great theaters, musical groups, and art schools as well as technical education institutions.

In the countryside, during maneuvers, collective-farm defense groups participate. The local farmers also arrange joint social affairs. Such get-togethers have become so much a part of the Soviet scene that they are a frequent subject for painting by Soviet artists. But the basic reason for this sense of identity between army and people is the Soviet concept of the people's war, with the civilian as much in it as the man bearing arms.

The relationship between subordinates and superiors in the Red Army is naturally based on discipline. This discipline, in turn, is based on the authority of the commanding personnel. The military salute is rigidly enforced, both on and off duty. From Red Army private to the upper ranks of officers every man knows that his superior is there because he has shown fitness and for no other reason. The political consciousness of the Red Army man is based on community of interests between subordinate and superior, upon the ideological sympathies of commanders and men, interests which naturally have been immensely developed with their technical and cultural progress.

The officers of the old Russian Army, being by and large a product of class selection, were as a body afflicted with the ills of the system. Many of them were inefficient, [for the simple reason that] they embraced their career not of free will, but because their caste status presumed them to be born to the sword. Others, taking advantage of the protection their epaulets gave them, behaved in an overbearing and provocative way. . . . When the Revolution occurred after a devastating war, the soldiers looked upon many of the officers and generals with hatred for their arrogance toward them, with contempt for their inefficiency, and with fear of them as innately counter-revolutionary: The Civil War proved that, as a rule, officers and generals sided with the forces of reaction.

The defects of the old Russian officer corps brought about a natural hatred of the masses for military rank in general. That is why it took eighteen years before some of the customary officers' ranks could be re-introduced into the Red Army. This was done in 1936 when a new generation had grown up which had forgotten the defects that went with the old army rank and was now ready to look upon an officer simply as a specially trained comrade. It was another four years before the ranks of general and admiral were reintroduced. Almost simultaneously the non-commissioned ranks of corporal and sergeant were reintroduced. The top rank of marshal had been created in 1935.

The reintroduction of these ranks further strengthened discipline and the authority of the commander. The introduction of impressive uniforms for the higher commanding personnel further enhanced their authority.

The Soviet generals are by and large very young men, their average age being about 42. This, together with the youthfulness of the draftees who are called up at the age of 19, and even in certain cases at 18, makes the Red Army perhaps the youngest in existence.

⋆ 8 ⋆

Education in the Soviet Union

THE EDUCATION AND CARE OF CHILDREN *

Soviet Russia treats child-life—all child-life—with profound respect, both for its own sake, that its latent powers may develop, and for the sake of the community; for well-trained citizens pull more than their own weight and augment communal wealth.

Soviet Russia begins child-care early: very early. Begins it with infancy and the pre-natal life, rightly arguing that if children are to develop into healthy men and women their earliest years and their mother's health have significance. Russia treats pregnant women with marked respect. Special seats in tramcars are reserved for their use, and as the time for delivery approaches the mother receives an adequate pension and retires from work: the pension continues for some weeks subsequent to the birth. [For a recent edict of the Supreme Soviet relating to mothers and children, see page 235.]

Birth increasingly takes place, not amidst the bustle and disturbance of a private house, for accommodation is still cramped in Russia, but in the quiet of a maternity hospital with doctors and nurses attending. From the maternity hospital the mother passes to the maternity home, where, until she is fit to return to normal duties, she receives proper care, whilst learning, through skilled instruction, how to tend an infant child.

The Russian infant becomes the care of the whole community; its fate never left to chance or to the whim or ignorance of the parent. According to Soviet law every child has the right to an equal start in life. Whatever the circumstances of its birth or the character of its parents, the child must be properly fed and receive all needed care.

Correct motherhood, according to modern standards, is seldom instinctive. Young mothers need instruction in child-care. Lack of elementary knowledge and skilled supervision produce avoidable risks and ills. In England the rich can hire skilled nurses and obtain skilled advice. Soviet mothers of every rank receive it gratuitously and as of right. Every week during the first ten months of its life the Russian mother takes her child to the doctor to be weighed and examined and herself to receive friendly advice.

* Hewlett Johnson, Dean of Canterbury, "The Education and Care of Children," in *The Secret of Soviet Strength* (New York: International Publishers, 1943), pp. 85–97.

Everything the mother sees and hears at the Consultative Centre has teaching value. Gay posters illustrate right and wrong child treatment. Models of beds and toilet tables, of suitable and unsuitable foods, suitable and unsuitable toys, hang on the walls for examination. The white overall and white headkerchief of the head nurse strike notes of cleanliness and hygiene; and if the baby has a cold or temperature mother and child enter a side-room divided by glass partitions into separate cubicles, each with its examining table for the child and chair for the mother. The doctor prescribes, and if necessary sends the infant for hospital treatment. The district nurse attends the examination and knows, when she later in the week visits the mother, what instructions were given and how they have been heeded.

Feeding receives peculiar attention and accounts for the healthy bodies of Russian children. Extra food is ordered if needed. If able to do so the parent meets half the cost; but in any event the child is assured of appropriate food.

Reforms were not effected without struggle. Crassest ignorance often opposed them. Peasant women resisted sanitary feeding and shrank in horror from putting a baby in a bath.

Maurice Hindus, speaking of the village beauty of his youth, whom, on his return to the village of his birth, he saw grown in thirty-five years into an old woman, seven of her nine children dead and another sickening, remarks, "It could not be otherwise, so long as the people live in ill-smelling, unventilated one-room huts, and share these with their pigs and chickens and calves. So long too as mothers seldom bathed their babies; and fed them, with unwashed fingers or through artificial nipples made of dirty linen, their own chewings of black bread and potatoes or the inevitable 'kasha' or gruel."

Patience and education however now tell their tale, with results registered in the fall of infantile mortality rates.

The Russian crèche is an educational institution, where a child learns to develop its muscles and exercise its senses. In the crèche the child grows up in the atmosphere of order, cleanliness and beauty, with gay colored toys at playtime and a sleeping bag on the balcony at regular hours of rest.

Life in the crèche is bright and methodical. Meals are varied, scientifically planned and ample. Breakfast has its omelette, cereal, cocoa and bread and butter; dinner its vegetable soup with sour cream—a favorite Russian dish—its meat soufflé, carefully prepared vegetables and vitaminized dessert; tea its cereals and biscuit with buttermilk or tea; supper its cereals with milk and stewed fruit.

Ailing children receive individual attention. Rickety children, for example, receive treatment with quartz or mercury lamps. All babies are inoculated against smallpox and diphtheria.

Great principles of life and conduct can never be taught too soon and find their way from the first into the crèche.

"Never do anything for this child which it can do for itself," is written over the door of the crèche.

The principle of individual initiative embodied in the slogan finds its exercise in a hundred ways. Don't hand the toy from the table when the child can't reach it. Suggest buffet or stool. Of course the child may use the buffet afterwards to reach the jam-jar or the favourite pipe. Doubtless it will. Individual initiative is the cause of much trouble. But it is an indispensable element in life and needs careful fostering. . . .

Complementary to independence and initiative is the principle of collective enterprise. Children are taught in their tenderest years the art of living togther. When, for instance, a child plays with building blocks, . . . it finds blocks of different sizes. Small blocks for individual use; others large, though light, demanding more than one pair of small hands to lift them. With these, children work together and undertake the serious task of co-operative building. For a small child's life is more serious than we are apt to think. What we call play are real tasks: toys are things to be held, balanced, fitted together. Houses, railway stations and bridges are things to be constructed. Soviet crèche and nursery schools wisely guide the self-chosen serious tasks of life's earliest and most creative years. A million children now attend crèche and nursery schools. Their numbers grow as accommodation increases.

The physical welfare of the child is a primary concern of the State. It is, in later years, the concern of a special State department which supervises school and home sanitation, regulates school regime, renders dispensary services and guards the child against mental and physical over-strain, with special provision by the state department for the mentally and nervously abnormal child.

Her treatment of her children registers a country's social health.

Does it differentiate between child and child, favoring this class to the disadvantage of that, or does it treat all alike? Does it place girls on an equality with boys? Does it foster virile minds in healthy bodies? Does it inspire childhood and adolescence with wise and generous ideals and provide, after school years are ended, an environment which leads to creative and purposeful careers for all of them?

In a word, treating each individual as an end in itself, does it train each to be independent, critical, beauty-loving and willing to fuse his personality with others in the creation of a healthy and united society?

Measured by these standards Tsarist Russia had lamentably failed. Periodic famines played havoc with childish physique. Intellectual starvation left the mind a blank. Education was wilfully neglected.

A spurt now and then towards a national educational system—such as that of Catharine the Great in 1782 beginning with the education of 20,000 children—quickly died down. Nicholas the First put an end to Catharine's experiment on discovering that education menaced autocracy. Secondary education was forbidden to all serfs, workers and peasants.

Ripples of educational activity stirred now and again across the ocean of ignorance and illiteracy and then subsided. With the shaking of political autocracy in 1905 liberal politicians seized the opportunity of pushing through educational reforms long overdue. That surface ruffle also died down, the Government's policy being crystallised in words of Tsar Alexander's Minister of Instruction:

"To teach the mass of the children, or even the majority of them, how to read will bring more harm than good." The Tsar approved.

Another member of the Tsarist Government put it bluntly thus:

"Children of the wealthy classes should be protected from an influx into the schools of children of the poor and middle classes."

The Soviet Government changed this policy instantly and completely. The new educational policy, so planned from the earliest days, aimed at developing vigorous bodies and vital minds, inspired by generous and high-souled impulses. In operation it fulfills its early promise, releasing unexpected ability in the masses of the people.

One of the first Soviet decrees made education universal and free to all, irrespective of race or creed. In that decree we find the key to the present colossal educational advance, which lifts Russia in two decades and a half from nineteenth to first place in world literacy. In 1914, eight million children attended Russian schools; more than thirty-six millions attend school today.

Lenin saw from the outset that high output and high culture are twin needs for a communist society. Hence education holds its prominent place beside industry in each succeeding Five-Year Plan.

Moral advance is perhaps the most significant feature and shows itself in innumerable ways. Discipline, for instance, is achieved without corporal punishment: canes are illegal and selfish competition discouraged. Class lists contain "excellents" and the reverse: they do not contain "first," "second" or "third" places. Competition of individuals within a class, encouraging anti-social concentration upon individual rewards, yields place to competition between class and class, decided by the number of "excellents" achieved and stimulating the clever child to aid rather than surpass his duller classmate. Teaching another child he must penetrate more deeply into the knowledge he would impart. He learns the art of instructing as well. It is a double gain.

Soviet education aims at producing the complete citizen. This demands, among other things, bridging the gulf between manual and intellectual activity, an end achieved by giving the child a thorough understanding of the nature of productive industry as part of the social whole.

The Soviet child is brought into close contact with some Soviet factory in order that, at first hand, it may learn what industry is and what it is for; what place any industry occupies in the social order; what effect industry has upon the worker; and what effect this or that product exerts upon the social body as a whole.

This is an admirable innovation, wholly different in principle from instruction in the use of particular tools or performance of technical tasks which will await the child later in industry. It is no industrial short cut, stealing school hours to supply industry with ready-trained "hands."

Technological training aims at making a many-sided social being; not a mere skilled worker, but a man or woman who understands not only the use of materials, nor even the scientific nature of the forces required to bring them to their final form—though that is a valuable part of the training—but in addition the man or woman who understands the effects of production, and particularly of new modes of production, upon the whole organization of life, and upon each human being who is employed. It aims at understanding not the parts of life, but life as a whole.

It is difficult to overstress the social importance of this. Let me illustrate the kind of social lesson it teaches. Take a child to a one- or two-man smithy; or to a tinker's shop worked by brothers. He can readily understand that the ownership of such tools as they employ is quite appropriate.

Take him, however, to a great factory, with its subdivision of labour and all its interlocked activities and he will quickly perceive how dangerous it would be for some individual, other than those whose co-operative effort made the machines and whose skill drives them, to own the machines and control the lives and welfare of those who work them. Readily the child understands why that which is socially produced and socially operated should be socially owned. He gets a social consciousness. He learns how to judge the relative social value of different operations. If he becomes a chemist he will enquire, not merely how to make a product, a scent or a poison, but what effect its production will have on society. If he becomes an engineer, he will enquire what is the social value of a railway he is invited to build. Social values will, in the case of this engineer, tend to take the place of monetary values.

Something remains to be said of out-of-school activities and of the treatment of the exceptional child.

No child born lacks a hobby, collecting stamps, eggs or cigarette cards, constructing wireless sets or model railways, photography, painting, singing or dancing.

The Soviet city makes extraordinary provision for the child and its hobby. Every city and many villages possess their Palaces of Pioneers, well equipped for eager amateurs: aviation workshops, fitted with air tunnels and precision machinery; laboratories where animals and animal breeding can be studied intensively; hot-houses where the student can create new varieties of plants. Art, dramatics, ballet dancing, music, painting, sculpture, chess and photography, taught and practised. I examined one building where 2,500 children were at work in 209 circles on sixty-nine different subjects. I have never seen its like in any other land.

THE SCHOOL SYSTEM *

Public education has always been given special attention in the U.S.S.R. Budget appropriations for this purpose have mounted yearly, the numbers of schools and pupils have vastly increased and the percentage of literacy has greatly risen as compared with 1914–1917.

In a declaration on the status of the unified Soviet school published on October 16, 1918, the following principles were laid down as bases for public education:

1. Democratization of public education—schools of all degrees to be placed within reach of the entire population and the latter to be widely drawn into the management of public education.

2. Enactment of universal, compulsory, free elementary education.

3. Principle of the unified school: a successive link between schools of various types and grades, a unified school system for all the peoples of the U.S.S.R.

4. Separation of the School from the Church. This was a natural consequence of the Decree of January 1, 1918, concerning the separation of the Church from the State. This edict declared the prohibition of any laws or decisions in the Soviet Republic "which would hinder or restrict the freedom of conscience, or establish whatever preferences or privileges on the basis of religious creed of the citizens" (paragraph 2). The 3rd paragraph of this decree declared that "every citizen is free to practise any religion or none at all. Any deprivation of rights in connection with practising any religious faith whatever or none at all is hereby repealed." In its decision of February 18, 1918, on schools, the People's Commissariat of Education explained: "Considering religion a matter of conscience of each individual person, the State remains neutral on the question of religion, that is to say, does not side with any religious creed, does not associate any special rights or preferences with creeds, does not offer material or moral support to any of them. From this it naturally ensues that the State cannot undertake any religious training of children."

5. Equal rights for men and women with regard to education (as also in other spheres of social life).

6. Instruction in the native language of the pupils; development of national culture.

The integrated school system today consists of the following links:

1. Pre-school social education for children up to 7 (kindergartens, pre-school homes for orphans, children's playgrounds).

2. Elementary school with a four-year course of instruction for children of both sexes aged from 7 to 11.

* Eugene Medynsky, "Schools and Education in the U.S.S.R.," *American Sociological Review*, June, 1944, Vol. IX, No. 3, pp. 287–93.

3. Junior secondary school with a seven-year course for children from 7 to 14.

4. Senior secondary school with a ten-year teaching course for children from 7 to 17.

5. Higher educational institutions (universities with a five-year course; institutes—technical, agricultural, medical, pedagogic, and other, with a four or four-and-a-half years' course of training).

On completing a junior secondary school boys and girls can transfer either to a senior secondary school, or to a secondary technical training institution with a three-year course (industrial and agricultural technicums, medical and pedagogical schools, etc.) for training workers of intermediate qualifications—technicians, assistant surgeons, elementary school teachers. After three years of practical work in their respective specialties, these workers, if they wish, can continue their education in a school of higher learning.

The following figures show the growth of the number of elementary and secondary schools and the number of pupils therein.

Before the Revolution, in 1914–1915—105,524 schools with 7,896,249 pupils.

In 1930–1931—152,813 schools with 17,614,537 pupils.

On the eve of World War II, in 1938–1939—171,579 schools with 31,517,375 pupils.

A particularly big increase occurred in the number of secondary schools and of pupils therein: there was an increase of 50.8 times in the number of pupils of junior secondary schools and 14.2 times in senior secondary schools. In 1914–1915 secondary schools were attended by only 635,591 pupils— children of the privileged strata of the urban population, while in 1938– 1939 this number reached 9,028,156. There was an especially great increase in the number of secondary schools in the countryside and in industrial settlements. Before the Soviet Revolution there were practically no such schools here.

From 231,000 in 1914–1915, the number of elementary and secondary school teachers reached 1,027,164—a 4.4-fold increase—by 1938–1939.

To appreciate fully such a huge growth of the school system and the number of pupils and teachers one should take into consideration the tremendous difficulties involved here: the construction of new schools had to be extensively developed, great numbers of teachers trained, and for many peoples of the U.S.S.R. (especially peoples of the East, such as Uzbeks, Tajiks, Kazakhs, Kirghizians, etc., as well as peoples of the North), whose education had been deliberately hindered by tsarism in the past days, new textbooks had to be compiled, and even written alphabets, since a number of nationalities of Russia had not any letters of their own before the Revolution. At present textbooks, books and newspapers are printed in about 150 languages of different peoples of the U.S.S.R.

The Soviet Government regarded the speedy introduction of universal compulsory free education as a matter of vital significance. Thanks to energetic measures, by 1938 this had been already introduced among all peoples of the U.S.S.R.: to the extent of four-year elementary schooling in countryside and junior secondary schooling (seven years, for children from 7 or 8 to 14 or 15) in town and industrial settlements. From 1944, compulsory education is established from the age of 7.

On December 26, 1919, on the initiative of Lenin was promulgated a decree on the elimination of illiteracy. . . . A huge number of special schools for adults were set up, attended by 5 million people yearly since this decree was published. In 1897 the percentage of literates aged over 9 was 24%, in 1939—81.2%.

The growth of literacy among the peoples in the East and North is particularly significant. Twenty years before the Soviet Revolution, in 1897, when an all-Russian census was held, the percentage of literacy among Kirghizians was 0.6%, among Tajiks—3.8%, among Uzbeks—1.6%. By the beginning of the 20th century this percentage had only slightly increased among all the peoples, and among the nationalities just mentioned it fluctuated between 2 and 5 per cent. As a result of the determined drive against illiteracy since the Soviet Revolution, the picture has sharply changed, especially so during the thirties: the percentage of literacy among the population aged over 9 increased between 1926 and 1939 as follows: Kirghizian Republic—from 15.1% to 71.7%; Uzbek Republic—from 10.6% to 67.8%.

The swift growth of the school system and the number of pupils caused unusual difficulty in training the requisite number of teachers.

Teachers for elementary schools are at present trained in teachers' colleges—intermediate training institutions with a three-year course which corresponds to normal schools in other countries. These colleges enroll students of both sexes from among the pupils who have completed junior (7-year) secondary schools. Teachers for classes V–VII of junior and senior secondary schools are trained at two-year teachers' institutes where students who have graduated from 9th and 10th class of secondary schools are eligible for enrollment. In 1943 there were 76 such institutes in the Soviet Union. Besides this, a considerable number of secondary school teachers are trained at universities.

Evening courses, and especially correspondence courses, are widely used in the U.S.S.R. for the purposes of pedagogic training, students thus continuing their main occupation uninterrupted. A special decision of the Soviet Government binds all practising teachers who have not received the required diploma to complete their pedagogic education by correspondence courses.

Teachers enjoy great respect and attention in the U.S.S.R. A considerable number of teachers have been elected deputies to the Supreme Soviets of the U.S.S.R. and the Union Republics. The title "Merited Teacher" has been instituted, this conferring the same privileges as those enjoyed by scientific workers. Special sanitoriums and rest homes have been established for teachers.

Universities of the U.S.S.R. have a five-year course and train workers for research institutions and teachers for elementary schools. University faculties include language and literature, history, geography, physico-mathematics, biology, chemistry, etc. In 1938 our universities enrolled 47,705 students. College-trained specialists are prepared in the U.S.S.R. at a four or four-and-a-half-year course of the institutes: industrial-technical, economic, etc. In 1943 there were 750 schools of higher learning in the U.S.S.R., including 23 universities.

The number of students of all higher educational institutions totalled 619,897. Since the Soviet Revolution of 1917 the number of these establishments increased seven fold (in 1914–1915 there were only 91) and the number of students grew six fold—112,000 in 1914–1915.

A still greater increase took place in intermediate vocational training institutions (technicums, etc.)—in 1914–1915 the total number was only 295, whereas by 1939 the figure had mounted to 3,732—an increase of 12.7 times.

For training of foremen and skilled workmen there exist trade, railway, and factory apprenticeship schools.

The management and administration of public education in each of the 16 Union Republics is effected by the People's Commissariat of Education of each Republic. These bodies organize pre-school educational establishments, general educational schools, universities, teachers' institutes, teachers' colleges, as well as cultural-educational work among adults (libraries, schools and courses for adults) in accordance with the specific national characteristics of each republic.

Vocational training institutions—secondary and higher—are under the jurisdiction of the appropriate People's Commissariats: medical schools fall within the province of the Health Commissariat, transport schools under the Railways Commissariat. The supervision over elementary vocational training institutions—trade, railway and factory apprenticeship schools—is within the province of a special department known as the Labour Reserves Board.

Thus there is no all-Union body in charge of general-educational elementary and secondary schools in the U.S.S.R. Each Union Republic is autonomous in building up its public education system. But the most important general directives concerning elementary and secondary schools in matters concerning the whole of the Soviet Union are established by the Council of People's Commissars of the U.S.S.R.

Organizationally, schools of higher learning are arranged somewhat differently—they are under the direct guidance of the corresponding People's

Commissariats. But the general supervision is effected by an All-Union body —the U.S.S.R. Committee on Higher Schools.

Despite all the hardships of wartime, the number of educational establishments, including the schools of higher learning, was not reduced in the U.S.S.R. On the contrary, the 1944 budget provides 21.1 billion rubles of appropriations for public education, this being a 66.1% increase over 1943. [The 1945 budget provided 28.6 billion rubles for public education, an increase of 39.9% over 1944.]

In all schools of the U.S.S.R. the term commences on September 1. There are three short vacations during the school term besides the long summer vacation of two or three months' duration.

Soon after the Soviet Revolution, in 1918, co-education was introduced in all types and grades of Soviet schools. This measure was necessitated by (1) the fact that at that time the question of establishing equal rights for men and women was one of most vital urgency, demanding priority, and (2) the necessity of placing schooling within the reach of the whole population.

Under these conditions one of the most important measures in the struggle for equal rights was the establishing of co-educational schools, because even identical curricula providing for general knowledge in girls' and boys' schools could not have surmounted undesirable traditions formed in girls' schools during the many decades before the revolutionary years, when the education of girls was far below the general educational requirements prevailing in boys' schools. The entire structure and curriculum of girls' schools was prone to cultivate a number of undesirable features; it was fenced off from reality and involved unwholesome isolation of boys and girls. Had segregated schooling been introduced at that time, it would have required many years to eliminate these negative features which had become so firmly rooted in girls' schools of pre-revolutionary days.

At that time there was an inadequate number of schools and the introduction of segregated schools in many inhabited places where there was only a boys' secondary school would have deprived many girls of a secondary education.

Thus co-education in that period played its desirable and progressive role. Co-education, however, entails certain shortcomings which, though duly appreciated at that time, still had to be left standing.

Co-education hinders the adaptation of the school program to the different rates of physiological development of boys and girls. It prevents adequate treatment of certain psychological differences, and the necessary differentiation of training of boys and girls for practical activities. Under co-education the composition of intermediate and senior classes of secondary schools becomes very heterogeneous, this negatively influencing the efficiency of the instructional program.

The full equality of women's rights and the general availability of education has been completely achieved during the quarter of a century that has elapsed since the Soviet Revolution. The number of schools has vastly increased. In all towns and industrial settlements universal compulsory seven-year secondary education has been introduced.

In view of all this and with the object of eliminating the shortcomings inherent in co-education, in all capitals of the U. S. S. Republics and in large industrial centers and cities (72 cities in all), as of autumn 1943, segregated education of boys and girls has been introduced in all of the ten classes of secondary schools by means of establishing separate schools for boys and girls. This was preceded by six months of experiment at segregated teaching in several Moscow schools during the spring term of 1943, yielding good results. In all other towns and in rural localities junior and senior secondary schools continue co-education.

As distinguished from the pre-revolutionary times, this segregated education provides for an identical level of general-educational knowledge for boys and girls, and involves no segregation in any extra-school activities. The principals of the schools concerned declared that during the first six months, the principle of segregated education introduced in 1943–1944 showed up favorably as indicated by achievement.

In moral training considerable attention is paid to cultivating the feeling of love for the country. This is achieved by means of lessons in history, native and Russian language and literature, geography, the Constitution of the U.S.S.R., extra class reading, social activities of the pupils, and meetings with Heroes of the Soviet Union. . . . This love for one's country and people is combined with cultivating international spirit—respect for other nations, fostering the spirit of equality of all nations.

Aesthetic training takes place by means of lessons in singing and drawing, excursions to art galleries and museums, out-of-town trips, amateur arts circles (drawing, singing, music, and theatricals). A number of towns and cities have special theatres for young spectators, and children's cinemas.

Physical training includes the training of children to observe the rules of hygiene; drill and physical culture lessons; gymnastics, games and sports.

An important role in the educational work of schools is played by the organization of Young Pioneers, which unites the most active pupils, who should and do provide an example to the rest of the children by their good programs at lessons, their discipline, their active social work and concern for the school's honor and good name.

Diversified experiences outside of lessons and school are an important part of educational work. These are achieved by voluntary activities in school and by creative endeavors of the pupils outside of school hours. These activities and experiences are provided by all kinds of circles (clubs), which may be classified as follows: (1) Educational (literature, history, biography); (2) Artistic (choirs, music, drawing, theatricals); (3) Domestic science and manual training (sewing, carpentry); (4) Physical culture; (5) Military.

Much attention is paid to reading done by pupils outside of school hours. School libraries recommend lists of books on the subjects being studied in lessons, on current events and on anniversary dates. Exhibitions of books are also arranged, besides which there are special circles of young readers.

Extracurricular institutions and activities are of exceptional diversity. First of all there are palaces and houses of Pioneers in all towns. Larger cities usually have a central Pioneers' House and several district houses complete with libraries, workshops, laboratories, and sports grounds.

With the object of cultivating in children love for nature and interest in farming there exist organizations as follows: (1) Young naturalists, whose activities are directed by the central station of young naturalists, at local stations which are established all over the Soviet Union; (2) Similar work in the sphere of technique and engineering effected by central and local stations of young technicians.

HIGHER EDUCATION *

It cannot be overemphasized that the school system of the Soviet Union, just as the entire life of the country, is undergoing a constant change.

I have a volume giving the most important laws and regulations pertaining to colleges in U.S.S.R. which were in force in 1940; almost none of these were promulgated earlier than in 1936; most of these laws were adopted in 1938 and later. Some of them are obsolete by now. The two-fold purpose of education, however, remains the same, namely, devotion to the task of building the type of human society as outlined by the leaders of the country and to the place in it the student is to occupy upon graduation on one hand, and training him for performance of a specific function in this society on the other hand.

Russian articles on the conditions in the colleges consistently stress that the turning point in the evolution of these schools was the national convention of professors and administrative officers of these schools, which took place in May, 1938, and culminated in a meeting with Stalin in the Kremlin. At this meeting, V. M. Molotov, then the head of the government, while taking pride in the fact that the number of students in college grade schools of U.S.S.R. at that time already exceeded that receiving education in the universities and other college type schools of Italy, Germany, England and France combined, pointed out that the quantitative, and even more the qualitative objectives in Soviet higher education have not yet been reached by far and specified the nearest tasks.

It would be impossible to enumerate all the individual changes which took place in Soviet schools from the time when progress of students was judged without examinations and students coming from workers' or peas-

* J. G. Tolpin, "Engineering Education in the Soviet Union," *Journal of Engineering Education,* October, 1943, Vol. XXXIV, No. 2, pp. 139–44.

ants' families were preferred for admission to schools for higher education over children of the middle class or aristocracy, to the present state, when no value is ascribed to the social origin of the student.

Special mention is deserved by the problem of women students. After the Revolution, the doors of all schools and professions were opened to women, and at the present time women are active in every field of industrial and social life of the Soviet Union. However, it is safe to assert that in those professions in which women were active also before the Revolution, such as medicine, their numbers are much greater than in others. There may be some women engaged in naval construction, for instance, but their number is certainly small; however, in 1939, 60 per cent of all physicians in U.S.S.R. were women; in some constituent republics the number of women physicians is still higher than this average; for instance among Bashkir physicians the number of women was stated to be 75 per cent.

Women direct research in many branches of chemistry and engineering. In some places they occupy administrative engineering positions of importance. Women amounted to 41 per cent of all students in colleges of U.S.S.R. in 1939; in the technical colleges they comprised 27 per cent. The greatest advance in this respect was made by the women of countries with a large percentage of Moslem population. Women of Uzbekistan, Azerbaidzhan and Turkmenia who did not dare to lift the veil from their face in the presence of men 25 years ago now study engineering, and in some cases teach engineering. Of all college educated engineers, 14.4 per cent were women in 1938. Of these, in the textile industry 32.8 per cent were women, in the food industry 31.1 per cent, but in coal mining only 8.7 per cent of the engineers were women, in oil production 9.3 per cent. The various branches of mechanical engineering had between 7.9 and 17.0 per cent women.

An education feature of recent years consisted in developing educational facilities in the various regions populated by national minorities. The number of students coming from these regions showed a consistent increase, and at the beginning of 1935 only 54.4 per cent of the university students were of Russian nationality, the others being Ukrainian, White Russian, Georgian, Armenian, etc. In the territories where languages other than Russian prevail schools were founded in which the native language and not Russian is the medium of education; Russian is only one of the more important subjects of instruction. Many secondary technical schools are also conducted in the native languages and some university courses in various subjects were offered in these languages in recent years. There are over 100 languages and dialects spoken on the territory of U.S.S.R.; over 60 of these are recognized for official use.

In 1939, the total number of professorships or chairs was close to 10,000, over half of them in the technical and agricultural colleges. The total teaching staff comprised 40,500 persons, against 5,800 in the universities and other college grade schools before the Revolution. Only 46 per cent of the persons occupying these chairs in 1939 were permanently appointed. The others were temporarily in their positions, and many chairs remained vacant.

Reading the Russian technical literature, you find internationally known experts with 50 or more years behind them in their chosen fields still active and reporting research work. A. N. Bakh, the leading biochemist of the Soviet Union, N. D. Zelinskiĭ, head of the Organic Chemistry Institute and A. E. Favorskiĭ, editor of the *Journal of General Chemistry,* are all octogenarians and all active in their fields, as are many others. The scientists, regardless of their political philosophy, longed for a chance to contribute to the development of the natural resources of the country. Many joined not only in the economic, but also in the political aims of Soviet education. The majority of the teaching personnel, however, is young, and for the most part educated under the Soviet regime.

Tuition in all schools of U.S.S.R. was free until recently and in 1939 89.7 per cent of students of all college grade schools received a state scholarship or stipend. A student of the first year was getting 130 rubles; second, 150 rubles; third and fourth, 175 rubles; fifth, 500 rubles. Aspirants, or post-graduate students in colleges and scientific research institutions carrying instruction duties were receiving 400 rubles per month shortly before the war. However, students who showed unsatisfactory progress in their work could suffer reduction of their stipends by 50 per cent. Dormitories, medical attention, and cultural needs of students were also provided. However, in October, 1940, a decree was issued eliminating free tuition in secondary and college grade schools, as well as payment of state stipends to all students, except those whose study received the mark "excellent." The tuition was set at from 150 rubles a year in the higher grades of secondary schools to 500 rubles a year in art colleges. Correspondence school students pay half of the regular tuition. An idea of the value of these payments may be gained by comparing them with the salaries of the teaching personnel, which ranged in 1940 from 1500 rubles per month for the head of a department in a college with a doctor's degree to 225 rubles per month for a laboratory assistant with only elementary school education.

The absolute expenditures for maintaining the schools for higher education may not be very indicative, as there is no way of correlating them with the expenditure in dollars. However, it may be of interest to say that it doubled within the five years from 1934 to 1938, at which time it exceeded 2,000,000,000 rubles.

Student activities in literature and politics have always been a characteristic feature of higher education in Russia. Some of these activities are preserved now in a greatly changed form. Politically the Communist youth organization occupies the foreground. Sport organizations come into increasing prominence, with American sports being very popular. Chess is the favorite game.

Apartment house for engineers and technicians

A seven-passenger car in the yard of an automobile factory in Moscow

On the beach in Moscow

A street near the Molotov Automobile Works

The apparent aim of the system of vocational education in the Soviet Union taken as a whole is to give a minimum of technical training to every employee of industry, from the common laborer up, and complaints are even voiced occasionally if in a certain industry a substantial number of workers is left without training. The scope of the program is indicated by the plan for the period 1938–1942, which called for training of over 9 million people for work in industry in different capacities. An American engineer who supervised in 1938 construction of a plant in the Soviet Union told me that in his estimation 50 per cent of the cost of the building went into the construction of social halls and classrooms.

Technical schools in U.S.S.R. aim at preparing engineers and also intermediate personnel. The first is done through schooling in college grade schools, the second involves study in secondary technical schools, called technicums, which occupy a position distinctly different from that of technical high schools in this country. They aim at preparation of assistant engineers. The secondary technical schools numbered 3,400 and had an enrollment of 700,000 in 1938; this enrollment was expected to reach 800,000 in 1942, at which time the number of technicums was to reach 3,500. For admission to a technicum 7 years preliminary schooling is required, as compared to 10 years' schooling necessary for admission to a college grade school. The course of instruction in a technicum is 4 years.

Factory schools perform an important function in training qualified workers. They showed an increase up to 1932, at which time they had 975,000 students in close to 4,000 institutions. Later, this type of school began to diminish in number. However, they were revived in a different form in October, 1940, when the decree was issued providing for creation of a labor reserve.

During the first five-year plan the factory schools trained 450,000 workers. This number was tripled in the second five-year industrialization period, during which 1,400,000 qualified workers were graduated from these schools. According to the third five-year plan 1.7 millions were to be trained in these schools. Along with purely vocational training, they give a certain amount of general and political education, and whenever the work at a particular plant requires it, for instance in the food industry, elementary rules of sanitation or information of similar value.

Industrial establishments in general served throughout the past 15 years as a training ground and it was estimated that in 1937 alone various schools and courses given at the plants graduated 3,000,000 out of 4,600,000 workers enrolled in them.

Correspondence courses leading to college degrees have been in existence in the Soviet Union for over 10 years in the field of social sciences, economics, law, agriculture, technology. Only in the field of medicine is instruction by correspondence courses prohibited by law. About 1,000 engineers and about 3,000 teachers have been graduated by this system between 1935 and 1940.

The students taking correspondence courses have to present themselves in person for practical laboratory and shop work for about a month a year, for which time they get leave from the plants where they are employed.

The system is sometimes criticized on the basis that there is lack of organization of its program and the difficulties connected with this method requiring extensive correspondence and occasional interviews with students who fall below the required level of progress.

In the rural districts a form of technical instruction has been recently made available consisting in Kolkhoz laboratories which are designed in the first place to aid the work of the farmer and improve the crops, but at the same time they disseminate much simple and rudimentary information on agriculture, soil chemistry and other subjects. There were 11,500 of these simple laboratories in the Ukraine in 1934, 125 in Turkmenia, and a substantial increase of them was planned.

There were at least 4 systematic courses of study in the Ukraine designed to prepare workers for these Kolkhoz laboratories; the experience of these laboratory workers rates much higher than their education, as a rule.

Admission to a university or technical college in the Soviet Union, the course of study and graduation regulations are largely governed by the Committee in Charge of Schools of Higher Education with headquarters in Moscow. In addition to graduation from a secondary school, i.e., a total of 10 years' preliminary schooling, the prerequisites for admission include also a competitive examination, and a number of students fail to pass this examination each year. Results of the examinations are published in the most important newspapers. Candidates graduated from the secondary schools with excellent marks may be excused from the entrance examinations.

The average age of a first year student at the present time is 19–20 years. The course of study of the engineering colleges is 5 years, with slight differences depending upon the branch of engineering.

MEDICAL EDUCATION IN THE SOVIET UNION *

Since the Revolution of 1917, the Soviet Union has undergone profound changes. Many of the basic concepts, however, have not been altered. Thus the Soviet social philosophy as it applies to medicine is expressed in Articles 120–122 of the Constitution of 1936:

> Citizens of the U.S.S.R. have the right to maintenance in old age and also in case of sickness or loss of working capacity. This right is ensured by the extensive development of social insurance of the workers and employees at state expense, free medical service for the working people, and the provision of a wide network of health resorts for the use of the working people. . . . Citizens

* Michael B. Shimkin, "Medical Education in the Soviet Union," *American Review of Soviet Medicine,* June, 1944, Vol. I, pp. 465–9, 475–80.

of the U.S.S.R. have the right to education. . . . Women in the U.S.S.R. are accorded equal rights with men. . . . Exercise of these rights is ensured . . . by state protection of the interests of mother and child, maternity leave with full pay, and the provision of a wide network of maternity homes, nurseries, and kindergartens.

The goal of medical care and preservation of health of all its citizens never has been relinquished by the Soviet Union. Methods of attaining it, on the other hand, have been modified and altered in several instances. These changes are well exemplified in the field of medical education.

The history of medical education under the Soviet system falls into three general periods: reconstruction, experimentation, and stabilization. Until 1922, the consequences of war, revolution, famine, and epidemics taxed the inadequate medical personnel and equipment that had remained from tsarist days. No changes were made in the curriculum, which continued on the five-year German plan with a large number of lectures, subjects, and didactic demonstrations. Restrictions against admission to medical schools based on sex, race, or religion were abolished, and preference was given during the early years to children of workers and peasants. Many students were inadequately prepared, equipment was insufficient, and there was a serious shortage of instructors. Examinations were either not given or reduced to formalities.

Between 1922 and 1930, there was a gradual improvement in the quality and the quantity of the schools. Examinations were resumed. The teaching of hygiene and preventive medicine was stressed.

In 1930, with the First Five-Year Plain, an accentuation in medical education was deemed essential, and radical changes were made in its administration and curriculum. Medical schools were removed from the jurisdiction of the Commissariat of Education and were placed under the Commissariat of Public Health. The medical course was shortened to four years. Subjects were reduced in number and coordinated, duplication was eliminated, recitations and lectures were restricted, and Latin terms were discontinued. Whereas the usual subjects of medicine were curtailed, hygiene and preventive medicine were allotted additional time. Social sciences, economics, physical culture, and military training occupied almost 40 per cent of the time. Students worked in groups and carried out collective tasks. Examinations were again abolished.

Since specialists were desired for collective farms, industries, maternity homes, nurseries, and health centers as well as for the usual clinical branches, three faculties of medicine were established: general medicine and prophylaxis, hygiene and sanitation, and pediatrics, including maternity and child protection. Three-fourths of the students took the general course. In the faculty of hygiene and sanitation which included 10 per cent of the students, the courses in all clinical subjects were reduced during this period to a total of less than 700 hours.

The results achieved from the new curriculum were not satisfactory, and revisions began shortly after its introduction. The plan was particularly criticized for its weakness in the preclinical sciences and for its premature overdevelopment of nontherapeutic specialties. . . .

By 1935, through various decisions of the Committee on Higher Education of the Council of People's Commissars and of the Commissariat of Public Health, the medical course was again lengthened to five years, lectures and recitations were increased, group projects were reduced, Latin was resumed for medical terms, and individual examinations and final board examinations were reintroduced. The medical course was gradually strengthened by increased time devoted to basic and clinical subjects, and by the addition of courses in medical specialties. Major differences between the three faculties of medicine were reduced until there remained only greater emphasis on the subjects of specialization. At the same time, the number of qualified instructors increased, the budget for medical education steadily became larger, and equipment and other physical facilities expanded.

In 1913, there were 19,785 physicians in Russia; in 1941, the number was 130,348. In 1913, there were 13 medical schools with 8,600 students; in 1941, 106,000 students were being trained in 51 medical schools. During the early years of the Soviet Union, such expansion could not have been accomplished without some compromises and difficulties. But the efficiency and the capabilities of the Soviet physicians have been well proven under fire and in disaster, and attest the soundness of their education and training. Despite severe losses, medical education continued without interruption during the war, and during the first 18 months, 32,000 graduates took their places in the ranks of military and civilian medicine of the Soviet Union.

The People's Commissariat of Public Health of the U.S.S.R. is the chief administrative body in all matters pertaining to medicine, including the education and training of physicians, dentists, pharmacists, and subprofessional medical personnel. It has six main divisions, including one on medical research and education. Under this division is a department of administration of medical educational institutions.

Matters of policy and the more important questions regarding education are considered also by the Committee on Higher Education of the Council of People's Commissars of the U.S.S.R.

The Commissariat of Public Health of the U.S.S.R. has direct supervision over but a few of the medical schools. The great majority of them are administered by the Commissariats of Public Health of the constituent republics of the Soviet Union, which are under the administration of the national commissariat. In 1941, there were 72 medical institutes in the Soviet Union.

Each republic of the Soviet Union has at least one medical school. The total enrollment of students in the medical schools in 1941 was approximately 106,000. The largest schools, with 2500 to 3500 students, were at the time in Moscow, Leningrad, Kiev, and Kharkov. The smaller schools have several hundred students enrolled in the five-year course. The plans of the curriculum, instruction, and examinations are uniform throughout the country.

The direction of medical education by the Commissariat of Public Health also involves postgraduate medical training of physicians, the training of specialists and research workers, and the education of the subprofessional medical assistants. There are 11 postgraduate institutes for physicians, and they are entirely separate from the medical schools. Specialists in clinical subjects and research workers are trained in the medical schools or in the many research institutes of the Union.

Graduates of medical schools are given certificates and the title of *vrach* (physician). All graduates, women as well as men, are given commissions in the Red Army or Navy Reserve. The new physicians appear before boards of the Commissariats of Public Health and, in order of their academic standing, choose assignments from a list of available posts. In 1939, 80–90 per cent of the graduates were sent to rural areas, where they were assigned to locations for one to three years. At the end of this period they may apply for another position or for further training. . . .

Outstanding graduates of medical schools and practicing physicians are permitted to study three years for the degree of Candidate of Medical Sciences. In non-clinical subjects, such as bacteriology or physiology, these students receive fellowships to work at medical schools or research institutions, including those of the Academy of Sciences. In clinical subjects, leading to specialization in surgery, internal medicine, etc., they must have had three years of rural practice or of service as hospital *ordinatori* (residents).

During the fellowship period the student-physicians are known as *aspirants*. They conduct original investigations, assist in research and in teaching. It is also required that they study a foreign language. Each aspirant submits a thesis at the end of his appointed term and defends it publicly against three "opponents" before a committee of professors who examine the qualifications of the aspirant and express their decision by secret ballot. The names of the successful candidates are then submitted for endorsement to the Commissariat of Public Health.

The highest medical degree is that of Doctor of Medical Sciences, which is obtained by additional work for an undesignated period—usually no less than three years—after the acquisition of the Candidate degree. It requires submission and publication of an extensive, original investigation. It is not conferred by an institute or medical school but by the Committee on Higher Education of the Council of People's Commissars.

Every physician in the Soviet Union is required to take from three to six months of postgraduate instruction every three years. . . . While in attendance, physicians are paid their regular salary, plus a stipend to offset extra expenses. During the war, the courses were shortened and limited to field surgery and other war topics.

The physicians of the Soviet Union are assisted by four types of subprofessional workers: feldshers (technical assistants), midwives, nurses, and laboratory technicians. The admission requirement to the "middle medical schools" is completion of seven years of primary education. The courses for feldshers and midwives are three years and those for nurses and technicians two years in length. Dentists and pharmacists are also trained in the middle medical schools, but higher qualifications may be obtained by completing a four-year course in the stomatologic and pharmacologic institutes, respectively. Ten years of education are required for admission to these higher schools.

The chief objective of medical education in the Soviet Union is to obtain an adequate supply of well-trained physicians for the entire population. A centralized plan under the complete direction of physicians appears to facilitate this accentuated production of personnel. It is not known by the author how the separation of medical schools from universities has affected medical education, but the essential collaboration of clinical medicine with the basic sciences depends more upon contacts between instructors and researchers than upon the administrative format.

The history of medical education in the Soviet Union is one of great expansion, with continually rising standards as material resources increase. In 1939, due to the great number of students, there was still a shortage of textbooks, electro-cardiographs, and other special equipment.

On the basis of the educational plan and the time devoted to it, it seems that premedical education in the Soviet Union is below American *pre-war* standards. A plan has already been made, however, to increase the post-war medical course to six years, with particular strengthening of the preclinical sciences and general education. This plan, in fact, was formulated in 1938 and was to have gone into effect in 1941 when the war intervened.

The general curriculum of the medical schools does not differ significantly from the American plans. There is greater emphasis on hygiene and sanitation, and a lesser number of hours is devoted to obstetrics and gynecology. Even in the pediatrics faculty, fewer hours are spent in obstetrics and gynecology than in most medical schools in the United States, although this is compensated by emphasis on these subjects during the practical work courses. The marked differences between the three faculties of medicine that existed in the 1930 plan have been reduced and are now of relatively minor importance. The trend has been obviously toward elimination of specialization during undergraduate medical training.

No formal provision is made in the Soviet plan for an interne year. After graduation, the best students may receive further training as residents in hospitals, or they may enter research institutes. The better students are assigned to districts where they have to rely on themselves, whereas gradu-

.tes of lower standing are sent to work as assistants to experienced
physicians.

It is interesting and significant that the Soviet plan of medical education,
.fter radical innovations in 1930, has returned gradually to the ideas fol-
owed in the United States. Group studies, complex courses combining
many phases of medical science, great emphasis on hygiene and sanitation
it the expense of courses in therapy, undergraduate specialization, and the
limination of examinations have all been tried and found wanting. Appar-
intly four years is the minimal time in which adequate medical education
:an be achieved, and the compression of courses into an accelerated program
vas not successful in the Soviet Union.

Soviet Law and Justice

THE INDIVIDUAL AND PROPERTY IN SOVIET LAW *

The theme running through Soviet law as it concerns the relationship between the state and the individual is that the state exists for the benefit of the individual, to guide him and protect him and to better his condition until such time as classes have disappeared and abundance has been achieved so that the state can "wither away."

Protection of the state from the individual who would overthrow it becomes one task of law. A second task is protection of the individual from unwarranted assumption of power by a state official or his failure to take measures designed to make certain that only the guilty are punished. Both tasks are important in considering the position of the individual in Soviet society.

The first task has been highly publicized outside the Soviet Union. The Soviet leaders have been severe in ridding the U.S.S.R. of individuals who were believed to be dangerous to the program directed toward socialism. These leaders have felt that the birth pangs of the dictatorship of the proletariat in the chaos of civil war and intervention following the first world war required harsh measures of protection. They have likewise felt that the long-standing hostility of other world powers which took concrete forms in refusal of recognition and culminated in the jockeying for position and ultimate catastrophe of the second world war, required unusual vigilance. Soviet law has therefore been strict during the twenty-six years of the Soviet state's existence.

The Soviet Criminal Code begins with all-inclusive chapters containing articles designed to protect the state from intentional and unintentional acts directed at the overthrow of the state or which might result in such a revolution. Omissions to act are likewise defined as dangerous to the state, and there is even included an article which provides that if an act is found to have been dangerous to the state, but is not specifically defined as a crime, it may be punished by analogy to the crime most nearly like it.

In the years from 1932 to 1937, the Soviet leaders apparently felt that Soviet society was becoming more thoroughly established and did not require the strictest application of the law. The article of the code permitting punishment by analogy was reserved for very unusual cases, and even in these

* John N. Hazard, "The Individual in Soviet Law," and "Property Rights in the Soviet Union," *American Sociological Review*, June, 1944, Vol. IX, pp. 251–6.

instances was used primarily to increase punishment for an act which was already clearly a crime, rather than to blanket a non-criminal act under some section of the code. Nevertheless, the strict features of the code were preserved and even expanded in cases where new problems arose to plague the state.

With the growing importance of state-owned and cooperatively-owned property following the successful development of collectivization and the first Five Year Plan, the protection of this type of property became of paramount importance. It gave rise to the law of August 7, 1932 which provided the death penalty for those who stole it. Likewise with the growth of juvenile crime in the mid-1930's, the state found it necessary to increase penalties and to withdraw some of the protection with which teen-age youngsters had previously been surrounded when they committed illegal acts.

While the state has not lagged in protecting itself, it has not ignored the other side of the medal—protection of the individual. It would probably be incorrect to say that law provides protection of the Soviet individual against his state, since Soviet law acknowledges no rule of law above the state. Law is believed to be the creation of the state and not its master. Nevertheless, the Soviet jurists believe that a strong state depends, in the last analysis, upon a contented citizenry, and this condition is achieved only when the majority believes that the inevitable restrictions and punishments set forth in the law are fairly administered.

Many of the measures designed to protect the individual against the unwarranted assumption of power by a state official, or against his failure to take measures designed to assure that only the guilty are punished, appear in the form of Constitutional guarantees.

The Constitution lays the basis for a procedure intended to give the individual accused of crime an opportunity to have a fair trial. Courts must comprise two lay judges in addition to the professional judge, so that the "horse sense" approach may be represented. Trials must be in the local language, with interpreters for those who do not understand. This is of utmost importance in a land of ethnic minorities. Cases must be heard openly for the public to attend, except in cases of sexual offenses or questions involving diplomatic or military matters.

The Prosecutor of the Union is charged with the duty of seeing that laws are exactly observed. An individual may telegraph or write if he is placed under arrest or otherwise penalized in what appears to be an illegal fashion. The Prosecutor maintains a special department to hear the complaints. While this procedure would hardly seem as protective as the writ of habeas corpus in common law, the Soviet jurists claim that it is designed to achieve the same purpose.

Inviolability of the person and the home is also guaranteed by the Constitution. While this guarantee does not prevent agencies of the law from arresting an individual, or entering a home, it prevents an individual without training or experience from making an unauthorized arrest or search. Penalties of the criminal code apply to those who violate this guarantee.

Protection of the innocent individual is one of the tasks of the Code of Criminal Procedure in each republic. The accused must be advised within a definite period of time why he is held, and must be given an attorney if he so desires and every opportunity to collect evidence in his own behalf. Failure to observe these procedural rules is cause for reversal on appeal, and reported decisions indicate that appellate courts pay close attention to observance of procedural rules. [Procedure is no longer relegated to the secondary position it held during the early days of the revolution.]

While the major principle of state ownership of the means of production has been preserved at all times since the revolution, the Soviet system has been sufficiently elastic to permit limited private enterprise when the national economy was hard pressed to meet the needs of the individual consumer. This happened in a large way during the crisis following upon the destructive early years of the revolution when the period known as the New Economic Policy was introduced in mid-1921 to last until the state was able to assume full responsibility for meeting the minimum economic needs of the people in the late 1920's. To a more limited extent private enterprise has already been called upon again to help out to meet an emergency. Existing law permitting collective farm households to use part of the land for a private garden plot has been emphasized, and city dwellers have been assigned land to use in gardening for the use of themselves and their groups. Private individuals have been encouraged to avail themselves of the law permitting them to obtain credit and gain access to materials to build their own homes.

Private ownership of consumers' goods has been recognized since the first days of the revolution. The Civil Code of 1922 provided extensively for their protection, control and inheritance. Subject always to the restriction set forth in Article One of the Civil Code to the effect that rights protected by the code could not be exercised to the detriment of the state, the right of private ownership of consumers' goods is generally parallel to this right under other systems of jurisprudence.

The trend has been to emphasize the right of private ownership of consumers' goods rather than to minimize it. The second federal Constitution, promulgated in 1936, set forth this right in precise terms, and even elevated to the level of Constitutional law the right of inheritance, as it had existed since 1923. Immediately after the revolution the right had been entirely abolished. Savings deposits are not only permitted, but encouraged by law which exempts them from inheritance taxation. Restrictions on the use of consumers' goods are directed only against obtaining property gain from them by their sale at unreasonable profit. Speculation is made a crime, and may include leasing a room in a privately owned dwelling, if this is done in violation of the restrictive provisions of a housing law based upon the most effective use for the benefit of all of the limited housing space available.

Control over the accumulation of property of a consumers' goods type is maintained not only by Article One of the Civil Code but by taxation on income and inheritance. Rates have risen during the war, but clearly not with the purpose of confiscating savings or consumers' goods.

Protection of property rights of the state in means of production and of individuals in consumers' goods is provided by the Criminal Code. Penalties for misuse of public funds or property are severe, and can even extend to the point of death in the event of larceny. Penalties for destruction or theft of the property of individuals are much less severe, but they form a chapter of the Criminal Code, and are rigidly enforced.

CITIZENS AT COURT *

The Soviet Constitution and the law relating to the court system in the USSR provide for cases in all courts to be heard in the presence of people's justices. The functions of a people's justice ordinarily occupy 10 days a year; the rest of his time he is free to devote to his usual work.

The Constitution establishes that people's justices serving in people's courts are elected, like the judges, by equal, direct, secret ballot for a term of three years, by the people of the territory within the jurisdiction of the given people's court, on the basis of the electoral districts.

People's justices serving in districts and regional courts are elected at sessions of the Soviet of Working People's Deputies; justices to the Supreme Courts of Union and Autonomous Republics and to the Supreme Court of the Soviet Union are elected at sessions of the corresponding Supreme Soviets.

The functions, rights and significance of the people's justices are very great. A people's justice is a member with equal rights in the court throughout the entire trial. All cases are decided by the judge together with the two people's justices, whether it is a matter of establishing guilt, applying the law, fixing punishment, calling additional witnesses or satisfying a plaintiff's claims.

Should both justices hold an opinion contrary to that of the judge, the sentence or judgment will be that of the justices. In such cases the judge has a right to express his minority opinion and affix it to the sentence or judgment. This dissenting opinion is not read out in court, and serves only as material for the higher court which checks the correctness of the sentence or judgment of the lower court. Either of the people's justices, should he be in the minority, has the same right to express dissent.

Should the right of the judge be impeached, i.e., should either party claim that he is not disinterested, it is the people's justices who decide whether

* A. S. Spectorov, "When Soviet Citizens Go to Court," Embassy of U.S.S.R. *Information Bulletin,* March 10, 1945, p. 7.

the impeachment is just. In such cases, should either people's justice hold that the claim is justified, the judge is held to be impeached.

During a trial the people's justices have the right to put any question to the witnesses, experts or the accused, which they may consider necessary to make the facts of the case clear or to establish the claims of objective justice. They may examine the material evidence and documents in court, as well as during the preliminary proceedings. This system guarantees the accused or the parties in the case full objectivity in passing judgment, and protects the court against errors.

In Tsarist Russia jurors were called only in the lower courts, and their rights were rigidly limited. Their only function was to decide whether or not the crime with which the accused was charged had been committed. Their answer could be only "Yes, it has been proved" or "No, it has not been proved." No discussion was permitted. In the higher courts, cases were decided without jurors.

In the Soviet Union, people's justices attend in all courts, from the People's Court to the Supreme Court of the USSR. All courts consist of a permanent judge who presides, and two justices, except in certain special cases established by law.

According to Soviet law, a people's justice has the right to substitute for the judge. In cases of his temporary absence through illness, or on vacation, the district Soviet of Working People's Deputies charges one of the people's justices with the duties of the judge.

The functions of the people's justices are varied. They take part in the trial of all sorts of cases relating to crimes committed against the life, health and reputation of citizens, charges of theft and embezzlement, civil cases relating to property claims, cases of infringement of labor laws or the theft of socialist property. Together with the judge, the people's justices receive the petitioners' applications and complaints, and give consultations. Not only do they take an active part in the work of the State's judiciary; they also receive instruction themselves in the administration of the State.

Many people's justices who have proved themselves capable and efficient have been elected as judges. There are thousands of them working as assistant judges. For example, A. Zhuravlev, a Moscow factory worker, who was elected a people's justice in 1935, has been working as an assistant judge since the summer of 1940. In this capacity he conducts preliminary investigations of cases brought to court, interviews both parties and examines material evidence. Leonova, a schoolteacher, who is a deputy to the Supreme Soviet of the USSR, serves as an assistant judge at the Supreme Court of the USSR.

The People's Commissariat of Justice organizes short-term courses to help the people's justices in their work by acquainting them with the basic laws of the Soviet code. They are active in defending the rights of servicemen's families. They strive to settle cases out of court wherever possible.

A people's justice is the elected representative of the people. He knows the needs of the people well, and is in a position to judge competently in both criminal and civil cases. Like the judge, he makes periodical reports on his activities to his constituents.

The fact that he is the elected representative of the people, his extensive rights, his close connection with his constituents and the fact that he is directly responsible to them, illustrate the democratic character of the Soviet judiciary system.

THE PUNISHMENT OF CRIME *

Within the span of one generation the Soviet Union has not only put into practice the most advanced theories of penology, but has also embarked on some daring experimentation with brilliant results.

What the Soviet Union has accomplished in this field . . . has significant implications. How a state treats its wayward and anti-social elements —society's most underprivileged members—tells volumes about that social order.

Tsarist penology was based exclusively on punishment; and in its application, the law discriminated between the rich and the under-privileged, between men and women, between the Russians and minority or national groups, often placed outside the law. The small consideration shown to juvenile offenders is best exemplified by the attitude of the Tsarist government to juvenile courts, two of which, following the world trend, had been established in 1912. These courts, as A. N. Akunev, the first children's court judge, took pains to impress on an all-Russian Conference, "cannot and must not serve to weaken the repressive measures applied to children who embark upon the path of crime." Equally clear in this frank public utterance are the implications toward the adult offender.

While the Soviet Government has abolished all distinctions based on the accident of birth, all distinctions based on national origin, religion, sex, or social status, Soviet jurisprudence recognizes the existence of distinctions among law violators. In inquiring into a crime, Soviet law enforcement machinery seeks to determine how "socially dangerous" is the act and what may have been the object or motives of the perpetrator. Soviet administrators also find it important to determine whether an offender has committed an offense out of ignorance, wilful malice, or hatred for the Soviet state. With this focussing upon motive, punishment in and for itself loses its meaning. It is not surprising, therefore, to find in the Soviet code this unique law, which provides that a person may not be punished for a crime if, at the time of trial, this act is no longer "socially dangerous," or if the offender has become a socially useful person. In other words, the state need

* Nathan Berman, "Soviet Progress in Penology," *Soviet Russia Today*, December, 1940, pp. 14–6, 33–4.

take no further steps to reform this person if he has since accomplished this end himself.

Similarly Soviet policy toward juvenile delinquency has been governed by the principle of the intent and objective of crime. Juveniles, the Soviet law ruled, could not be consciously anti-Soviet, regardless of the nature or gravity of their offenses. As early as 1918 special commissions were set up to handle juvenile offenders along "medico-pedagogical" lines only. They were not to be prosecuted or punished, but educated, supervised and trained in constructive living. This approach remained in force for over seventeen years, through the most difficult period of Soviet existence. Though this set-up was abolished in 1935, the change was primarily one of form; the fundamental principles . . . remained intact.

It depends on the operation of the law enforcement machinery whether laws are translated into real justice. The make-up of the Soviet people's courts is as follows. The presiding judge, in accordance with the provisions of the Soviet Constitution, is elected by direct and secret vote for three years. The two associate judges who, together with him, make up the court and have an equal vote in rendering a verdict, are chosen from a panel of dependable and qualified workers submitted by various organizations in the community. The right to defense counsel, for a small fee or without it, is guaranteed by the Constitution (the Supreme Court of the USSR has ordered new trials in cases where no defense counsel was provided). This includes appeals to the higher courts, if necessary. Such services as psychiatric or other expert opinion are equally accessible to defendant and state.

One has to have experience with the workings of other courts to appreciate some of the features of the Soviet people's courts. There is a simplicity and informality one just does not associate with a court of law. No oath is administered; contempt of court, which muzzles many a poor defendant, is unknown. There is no battle over technicalities that the people most concerned can rarely follow.

But even more important are the close ties between the court personnel and the community. Elected for a three year term, the judge is expected to keep in close and continuous touch with the electors and their organizations. He meets with the community to carry out his correlated job of educating the citizens and to hear criticism of his or her conduct on the bench. Soviet criminological journals stress this. Harsh, straight-from-the-shoulder words are spoken about judges who have neglected this angle of their work.

The Soviet lawyer also has this dual responsibility. Besides representing clients in court, or otherwise rendering legal advice, he helps Soviet citizens familiarize themselves with their rights and responsibilities. In 1938, Soviet lawyers, through their associations, represented 64,000 cases in court free of charge, gave half a million free consultations and aided nearly that many more in drawing up documents, gratis. They also delivered over 58,000 popular lectures and talks before labor and farmer groups. Soviet judicial machinery is thus organically connected with society.

Soviet correctional institutions are agencies of reform in the best sense of the word. They operate on the most progressive principles in the field. Soviet law forbids any form of physical punishment, including reduction of normal diet, as a disciplinary measure. Instead, social pressure, privileges and reduction of time for good behavior are employed to stimulate adjustment and cooperation. Soviet correctional institutions, moreover, practice to a very high degree normal living and useful employment. With a scarcity of labor in the country in general, useful productive work by inmates in correctional institutions is more than welcome. They are paid, in some places at the prevailing union rate.

All Soviet correctional institutions have some sort of self-government in operation; not make-believe affairs but real functioning bodies which, while aiding in the operation of the institution, help train the inmates in the principles and rules of social living. These institutions not only have their cultural and athletic clubs, but publish their own newspapers, dealing with national and international political events, as well as with problems of their own production and the management or mismanagement of the place. The authorities get their information of an institution from its newspaper as well as from the director's report. The Soviet Government encourages such self-expression among the inmates of its correctional institutions.

The most progressive penological form in the Soviet Union is the "labor-correctional" commune. The first to be organized, the Bolshevo Commune, soon became known all over the world. This daring experiment in the rehabilitation of criminals by means of voluntary, self-regulated, normal community living, caught the outside world in disbelieving bewilderment. Its immediate and complete success resulted in the extension of the commune idea all over the Soviet Union. 1939 was another landmark in its history. After 15 years of successful operation as a correctional community, Bolshevo and several others were given official status as normal communities, which, in fact, they had been for years. This change was perhaps unavoidable since the number of "graduated" inmates who preferred to continue living there with their families and friend far outnumbered the "undergraduates." This event not only spells the success of the commune idea as such, but reemphasizes the universal progressive belief that antisocial elements can most successfully be reclaimed to society primarily through humane treatment and constructive living.

The "correctional-labor" sentence is another penological practice of the Soviet Union. Such a sentence provides that a defendant is to work for a stipulated period, most frequently at his own job, at reduced pay. The periodic deductions themselves are believed to have the effect of repeated reprimands. Even if this meant nothing more than the imposition of a fine paid out in installments, as some claim, it still is an achievement. . . .

Another correctional method used by the Soviets calls for mention here —the special construction project camps. The best known were established during the building of the Baltic-White Sea Canal (Belomor) and the Moscow-Volga Canal. Involuntary labor was extensively used on these gigantic projects. Soviet authorities proudly point to the fact that while doing work benefiting the whole country thousands of anti-social individuals themselves became industrious and socially useful people, regaining their freedom and self-respect. (It might be added that such hardships as these workers experienced in the building of the canals were in no way different from those of free Soviet citizens who pioneered in the building of the industrial city of Dnieprostroy or, more recently, Komsomolsk, built almost exclusively by Soviet youth, and which is characteristic of pioneering work anywhere.)

The results are reflected in the steady and rapid fall in the crime rate which of course, at the same time, reflects the general improvement in social and economic conditions. In the two years between 1935-37, convictions for crime fell 28 per cent.

There are still crime and criminals in the Soviet Union, just as there still exist problems of personality and social adjustment. Because the Soviet Union is a constantly changing, highly dynamic society, there are numbers of people who find it difficult, or are simply unwilling to keep pace. This has necessitated not only the continued operation of the law enforcement machinery, but also the need for its constant adjustment to changing situations and problems.

On April 7, 1935, it was decreed that juvenile delinquents over twelve years of age, charged with the commission of more serious offenses, be tried by regular People's Courts and may be punished in accordance with the provisions of the criminal code. The decree also provides specifically for punishment of adults, whether they be parents or others, found guilty of contributing to the delinquency of minors. It is significant to note that while in the case of a juvenile, the provision is that he may be punished in accordance with the law covering the offense he is charged with, the punishments for any adults involved is very specific—not less than five years' imprisonment.

The full meaning of this law can only be grasped when considered together with the set of decrees passed on May of that year dealing with the same subject. These authorized large appropriations for the improvement and extension of children's homes; called upon the trade unions, educational and political organizations to assign immediately hundreds of their best members to assist in the delinquency prevention and child welfare program; and urged and warned organizations, educators, Party and law enforcement workers, parents and guardians, to pay closer attention to the needs and problems of the Soviet child. From the law enforcement point of view, the more serious juvenile offender is now under the jurisdiction of the Commissariat of Justice instead of the Commissariat of Education. The procedure has this advantage, that while educational facilities for the reclamation of the youth remain, the courts have jurisdiction over the adult contributor as well as the juvenile offender.

Soviet legal machinery is not without its shortcomings and handicaps, of which, incidentally, the government is the strictest judge and critic. The problem is primarily one of inadequate personnel. Those charged with the execution of the law are not always best equipped by temperament or ability for the job—there simply are not enough well qualified and properly trained people to do this work. Secondly, it is more difficult by far to be a law-enforcing worker, especially a judge, in the Soviet Union than elsewhere.

The Soviet Union's achievements in the field of delinquency and crime prevention and treatment, after due allowance for avoidable and unavoidable past shortcomings, constitute one of the most valuable chapters in the annals of criminology and penology in our times.

Appendices

APPENDIX I

THE CONSTITUTION OF THE SOVIET UNION *

CHAPTER I. THE ORGANIZATION OF SOCIETY

ARTICLE 1. The Union of Soviet Socialist Republics is a socialist state of workers and peasants.

ARTICLE. 2. The Soviets of Working People's Deputies, which grew and attained strength as a result of the overthrow of the landlords and capitalists and the achievement of the dictatorship of the proletariat, constitute the political foundations of the U.S.S.R.

ARTICLE 3. In the U.S.S.R. all power belongs to the working people of town and country as represented by the Soviets of Working People's Deputies.

ARTICLE 4. The socialist system of economy and the socialist ownership of the means and instruments of production firmly established as a result of the abolition of the capitalist system of economy, the abrogation of private ownership of the means and instruments of production and the abolition of the exploitation of man by man, constitute the economic foundation of the U.S.S.R.

ARTICLE 5. Socialist property in the U.S.S.R. exists either in the form of state property (the possession of the whole people), or in the form of cooperative and collective-farm property (property of a collective farm or property of a cooperative association).

ARTICLE 6. The land, its natural deposits, waters, forests, mills, factories, mines, rail, water and air transport, banks, post, telegraph and telephones, large state-organized agricultural enterprises (state farms, machine and tractor stations and the like) as well as municipal enterprises and the bulk of the dwelling houses in the cities and industrial localities, are state property, that is, belong to the whole people.

ARTICLE 7. Public enterprises in collective farms and cooperative organizations, with their livestock and implements, the products of the collective farms and cooperative organizations, as well as their common buildings, constitute the common, socialist property of the collective farms and cooperative organizations.

In addition to its basic income from the public, collective-farm enterprise, every household in a collective farm has for its personal use a small plot of land attached to the dwelling and, as its personal property, a subsidiary establishment on the plot, a dwelling house, livestock, poultry and minor agricultural implements—in accordance with the statutes of the agricultural artel.

ARTICLE 8. The land occupied by collective farms is secured to them for their use free of charge and for an unlimited time, that is, in perpetuity.

ARTICLE 9. Alongside the socialist system of economy, which is the predominant form of economy in the U.S.S.R., the law permits the small private economy of individual peasants and handicraftsmen based on their personal labor and precluding the exploitation of the labor of others.

* Based on the English edition of the Constitution adopted in December, 1936, as published in 1938 by the State Political Publishing House of the U.S.S.R., with the amendments adopted at the 1st, 2nd, 3rd, 6th, 7th, 8th and 10th Sessions of the Supreme Soviet of the U.S.S.R.

ARTICLE 10. The right of citizens to personal ownership of their incomes from work and of their savings, of their dwelling houses and subsidiary household economy, their household furniture and utensils and articles of personal use and convenience, as well as the right of inheritance of personal property of citizens, is protected by law.

ARTICLE 11. The economic life of the U.S.S.R. is determined and directed by the state national economic plan with the aim of increasing the public wealth, of steadily improving the material conditions of the working people and raising their cultural level, of consolidating the independence of the U.S.S.R. and strengthening its defensive capacity.

ARTICLE 12. In the U.S.S.R. work is a duty and a matter of honor for every able-bodied citizen, in accordance with the principle: "He who does not work, neither shall he eat."

The principle applied in the U.S.S.R. is that of socialism: "From each according to his ability, to each according to his work."

CHAPTER II. THE ORGANIZATION OF THE STATE

ARTICLE 13. The Union of Soviet Socialist Republics is a federal state, formed on the basis of the voluntary association of Soviet Socialist Republics having equal rights, namely:
The Russian Soviet Federated Socialist Republic
The Ukrainian Soviet Socialist Republic
The Byelorussian Soviet Socialist Republic
The Azerbaidjan Soviet Socialist Republic
The Georgian Soviet Socialist Republic
The Armenian Soviet Socialist Republic
The Turkmen Soviet Socialist Republic
The Uzbek Soviet Socialist Republic
The Tadjik Soviet Socialist Republic
The Kazakh Soviet Socialist Republic
The Kirghiz Soviet Socialist Republic
The Karelo-Finnish Soviet Socialist Republic
The Moldavian Soviet Socialist Republic
The Lithuanian Soviet Socialist Republic
The Latvian Soviet Socialist Republic
The Estonian Soviet Socialist Republic.

ARTICLE 14. The jurisdiction of the Union of Soviet Socialist Republics, as represented by its highest organs of state authority and organs of government, covers:
a) Representation of the Union in international relations, conclusion and ratification of treaties with other states, and the establishment of the general character of the relations between the Union Republic and foreign States;
b) Questions of war and peace;
c) Admission of new republics into the U.S.S.R.;
d) Control over the observance of the Constitution of the U.S.S.R. and ensuring conformity of the Constitutions of the Union Republics with the Constitution of the U.S.S.R.;
e) Confirmation of alterations of boundaries between Union Republics;
f) Confirmation of the formation of new Territories and Regions and also of new Autonomous Republics within Union Republics;
g) Organization of the defense of the U.S.S.R. and direction of all the armed forces of the U.S.S.R.; the establishment of the guiding principles of the organization of the military formations of the Union Republics;
h) Foreign trade on the basis of state monopoly;
i) Safeguarding the security of the state;
j) Establishment of the national economic plans of the U.S.S.R.;
k) Approval of the single state budget of the U.S.S.R. as well as of the taxes and revenues which go to the all-Union, Republican and local budgets;
l) Administration of the banks, industrial and agricultural establishments and enterprises and trading enterprises of all-Union importance;

m) Administration of transport and communications;

n) Direction of the monetary and credit system;

o) Organization of state insurance;

p) Raising and granting of loans;

q) Establishment of the basic principles for the use of land as well as for the use of natural deposits, forests and waters;

r) Establishment of the basic principles in the spheres of education and public health;

s) Organization of a uniform system of national economic statistics;

t) Establishment of the principles of labor legislation;

u) Legislation on the judicial system and judicial procedure; criminal and civil codes;

v) Laws on citizenship of the Union; laws on the rights of foreigners;

w) Issuing of all-Union acts of amnesty.

ARTICLE 15. The sovereignty of the Union Republics is limited only within the provisions set forth in Article 14 of the Constitution of the U.S.S.R. Outside of these provisions, each Union Republic exercises state authority independently. The U.S.S.R. protects the sovereign rights of the Union Republics.

ARTICLE 16. Each Union Republic has its own Constitution, which takes account of the specific features of the Republic and is drawn up in full conformity with the Constitution of the U.S.S.R.

ARTICLE 17. To every Union Republic is reserved the right freely to secede from the U.S.S.R.

ARTICLE 18. The territory of a Union Republic may not be altered without its consent.

a) Each Union Republic has the right to enter into direct relations with foreign states, to conclude agreements with them and exchange diplomatic and consular representatives with them.

b) Each Union Republic has its republican military formation.

ARTICLE 19. The laws of the U.S.S.R. have the same force within the territory of every Union Republic.

ARTICLE 20. In the event of a discrepancy between a law of a Union Republic and an all-Union law, the all-Union law prevails.

ARTICLE 21. A single Union citizenship is established for all citizens of the U.S.S.R. Every citizen of a Union Republic is a citizen of the U.S.S.R.

[Articles 22 to 29b contain names of the Republics, regions and districts listed in the table by Corliss Lamont, pp. 222–3.]

CHAPTER III. THE HIGHEST ORGANS OF STATE AUTHORITY OF THE UNION OF SOVIET SOCIALIST REPUBLICS

ARTICLE 30. The highest organ of state authority of the U.S.S.R. is the Supreme Soviet of the U.S.S.R.

ARTICLE 31. The Supreme Soviet of the U.S.S.R. exercises all rights vested in the Union of Soviet Socialist Republics in accordance with Article 14 of the Constitution, in so far as they do not, by virtue of the Constitution, come within the jurisdiction of organs of the U.S.S.R. that are accountable to the Supreme Soviet of the U.S.S.R., that is, the Presidium of the Supreme Soviet of the U.S.S.R., the Council of People's Commissars of the U.S.S.R. and the People's Commissariats of the U.S.S.R.

ARTICLE 32. The legislative power of the U.S.S.R. is exercised exclusively by the Supreme Soviet of the U.S.S.R.

ARTICLE 33. The Supreme Soviet of the U.S.S.R. consists of two Chambers: the Soviet of the Union and the Soviet of Nationalities.

ARTICLE 34. The Soviet of the Union is elected by the citizens of the U.S.S.R. according to electoral areas on the basis of one deputy for every 300,000 of the population.

ARTICLE 35. The Soviet of Nationalities is elected by the citizens of the U.S.S.R. according to Union and Autonomous Republics, Autonomous Regions and national areas on the basis of twenty-five deputies from each Union Republic, eleven deputies from each Autonomous Republic, five deputies from each Autonomous Region and one deputy from each national area.

ARTICLE 36. The Supreme Soviet of the U.S.S.R. is elected for a term of four years.

ARTICLE 37. Both Chambers of the Supreme Soviet of the U.S.S.R., the Soviet of the Union and the Soviet of Nationalities, have equal rights.

ARTICLE 38. The Soviet of the Union and the Soviet of Nationalities have an equal right to initiate legislation.

ARTICLE 39. A law is considered adopted if passed by both Chambers of the Supreme Soviet of the U.S.S.R. by a simple majority vote in each.

ARTICLE 40. Laws passed by the Supreme Soviet of the U.S.S.R. are published in the languages of the Union Republics over the signatures of the President and Secretary of the Presidium of the Supreme Soviet of the U.S.S.R.

ARTICLE 41. Sessions of the Soviet of the Union and the Soviet of Nationalities begin and terminate simultaneously.

ARTICLE 42. The Soviet of the Union elects a Chairman of the Soviet of the Union and two Vice-Chairmen.

ARTICLE 43. The Soviet of Nationalities elects a Chairman of the Soviet of Nationalities and two Vice-Chairmen.

ARTICLE 44. The Chairmen of the Soviet of the Union and the Soviet of Nationalities preside over the sittings of the respective Chambers and direct the procedure of these bodies.

ARTICLE 45. Joint sittings of both Chambers of the Supreme Soviet of the U.S.S.R. are presided over alternately by the Chairman of the Soviet of the Union and the Chairman of the Soviet of Nationalities.

ARTICLE 46. Sessions of the Supreme Soviet of the U.S.S.R. are convened by the Presidium of the Supreme Soviet of the U.S.S.R. twice a year.

Special sessions are convened by the Presidium of the Supreme Soviet of the U.S.S.R. at its discretion or on the demand of one of the Union Republics.

ARTICLE 47. In the event of disagreement between the Soviet of the Union and the Soviet of Nationalities, the question is referred for settlement to a conciliation commission formed on a parity basis. If the conciliation commission fails to arrive at an agreement, or if its decision fails to satisfy one of the Chambers, the question is considered for a second time by the Chambers. Failing agreement between the two Chambers, the Presidium of the Supreme Soviet of the U.S.S.R. dissolves the Supreme Soviet of the U.S.S.R. and orders new elections.

ARTICLE 48. The Supreme Soviet of the U.S.S.R. at a joint sitting of both Chambers elects the Presidium of the Supreme Soviet of the U.S.S.R., consisting of a President of the Presidium of the Supreme Soviet of the U.S.S.R., sixteen Vice-Presidents, a Secretary of the Presidium and twenty-four members of the Presidium.

The Presidium of the Supreme Soviet of the U.S.S.R. is accountable to the Supreme Soviet of the U.S.S.R. for all its activities.

ARTICLE 49. The Presidium of the Supreme Soviet of the U.S.S.R.:
a) Convenes the sessions of the Supreme Soviet of the U.S.S.R.;
b) Interprets laws of the U.S.S.R. in operation, issues decrees;

c) Dissolves the Supreme Soviet of the U.S.S.R. in conformity with Article 47 of the Constitution of the U.S.S.R. and orders new elections;

d) Conducts referendums on its own initiative or on the demand of one of the Union Republics;

e) Annuls decisions and orders of the Council of People's Commissars of the U.S.S.R. and of the Councils of People's Commissars of the Union Republics in case they do not conform to law;

f) In the intervals between sessions of the Supreme Soviet of the U.S.S.R., relieves of their posts and appoints People's Commissars of the U.S.S.R. on the recommendation of the Chairman of the Council of People's Commissars of the U.S.S.R., subject to subsequent confirmation by the Supreme Soviet of the U.S.S.R.;

g) Awards decorations and confers titles of honor of the U.S.S.R.;

h) Exercises the right of pardon;

i) Appoints and removes the higher commands of the armed forces of the U.S.S.R.;

j) In the intervals between sessions of the Supreme Soviet of the U.S.S.R., proclaims a state of war in the event of armed attack on the U.S.S.R., or whenever necessary to fulfill international treaty obligations concerning mutual defense against aggression;

k) Orders general or partial mobilization;

l) Ratifies international treaties;

m) Appoints and recalls plenipotentiary representatives of the U.S.S.R. to foreign states;

n) Receives the credentials and letters of recall of diplomatic representatives accredited to it by foreign states;

o) Proclaims martial law in separate localities or throughout the U.S.S.R. in the interests of the defense of the U.S.S.R. or for the purpose of ensuring public order and state security.

ARTICLE 50. The Soviet of the Union and the Soviet of Nationalities elect Credentials Commissions which verify the credentials of the members of the respective Chambers.

On the recommendation of the Credentials Commissions, the Chambers decide either to endorse the credentials or to annul the election of the deputies concerned.

ARTICLE 51. The Supreme Soviet of the U.S.S.R., when it deems necessary, appoints commissions of inquiry and investigation on any matter.

It is the duty of all institutions and public servants to comply with the demands of these commissions and to submit to them the necessary materials and documents.

ARTICLE 52. A member of the Supreme Soviet of the U.S.S.R. may not be prosecuted or arrested without the consent of the Supreme Soviet of the U.S.S.R., and during the period when the Supreme Soviet of the U.S.S.R. is not in session, without the consent of the Presidium of the Supreme Soviet of the U.S.S.R.

ARTICLE 53. On the expiration of the term of office of the Supreme Soviet of the U.S.S.R., or after the dissolution of the Supreme Soviet prior to the expiration of its term of office, the Presidium of the Supreme Soviet of the U.S.S.R. retains its powers until the formation of a new Presidium of the Supreme Soviet of the U.S.S.R. by the newly-elected Supreme Soviet of the U.S.S.R.

ARTICLE 54. On the expiration of the term of office of the Supreme Soviet of the U.S.S.R., or in the event of its dissolution prior to the expiration of its term of office, the Presidium of the Supreme Soviet of the U.S.S.R. orders new elections to be held within a period not exceeding two months from the date of expiration of the term of office or dissolution of the Supreme Soviet of the U.S.S.R.

ARTICLE 55. The newly-elected Supreme Soviet of the U.S.S.R. is convened by the outgoing Presidium of the Supreme Soviet of the U.S.S.R. not later than one month after the elections.

ARTICLE 56. The Supreme Soviet of the U.S.S.R. at a joint sitting of both Chambers, appoints the Government of the U.S.S.R., namely, the Council of People's Commissars of the U.S.S.R.

CHAPTER IV. THE HIGHEST ORGANS OF STATE AUTHORITY OF THE UNION REPUBLICS

ARTICLE 57. The highest organ of state authority of a Union Republic is the Supreme Soviet of the Union Republic.

ARTICLE 58. The Supreme Soviet of a Union Republic is elected by the citizens of the Republic for a term of four years.

The basis of representation is established by the Constitution of the Union Republic.

ARTICLE 59. The Supreme Soviet of a Union Republic is the sole legislative organ of the Republic.

ARTICLE 60. The Supreme Soviet of a Union Republic:

a) Adopts the Constitution of the Republic and amends it in conformity with Article 16 of the Constitution of the U.S.S.R.;

b) Confirms the Constitution of the Autonomous Republics forming part of it and defines the boundaries of their territories;

c) Approves the national economic plan and also the budget of the Republic;

d) Exercises the right of amnesty and pardon of citizens sentenced by the judicial organs of the Union Republic;

e) Establishes the representation of the Union Republics in international relations;

f) Establishes the method of the creation of military formations of the Union Republic.

ARTICLE 61. The Supreme Soviet of a Union Republic elects the Presidium of the Supreme Soviet of the Union Republic, consisting of a Chairman of the Presidium of the Supreme Soviet of the Union Republic, Vice-Chairmen, a Secretary of the Presidium and members of the Presidium of the Supreme Soviet of the Union Republic.

The powers of the Presidium of the Supreme Soviet of a Union Republic are defined by the Constitution of the Union Republic.

ARTICLE 62. The Supreme Soviet of a Union Republic elects a Chairman and Vice-Chairmen to conduct its sittings.

ARTICLE 63. The Supreme Soviet of a Union Republic appoints the Government of the Union Republic, namely, the Council of People's Commissars of the Union Republic.

CHAPTER V. THE ORGANS OF GOVERNMENT OF THE UNION OF SOVIET SOCIALIST REPUBLICS

ARTICLE 64. The highest executive and administrative organ of state authority of the Union of Soviet Socialist Republics is the Council of People's Commissars of the U.S.S.R.

ARTICLE 65. The Council of People's Commissars of the U.S.S.R. is responsible to the Supreme Soviet of the U.S.S.R. and accountable to it; and in the intervals between sessions of the Supreme Soviet it is responsible and accountable to the Presidium of the Supreme Soviet of the U.S.S.R.

ARTICLE 66. The Council of People's Commissars of the U.S.S.R. issues decisions and orders on the basis and in pursuance of the laws in operation, and supervises their execution.

ARTICLE 67. Decisions and Orders of the Council of People's Commissars of the U.S.S.R. are binding throughout the territory of the U.S.S.R.

ARTICLE 68. The Council of People's Commissars of the U.S.S.R.:

a) Coordinates and directs the work of the All-Union and Union-Republican People's Commissariats of the U.S.S.R. and of other institutions, economic and cultural, under its administration;

b) Adopts measures to carry out the national economic plan and the state budget, and to strengthen the credit and monetary system;

c) Adopts measures for the maintenance of public order, for the protection of the interests of the state, and for the safeguarding of the rights of citizens;

d) Exercises general guidance in respect of relations with foreign states;

e) Fixes the annual contingent of citizens to be called up for military service and directs the general organization and development of the armed forces of the country;

f) Sets up, whenever necessary, special committees and Central Administrations under the Council of People's Commissars of the U.S.S.R. for matters concerning economic, cultural and defense organization and development.

ARTICLE 69. The Council of People's Commissars of the U.S.S.R. has the right, in respect of those branches of administration and economy which come within the jurisdiction of the U.S.S.R., to suspend decisions and orders of the Councils of People's Commissars of the Union Republics and to annul orders and instructions of People's Commissars of the U.S.S.R.

ARTICLE 70. The Council of People's Commissars of the U.S.S.R. is appointed by the Supreme Soviet of the U.S.S.R. and consists of:

The Chairman of the Council of People's Commissars of the U.S.S.R.;
The Vice-Chairmen of the Council of People's Commissars of the U.S.S.R.;
The Chairman of the State Planning Commission of the U.S.S.R.;
The People's Commissars of the U.S.S.R.;   .
The Chairman of the Committee on Arts;
The Chairman of the Committee on Higher Education;
The Chairman of the Board of the State Bank.

ARTICLE 71. The Government of the U.S.S.R. or a People's Commissar of the U.S.S.R. to whom a question of a member of the Supreme Soviet of the U.S.S.R. is addressed must give a verbal or written reply in the respective Chamber within a period not exceeding three days.

ARTICLE 72. The People's Commissars of the U.S.S.R. direct the branches of state administration which come within the jurisdiction of the U.S.S.R.

ARTICLE 73. The People's Commissars of the U.S.S.R. issue, within the limits of the jurisdiction of the respective People's Commissariats, orders and instructions on the basis and in pursuance of the laws in operation, and also of decisions and orders of the Council of People's Commissars of the U.S.S.R., and supervise their execution.

ARTICLE 74. The People's Commissariats of the U.S.S.R. are either All-Union or Union-Republican Commissariats.

ARTICLE 75. The All-Union People's Commissariats direct the branches of state administration entrusted to them throughout the territory of the U.S.S.R. either directly or through bodies appointed by them.

ARTICLE 76. The Union-Republican People's Commissariats, as a rule, direct the branches of state administration entrusted to them through the corresponding People's Commissariats of the Union Republics; they administer directly only a definite and limited number of enterprises according to a list confirmed by the Presidium of the Supreme Soviet of the U.S.S.R.

ARTICLE 77. The following People's Commissariats are All-Union People's Commissariats:

Foreign Trade, Railways, Post and Telegraph and Telephones, Maritime Transport, River Transport, Coal Industry, Oil Industry, Power Stations, Electrical Industry, Iron and Steel Industry, Non-Ferrous Metallurgy, Chemical Industry, Aviation Industry, Shipbuilding Industry, Munitions, Armaments, Heavy Machine-building, Medium Machine-building. [During the war converted into People's Commissariat of Tank Industry.] General Machine-building. [During the war converted into People's Commissariat of Mortar Armament.] Navy, Agricultural Procurement, Construction, Paper and Cellulose Industry. [In 1946, these Commissariats, as well as about a dozen new ones, were renamed "Ministries," and made parts of a new Council of Ministers.]

ARTICLE 78. The following People's Commissariats are Union-Republican People's Commissariats:

Defense, Foreign Affairs, Food Industry, Fish Industry, Meat and Dairy Industry, Light Industry, Textile Industry, Timber Industry, Agriculture, State Grain and Livestock Farms, Finance, Trade, Internal Affairs, State Security. [The Commissariats of Internal Affairs and State Security have since been merged into the People's Commissariat of Internal Affairs. (*New York Times,* July 21, 1941.)] Justice, Public Health, Building Materials Industry, State Control.

CHAPTER VI. THE ORGANS OF GOVERNMENT OF THE UNION REPUBLICS

ARTICLE 79. The highest executive and administrative organ of state authority of a Union Republic is the Council of People's Commissars of the Union Republic.

ARTICLE 80. The Council of People's Commissars of a Union Republic is responsible to the Supreme Soviet of the Union Republic and accountable to it; and in the intervals between sessions of the Supreme Soviet of the Union Republic it is responsible and accountable to the Presidium of the Supreme Soviet of the respective Union Republic.

ARTICLE 81. The Council of People's Commissars of a Union Republic issues decisions and orders on the basis and in pursuance of the laws in operation of the U.S.S.R. and of the Union Republic, and of the decisions and orders of the Council of People's Commissars of the U.S.S.R., and supervises their execution.

ARTICLE 82. The Council of People's Commissars of a Union Republic has the right to suspend decisions and orders of Councils of People's Commissars of Autonomous Republics, and to annul decisions and orders of Executive Committees of Soviets of Working People's Deputies of Territories, Regions and Autonomous Regions.

ARTICLE 83. The Council of People's Commissars of a Union Republic is appointed by the Supreme Soviet of the Union Republic and consists of:

The Chairman of the Council of People's Commissars of the Union Republic;
The Vice-Chairmen;
The Chairman of the State Planning Commission;
The People's Commissars of:

Food Industry, Fish Industry, Meat and Dairy Industry, Light Industry, Textile Industry, Timber Industry, Building Materials Industry, Agriculture, State Grain and Livestock Farms, Finance, Trade, Internal Affairs, State Security, Justice, Public Health, State Control, Education, Local Industry, Municipal Economy, Social Maintenance, Automobile Transport, The Chief of the Arts Administration, The Representatives of the All Union People's Commissariats. Under the amendments to the Constitution adopted by the 10th Session of the Supreme Soviet of the U.S.S.R., February 2, 1944, the Union Republics now have the right to appoint Commissars of Defense and Foreign Affairs to their Councils of People's Commissars.

ARTICLE 84. The People's Commissars of a Union Republic direct the branches of state administration which come within the jurisdiction of the Union Republic.

ARTICLE 85. The People's Commissars of a Union Republic issue, within the limits of the jurisdiction of their respective People's Commissariats, orders and instructions on the basis and in pursuance of the laws of the U.S.S.R. and of the Union Republic, of the decisions and orders of the Council of People's Commissars of the U.S.S.R. and that of the Union Republic, and of the orders and instructions of the Union Republican People's Commissariats of the U.S.S.R.

ARTICLE 86. The People's Commissariats of a Union Republic are either Union-Republican or Republican Commissariats.

ARTICLE 87. The Union-Republican People's Commissariats direct the branches of state administration entrusted to them, and are subordinate both to the Council of People's Commissars of the Union Republic and to the corresponding Union-Republican People's Commissariats of the U.S.S.R.

ARTICLE 88. The Republican People's Commissariats direct the branches of state administration entrusted to them and are directly subordinate to the Council of People's Commissars of the Union Republic.

CHAPTER VII. THE HIGHEST ORGANS OF STATE AUTHORITY OF THE AUTONOMOUS SOVIET SOCIALIST REPUBLICS

ARTICLE 89. The highest organ of state authority of an Autonomous Republic is the Supreme Soviet of the respective Autonomous Soviet Socialist Republic.

ARTICLE 90. The Supreme Soviet of an Autonomous Republic is elected by the citizens of the Republic for a term of four years on the basis of representation established by the Constitution of the Autonomous Republic.

ARTICLE 91. The Supreme Soviet of an Autonomous Republic is the sole legislative organ of the Autonomous Soviet Socialist Republic.

ARTICLE 92. Each Autonomous Republic has its own Constitution, which takes account of the specific features of the Autonomous Republic and is drawn up in full conformity with the Constitution of the Union Republic.

ARTICLE 93. The Supreme Soviet of an Autonomous Republic elects the Presidium of the Supreme Soviet of the Autonomous Republic and appoints the Council of People's Commissars of the Autonomous Republic, in accordance with its Constitution.

CHAPTER VIII. THE LOCAL ORGANS OF STATE AUTHORITY

ARTICLE 94. The organs of state authority in territories, regions, autonomous regions, areas, districts, cities and rural localities (stanitsas, villages, hamlets, kishlaks, auls) are the Soviets of Working People's Deputies.

ARTICLE 95. The Soviets of Working People's Deputies of territories, regions, autonomous regions, areas, districts, cities and rural localities (stanitsas, villages, hamlets, kishlaks, auls) are elected by the working people of the respective territories, regions, autonomous regions, areas, districts, cities or rural localities for a term of two years.

ARTICLE 96. The basis of representation for Soviets of Working People's Deputies is defined by the Constitutions of the Union Republics.

ARTICLE 97. The Soviets of Working People's Deputies direct the work of the organs of administration subordinate to them, ensure the maintenance of public order, the observance of the laws and the protection of the rights of citizens, direct local economic and cultural organization and development and draw up the local budgets.

ARTICLE 98. The Soviets of Working People's Deputies adopt decisions and issue orders within the limits of the powers vested in them by the laws of the U.S.S.R. and of the Union Republic.

ARTICLE 99. The executive and administrative organs of the Soviets of Working People's Deputies of territories, regions, autonomous regions, areas, districts, cities and rural localities are the Executive Committees elected by them, consisting of a Chairman, Vice-Chairmen, a Secretary and members.

ARTICLE 100. The executive and administrative organ of rural Soviets of Working People's Deputies in small localities, in accordance with the Constitutions of the Union Republics, is the Chairman, the Vice-Chairman, and the Secretary elected by them.

ARTICLE 101. The executive organs of the Soviets of Working People's Deputies are directly accountable both to the Soviets of Working People's Deputies which elected them and to the executive organ of the superior Soviet of Working People's Deputies.

CHAPTER IX. THE COURTS AND THE PROCURATOR'S OFFICE

ARTICLE 102. In the U.S.S.R. justice is administered by the Supreme Court of the U.S.S.R., the Supreme Courts of the Union Republics, the Territorial and the Regional courts, the courts of the Autonomous Republics and the Autonomous Regions, the Area courts, the special courts of the U.S.S.R. established by decision of the Supreme Soviet of the U.S.S.R., and the People's Courts.

ARTICLE 103. In all courts cases are tried with the participation of people's assessors, except in cases specially provided for by law.

ARTICLE 104. The Supreme Court of the U.S.S.R. is the highest judicial organ. The Supreme Court of the U.S.S.R. is charged with the supervision of the judicial activities of all the judicial organs of the U.S.S.R. and of the Union Republics.

ARTICLE 105. The Supreme Court of the U.S.S.R. and the special courts of the U.S.S.R. are elected by the Supreme Soviet of the U.S.S.R. for a term of five years.

ARTICLE 106. The Supreme Courts of the Union Republics are elected by the Supreme Soviets of the Union Republics for a term of five years.

ARTICLE 107. The Supreme Courts of the Autonomous Republics are elected by the Supreme Soviets of the Autonomous Republics for a term of five years.

ARTICLE 108. The Territorial and the Regional courts, the courts of the Autonomous Regions and the Area courts are elected by the Territorial, Regional or Area Soviets of Working People's Deputies or by the Soviets of Working People's Deputies of the Autonomous Regions for a term of five years.

ARTICLE 109. People's Courts are elected by the citizens of the district on the basis of universal, direct and equal suffrage by secret ballot for a term of three years.

ARTICLE 110. Judicial proceedings are conducted in the language of the Union Republic, Autonomous Republic or Autonomous Region, persons not knowing this language being guaranteed every opportunity of fully acquainting themselves with the material of the case through an interpreter and likewise the right to use their own language in court.

ARTICLE 111. In all courts of the U.S.S.R. cases are heard in public, unless otherwise provided for by law, and the accused is guaranteed the right to be defended by Counsel.

ARTICLE 112. Judges are independent and subject only to the law.

ARTICLE 113. Supreme supervisory power over the strict execution of the laws by all People's Commissariats and institutions subordinated to them, as well as by public servants and citizens of the U.S.S.R., is vested in the Procurator of the U.S.S.R.

ARTICLE 114. The Procurator of the U.S.S.R. is appointed by the Supreme Soviet of the U.S.S.R. for a term of seven years.

ARTICLE 115. Procurators of Republics, Territories and Regions, as well as Procurators of Autonomous Republics and Autonomous Regions, are appointed by the Procurator of the U.S.S.R. for a term of five years.

ARTICLE 116. Area, district and city procurators are appointed for a term of five years by the Procurators of the Union Republics, subject to the approval of the Procurator of the U.S.S.R.

ARTICLE 117. The organs of the Procurator's Office perform their functions independently of any local organs whatsoever, being subordinate solely to the Procurator of the U.S.S.R.

CHAPTER X. FUNDAMENTAL RIGHTS AND DUTIES OF CITIZENS

ARTICLE 118. Citizens of the U.S.S.R. have the right to work, that is, are guaranteed the right to employment and payment for their work in accordance with its quantity and quality.

The right to work is ensured by the socialist organization of the national economy, the steady growth of the productive forces of Soviet society, the elimination of the possibility of economic crises, and the abolition of unemployment.

ARTICLE 119. Citizens of the U.S.S.R. have the right to rest and leisure.

The right to rest and leisure is ensured by the reduction of the working day to seven hours for the overwhelming majority of the workers, the institution of annual vacations with full pay for workers and employees and the provision of a wide network of sanatoria, rest homes and clubs for the accommodation of the working people.

ARTICLE 120. Citizens of the U.S.S.R. have the right to maintenance in old age and also in case of sickness or loss of capacity to work.

This right is ensured by the extensive development of social insurance of workers and employees at state expense, free medical service for the working people and the provision of a wide network of health resorts for the use of the working people.

ARTICLE 121. Citizens of the U.S.S.R. have the right to education.

This right is ensured by universal, compulsory elementary education; by education, including higher education, being free of charge; by the system of state stipends for the overwhelming majority of students in the universities and colleges; by instruction in schools being conducted in the native language, and by the organization in the factories, state farms, machine and tractor stations and collective farms of free vocational, technical and agronomic training for the working people.

ARTICLE 122. Women in the U.S.S.R. are accorded equal rights with men in all spheres of economic, state, cultural, social and political life.

The possibility of exercising these rights is ensured to women by granting them an equal right with men to work, payment for work, rest and leisure, social insurance and education, and by state protection of the interests of mother and child, pre-maternity and maternity leave with full pay, and the provision of a wide network of maternity homes, nurseries and kindergartens.

ARTICLE 123. Equality of rights of citizens of the U.S.S.R., irrespective of their nationality or race, in all spheres of economic, state, cultural, social and political life, is an indefeasible law.

Any direct or indirect restriction of the rights of, or, conversely, any establishment of direct or indirect privileges for, citizens on account of their race or nationality, as well as any advocacy of racial or national exclusiveness or hatred and contempt, is punishable by law.

ARTICLE 124. In order to ensure to citizens freedom of conscience, the church in the U.S.S.R. is separated from the state, and the school from the church. Freedom of religious worship and freedom of anti-religious propaganda is recognized for all citizens.

ARTICLE 125. In conformity with the interests of the working people, and in order to strengthen the socialist system, the citizens of the U.S.S.R. are guaranteed by law:
  a) freedom of speech;
  b) freedom of the press;
  c) freedom of assembly, including the holding of mass meetings;
  d) freedom of street processions and demonstrations.
These civil rights are ensured by placing at the disposal of the working people and their organizations printing presses, stocks of paper, public buildings, the streets, communications facilities and other material requisites for the exercise of these rights.

ARTICLE 126. In conformity with the interests of the working people, and in order to develop the organizational initiative and political activity of the masses of the people, citizens of the U.S.S.R. are ensured the right to unite in public organizations—trade unions, cooperative associations, youth organizations, sport and defense organizations, cultural, technical and scientific societies; and the most active and politically most conscious citizens in the ranks of the working class and other sections of the working people unite in the Communist Party of the Soviet Union (Bolsheviks), which is the vanguard of the working people in their struggle to strengthen and develop the socialist system and is the leading core of all organizations of the working people, both public and state.

ARTICLE 127. Citizens of the U.S.S.R. are guaranteed inviolability of the person. No person may be placed under arrest except by decision of a court or with the sanction of a procurator.

ARTICLE 128. The inviolability of the homes of citizens and privacy of correspondence are protected by law.

ARTICLE 129. The U.S.S.R. affords the right of asylum to foreign citizens persecuted for defending the interests of the working people, or for their scientific activities, or for their struggle for national liberation.

ARTICLE 130. It is the duty of every citizen of the U.S.S.R. to abide by the Constitution of the Union of Soviet Socialist Republics, to observe the laws, to maintain labor discipline, honestly to perform public duties, and to respect the rules of socialist intercourse.

ARTICLE 131. It is the duty of every citizen of the U.S.S.R. to safeguard and strengthen public, socialist property as the sacred and inviolable foundation of the Soviet system, as the source of the wealth and might of the country, as the source of the prosperous and cultured life of all the working people.

Persons committing offenses against public, socialist property are enemies of the people.

ARTICLE 132. Universal military service is law.

Military service in the Workers' and Peasants' Red Army is an honorable duty of the citizens of the U.S.S.R.

ARTICLE 133. To defend the fatherland is the sacred duty of every citizen of the U.S.S.R. Treason to the country—violation of the oath of allegiance, desertion to the enemy, impairing the military power of the state, espionage—is punishable with all the severity of the law as the most heinous of crimes.

CHAPTER XI. THE ELECTORAL SYSTEM

ARTICLE 134. Members of all Soviets of Working People's Deputies—of the Supreme Soviet of the U.S.S.R., the Supreme Soviets of the Union Republics, the Soviets of Working People's Deputies of the Territories and Regions, the Supreme Soviets of the Autonomous Republics, and Soviets of Working People's Deputies of Autonomous Regions, area, district, city and rural (stanitsa, village, hamlet, kishlak, aul) Soviets of Working People's Deputies—are chosen by the electors on the basis of universal, direct and equal suffrage by secret ballot.

ARTICLE 135. Elections of deputies are universal: all citizens of the U.S.S.R. who have reached the age of eighteen, irrespective of race or nationality, religion, educational and residential qualifications, social origin, property status or past activities, have the right to vote in the election of deputies and to be elected, with the exception of insane persons and persons who have been convicted by a court of law and whose sentences include deprivation of electoral rights.

ARTICLE 136. Elections of deputies are equal: each citizen has one vote; all citizens participate in elections on an equal footing.

ARTICLE 137. Women have the right to elect and be elected on equal terms with men.

ARTICLE 138. Citizens serving in the Red Army have the right to elect and be elected on equal terms with all other citizens.

ARTICLE 139. Elections of deputies are direct: all Soviets of Working People's Deputies, from rural and city Soviets of Working People's Deputies to the Supreme Soviet of the U.S.S.R., inclusive, are elected by the citizens by direct vote.

ARTICLE 140. Voting at elections of deputies is secret.

ARTICLE 141. Candidates for election are nominated according to electoral areas.

The right to nominate candidates is secured to public organizations and societies of the working people: Communist Party organizations, trade unions, cooperatives, youth organizations and cultural societies.

ARTICLE 142. It is the duty of every deputy to report to his electors on his work and on the work of the Soviet of Working People's Deputies, and he is liable to be recalled at any time in the manner established by law upon decision of a majority of the electors.

CHAPTER XII.   ARMS, FLAG, CAPITAL

ARTICLE 143.   The arms of the Union of Soviet Socialist Republics consist of a sickle and hammer against a globe depicted in the rays of the sun and surrounded by ears of grain with the inscription "Workers of All Countries, Unite!" in the languages of the Union Republics.   At the top of the arms is a five-pointed star.

ARTICLE 144.   The state flag of the Union of Soviet Socialist Republics is of red cloth with the sickle and hammer depicted in gold in the upper corner near the staff and above them a five-pointed red star bordered in gold. The ratio of the width to the length is 1:2.

ARTICLE 145.   The capital of the Union of the Soviet Socialist Republics is the City of Moscow.

CHAPTER XIII.   PROCEDURE FOR AMENDING THE CONSTITUTION

ARTICLE 146.   The Constitution of the U.S.S.R. may be amended only by decision of the Supreme Soviet of the U.S.S.R. adopted by a majority of not less than two-thirds of the votes cast in each of its Chambers.

APPENDIX II

THE SOVIET CENSUS OF 1939 *

On January 17, 1939, the total population of the U.S.S.R. was 170,467,186, an increase of 15.9 per cent as compared with the population on December 17, 1926, when the last All-Union census was taken. During this same period the population of Europe increased by approximately thirty-two million, or 8.7 per cent. . . . The Soviet Union has developed into a powerful industrial nation and its small-scale agriculture has been converted into large-scale collectivized agriculture. In the same period the national income of the U.S.S.R. increased from 21.7 billion rubles in 1926 to 105 billion rubles in 1938; per capita national income increased 4.2 times. This growth in the industrial strength of the country finds reflection in the increased production of industrial goods, rising from 15.9 billion rubles in 1926 to 106.8 billion in 1938, while the per capita production rose from 108 rubles in 1926 to 624 in 1938.

At the same time the rural areas have changed substantially. In 1926 only 1.7 per cent of the peasant households were collectivized, but in 1938 collectivization had taken in 93.5 per cent. The sown area had increased from 110.3 million hectares in 1926 to 136.9 million in 1938, and the growing efficiency of agriculture has made possible the extension of cultivated land and the increase of output, so that the harvest well exceeds the maximum harvest of old Russia. The present organization of agriculture makes it less and less affected by unfavorable weather conditions, so that, for instance, despite bad weather in 1938 and 1939 in many parts of the Union, the harvest was larger than the best harvests of old Russia. With a decrease in the rural population of 6.2 million, agricultural production was 25 per cent greater in 1938 than in 1926.

The enlargement of old industrial centers and the establishment of new ones in all republics have brought a rise of 29.6 million in urban population, more than doubling the number in 1926. This increase is caused not only by the natural growth in urban population but by a considerable redistribution of population between the rural districts and the cities. In 1926 there were 709 cities and 125 towns. Now there are 922 cities and 1,448 towns. The table below shows the classification of these cities.

* *The American Quarterly on the Soviet Union,* November, 1940, Vol. III, pp. 89–100.

NUMBER AND POPULATION OF SOVIET CITIES AND TOWNS, 1926 AND 1939

	DEC. 17, 1926		JAN. 17, 1939	
	No. of cities	Population 1,000	No. of cities	Population 1,000
Moscow	1	2,029.4	1	4,137.1
Leningrad	1	1,690.1	1	3,191.3
Cities from 500,000 to 1,000,000 inhabitants	1	513.6	9	5,852.5
Cities from 400,000 to 500,000 inhabitants	3	1,291.5	5	2,140.7
Cities from 300,000 to 400,000 inhabitants	2	631.7	3	1,093.0
Cities from 200,000 to 300,000 inhabitants	4	972.7	20	4,949.2
Cities from 100,000 to 200,000 inhabitants	21	2,860.4	43	6,069.0
Total cities with more than 100,000 inhabitants				
Cities from 50,000 to 100,000	33	9,989.4	82	27,432.8
Total cities with more than 50,000	57	3,903.2	92	6,703.8
inhabitants	90	13,892.6	174	34,136.6
Cities and towns with up to 50,000 inhabitants	744	12,421.5	2,196	21,773.3
Grand Total	834	26,314.1	2,370	55,909.9

Source: *Problemy Ekonomiki*, No. 5, 1939, p. 42.

From 1926 to 1939 the natural increase in rural population was 18.2 million people but during the same period 24.4 million people migrated from the rural areas to the cities, leaving a net decrease of 6.2 million. In Soviet society the migration from village to city assumes particular importance as an integral part of the industrialization of the country. It is planned to obtain 1.5 million workers per year from the collective farms where their labor is no longer necessary because of the increased efficiency of modern mechanized agriculture. For instance in 1939, 1.9 million workers used tractors and combines on the collective farms. Without the help of the machine-tractor-stations the same work would have necessitated 9.9 million farmers. From 1922 to 1925 the culti-vation of one hectare of sown area on individual farms necessitated 20.8 man-days the production of one centner of grain—3.2 man-days. On the collective farms in 1939 one hectare of sown area absorbed 10.5 man-days and one centner of grain 1 man-day. These figures give an indication of the possibilities of transferring the rural population to the industrial areas, while at the same time increasing agricultural output.

With the general increase in population, there have been considerable variations between different republics and regions in the rate of growth. While the average for the whole U.S.S.R. was a 15.9 per cent increase, the Table below indicates the much more rapid rise in some areas.

PER CENT INCREASE IN POPULATION BY AREA, 1926–1939

Kirghiz S.S.R.	45.7
Armenian S.S.R.	45.4
Tadzhik S.S.R.	43.9
Azerbaidzhan S.S.R.	38.7
Uzbek S.S.R.	37.6
Georgian S.S.R.	32.3
Turkmen S.S.R.	25.6
Sverdlovsk Oblast	53.0
Novosibirsk Oblast	53.0
Irkutsk Oblast	49.0
Chitinsk Oblast	73.0
Khabarovsk Krai	136.0
Moscow Oblast	74.0
Leningrad Oblast	44.0
Stalinsk Oblast (Ukraine)	91.0

Source: *Bolshevik*, No. 10, 1940, p. 16.

The areas gaining most rapidly in population are seen to be the Far East, the Central
sian Republics, the Far North and the great industrial centers. To offset this, there has
en a decrease of 10 to 15 per cent in the population of the crowded agricultural dis-
cts of Central Russia.

The change in the social groupings within the Soviet population is given in the Table
low.

COMPOSITION OF THE POPULATION IN SELECTED YEARS

	1913	1928	1937	1939
Workers and employees	16.7	17.3	34.7	49.73
Collective farmers and cooperative hand-icraftsmen	None	2.9	55.5	46.9
Individual farmers and non-cooperative handicraftsmen	65.1	72.9	5.6	2.6
Bourgeoisie (landlords, merchants, ku-laks)	15.9	4.5	..	..
Others (students, pensioners, Army) ..	2.3	2.4	4.2	..
Non-working population	No data	No data	No data	0.04
Not listed	No data	No data	No data	0.73

Source: *Bolshevik*, No. 15–16, 1939, p. 113 and *Bolshevik* No. 10, 1940, p. 17.

The present census is the first which gives accurate data on the nationality compo-
tion of the population. The 1926 census asked for information on national origin
arodnost) instead of on nationality (*natsionalnost*). Although the 1920 census of the
SFSR contained a question regarding nationality as in 1939, the results of this census
ere never published in full. Consequently there is no accurate basis of comparison re-
rding nationality groupings. When the census material from the Far North is com-
eted, there will be for the first time exhaustive data on all the nationalities of the
untry, including information on the age groupings, literacy, and occupation.

Some indication of a leveling-up process which is leading to the complete elimination
social differences between nationalities is the increasing number of intermarriages be-
een different national groups: in 1927 only 7.5 per cent of the marriages in the
krainian SSR were between people of different nationality; by 1937 this figure had in-
eased to 19 per cent. In the Armenian SSR the corresponding percentages were 1 per
nt in 1927 and 7.4 per cent in 1937. Among the Kazakh people, intermarriages were
6 per cent of the total in 1936 and 7 per cent in 1937.

Data on the occupational distribution within the population is not yet complete, but
ready it reflects clearly the changes taking place in Soviet economy. The first Table
low, for instance, gives figures on the persons engaged in metal trades and the sec-
d Table shows the number in agricultural specialties.

METAL WORKERS, 1926 AND 1939

	(In Thousands)	
	1926	*1939*
otal Metal Workers	981.0	4,331.1
rners	63.5	432.3
lling Machine Operators	5.0	65.2
her Lathe Operators	14.9	240.5
ectro-Automatic Welders	....	109.5
oulders	11.3	137.6
ess and Stamp Operators	8.9	55.2

urce: *Bolshevik*, No. 10, 1940, p. 19.

WORKERS IN AGRICULTURAL SPECIALTIES, 1939

(In Thousand

Chairmen of Special Meat & Dairy Farm Divisions (*Kolkhoznie Tovarnie Fermi*)	200.5
Heads of Tractor Brigade	97.6
Heads of Field Brigade	549.6
Heads of Livestock Brigade	103.1
Brigade Heads	89.3
Section Heads	466.5
Heads of Farm Laboratories, Seed Selection and Yarovization	16.9
Tractor Drivers	803.1
Combine Operators	131.2
Total	2457.8

Source: *Bolshevik,* No. 10, 1940, p. 19.

In 1926 many of these professions did not exist and there were only about 4,2 tractor drivers in all. Similarly in many industries, as for instance in the building trad there were none of the modern technical professions. Conversely, in mining and in t oil industry many of the occupations involving manual labor which were enumerat in past censuses have been displaced completely.

The census of 1939 bears witness to the improved cultural level of the populatic 81.2 per cent of those over 9 years of age are now literate, as compared with 51.1 cent in 1926 and 24 per cent in 1897. This increase has been particularly rapid in national republics. Furthermore, it has not been confined to the urban population, a the gap in literacy between men and women is being closed in the Central Asian F publics. For instance, in 1926 the figures for literacy among women were: Tadzhik S.S —less than 1 per cent; Uzbek S.S.R.—6.5 per cent; Kirgiz S.S.R.—7.4 per cent; a Turkmen S.S.R.—7.7 per cent. The present level of literacy for women in the sa republics is 65.2 per cent; 61.6 per cent; 63 per cent, and 60.6 per cent, respective These figures are, of course, related directly to those on education. There are now 2 students per thousand population in the U.S.S.R. and the highest levels are again the non-Russian republics, with the Tadzhik S.S.R. reaching 394 per thousand. T great bulk of these students throughout the country are in elementary and second. schools—totalling 31 million out of 37.9 million. Another five million are in the g eral elementary courses for adults, and the remaining study in the higher educatio institutions. It is interesting to note that 89.4 per cent of the population with second education are under 39 years of age, which means that they received their educati under the Soviet regime. Similarly, 70 per cent of those with higher education are the same age group. The resulting increase in the Intelligentsia is indicated in Table below.

PROFESSIONAL WORKERS, 1926 AND 1939

(In Thousan

	1926	193
Engineers, Architects and Construction Supervisors	32	30
Middle Technical Personnel	175	83
Agronomists	18	9
Other Agro-Technical Personnel	13	11
Scientific Workers (Including Professors and Teachers of Higher Educational Institutes)	14	9
Teachers	348	120
Cultural-Educational Workers (Journalists, Librarians, Club Directors)	59	49
Art Workers	54	17
Doctors	70	15
Middle Medical Personnel (Feldshers, Nurses, etc.)	130	60
Bookkeepers, Accountants, etc.	375	176

Source: *Bolshevik,* No. 10, 1940, p. 22.

In summary, the 1939 census shows the following characteristics of population changes in the Soviet Union. First of all there is the very rapid natural increase in population. While the birthrate figures are not complete, some preliminary figures can be given. In 1938, the birthrate per thousand was 28.5 in Moscow, 27.4 in Leningrad and Kiev, 27.7 in Kharkov, 33.9 in Baku. This compares with 1936 figures of 13.5 in New York, 14.1 in Berlin, 11.5 in Paris, 13.6 in London, 21.7 in Rome. For the USSR as a whole the birthrate exceeded the deathrate in 1938 by 115.7 per cent as compared with 71 per cent in the United States. For some republics in the USSR this figure is much higher, as for example, 266.7 per cent in White Russia, and 234 per cent in Georgia and Armenia.

The second characteristic of the population as indicated by the census, is that the overwhelming preponderance of the people have been brought up and received their education under the Soviet regime. Finally, some of the most interesting material relates to the development of the non-Russian nationalities, both from the point of view of their economic and technical improvement and of their cultural level. Although the educational and health level in the Central Asian Republics still lags considerably behind the other regions, the rate of improvement is higher than elsewhere. These changes, taken with the redistribution of population as between town and country and as between west and east which is revealed in the Census returns, mirror the Soviet planning of the geographical allocation of productive enterprises, both agricultural and industrial.

AGE COMPOSITION OF THE POPULATION OF THE USSR ACCORDING TO THE 1939 CENSUS

(Excluding Western Ukraine and Western Byelorussia)

Age Group	Number of Individuals	Per Cent Total
Up to 7 Years	31,412,232	18.6
8–11	16,409,098	9.7
12–14	13,336,151	7.9
15–19	15,124,176	8.9
20–29	30,639,041	18.0
30–39	25,332,993	14.9
40–49	15,235,864	9.0
50–59	10,867,408	6.4
60 Years and Older	11,129,290	6.6
Age Not Indicated	32,874	0.0
Total	169,519,127	100.

POPULATION OF USSR (WITH FAMILIES) BY SOCIAL GROUPS
(Excluding Western Ukraine and Western White Russia)

Social groups	Number of persons including families	Per cent of total
Workers, city and rural	54,566,283	32.19
Employees, city and rural	29,758,484	17.54
Collective farm members	75,616,388	44.61
Cooperative handicraft workers	3,888,434	2.29
Noncooperative handicraft workers	1,396,203	0.82
Individual peasants	3,018,050	1.78
Nonworkers	60,006	0.04
Those not indicating social group	1,235,279	0.73
Total	169,519,127	100.00

APPENDIX III

TABLE OF SOVIET NATIONALITIES *

Republic, Region or District	Date of Formation	Population (Estimated as of July 1, 1941)	Predominant Ethnic Strain	National Origins [1] (In per cent of total as of 1926 census)	Total of Dominant Nationality in All U.S.S.R. [2] (1941 estimate)	Area (In sq. miles est. Nov. 1, 1945)	Location	Capital
RUSSIAN SOVIET FEDERATED SOCIALIST REPUBLIC (RSFSR)	1918	114,337,428	Slav	Russian, 73.4%; Ukrainian, 7.8%; Kazak, 3.8%; Tatar, 2.8%	104,833,638	6,612,601	Soviet Europe and Siberia	Moscow
Autonomous Soviet Socialist Republics								
BASHKIR ASSR	1919	3,304,476	Turco-Tatar	Bashkir, 23.5%; Russian, 39.0%	Bashkir 885,747	54,233	Southwest Urals	Ufa
BURYAT-MONGOLIAN ASSR	1923	569,713	Mongol	Buryat, 43.8%; Russian, 52.7%	Buryat 249,534	127,020	Southeastern Siberia	Ulan-Ude
CHUVASH ASSR	1925	1,133,300	Turco-Tatar	Chuvash, 80%; Russian, 15.8%	1,437,424	6,909	Middle Volga River	Cheboksary
DAGHESTAN ASSR	1921	977,800	Japhetic	Gortsy, 64.5%; Russian, 12.5%	900,928	13,124	Northeast Caucasus	Makhach-Kala
KABARDINO-BALKARIAN ASSR	1936	377,485	Japhetic	Kabardin, 60%; Balkar, 16.3%	172,442	4,747	Caucasus	Nalchik
KOMI ASSR	1936	335,172	Finno-Ugrian	Komi, 92.3%; Russian, 6.1%	420,487	144,711	Northwest Urals	Syktyvkar
MARI ASSR	1936	608,904	Finno-Ugrian	Mari, 51.4%; Russian, 43.6%	505,711	8,993	Middle Volga River	Ioshkar-Ola
MORDOVIAN ASSR	1934	1,248,982	Finno-Ugrian	Mordovian, 37.4%; Russian, 57.3%	Mordov. 1,525,166	9,843	Middle Volga Basin	Saransk
NORTH OSSETIAN ASSR	1936	345,592	Iranian	Ossetian, 84.2%; Ukrainian, 6.8%	372,557	2,393	Caucasus	'Dzaudzhikau
TATAR ASSR	1920	3,067,740	Turco-Tatar	Tatar, 50.4%; Russian, 41.8%	4,518,808	25,900	Middle Volga River	Kazan
UDMURSK ASSR	1934	1,281,987	Finno-Ugrian	Udmursk, 52.3%; Russian, 43.3%	636,442	15,015	Middle Volga Basin	Izhevsk
YAKUTSK ASSR	1922	420,892	Turco-Tatar	Yakut, 81.6%; Russian, 10.4%	324,000	1,169,927	Northeast Siberia	Yakutsk
Autonomous Regions								
ADYGEI AR	1922	254,055	Japhetic	Cherkess, 47.8%; Russian, 25.6%	92,441	1,505	Northwest Caucasus	Maikop
CHERKESS AR	1928	97,333	Japhetic	Kabardin, 33.3%; Beskeskabaz, 29.7%; Nogaitsi, 16.8%; Cherkess, 7.2%	172,442	1,273	Caucasus	Sulimov
JEWISH AR	1934	113,925	Jewish	Jew, 40% (est. 1936)	5,334,824	14,204	Southern Far East	Birobidzhan
KHAKASS AR	1930	284,404	Turkic & Mongol	Khakass, 51.7%; Russian, 48.3%	55,274	19,261	South Central Siberia	Abakan
OIROT AR	1922	169,631	Turco-Tatar	Oirot & Altai, 37.2%; Russian, 52%	Oirot 50,140	35,936	South Central Siberia	Oirot-Tura
TUVA AR	1945	86,400	Mongol	Tuvan, 86%; Russian, 14%	74,304	78,120	South Central Siberia	Kyzyl
National Districts								
AGIN BURYAT MONGOL ND	1937	32,000*	Mongol	*Figures not available*	*Figures not available*	10,730	Southeastern Siberia	Aginskoe
CHUKOTSKY ND	1930	14,983*	Paleo-Asiatic			254,991	Bering Strait	Anadyr
EVENKI ND	1930	38,804*	Mongol			209,057	North Central Siberia	Tura
KOMI-PERMIAK ND	1925	201,000*	Finno-Ugrian			8,916	Northwest Siberia	Kudymkar
KORIAK ND	1930	12,500*	Paleo-Asiatic			119,968	North Far East	Palana
NENETS ND	1929	28,125*	Mongol			82,797	Northeast Soviet Europe	Naryan Mar
OSTYAGO VOGULSK ND	1930	102,200*	Finno-Ugrian			293,366	Northwest Siberia	Ostyago Vogulsk
TAIMYR ND	1930	8,000*	Mongol			286,643	North Central Siberia	Dudinka
UST ORDIN BURYAT MONGOL ND	1937	110,000*	Mongol			10,923	Southeastern Siberia	Ust-Orda
YAMAL-NENETSKY ND	1930	12,753*	Mongol			179,876	Northwest Siberia	Sale Khard

Republic	Year	Linguistic family	National origin[1]	Population	National group total[2]	Area	Region	Capital
UKRAINIAN SOVIET SOCIALIST REPUBLIC	1919	Slav	Ukrainian, 80%; Russian, 9.2%; Jew, 5.4%	42,272,943	226,792	236,544	Southwest Soviet Europe	Kiev
BELORUSSIAN SSR	1919	Slav	Byelo-Russian, 80.6%; Jew, 8.2%	10,525,511	8,595,036	82,131	West Soviet Europe	Minsk
KARELO-FINNISH SSR	1940	Finno-Ugrian	Karelian and Finn, 43%; Russian, 57%	512,977	Karel. 265,431; Finn 170,341	76,440	Northwest Soviet Europe	Petrozavodsk
ESTONIAN SSR	1940	Finno-Ugrian	Estonian, 87.7%; Russian, 8.2%	1,120,000	1,124,102	18,525	Baltic Sea	Tallinn
LATVIAN SSR	1940	Baltic	Latvian, 75.6%; Russian, 12.3% (est. 1941)	1,950,502	1,607,925	25,662	Baltic Sea	Riga
LITHUANIAN SSR	1940	Baltic	Lithuanian, 85%; Russian, 2.5% (est. 1941)	3,134,970	2,697,942	24,382	Baltic Sea	Vilnius
MOLDAVIAN SSR	1940	Romanian	Moldavian, 70%	2,321,225	1,624,857	13,143	Southwest Soviet Europe	Kishinev
GEORGIAN SSR[3]	1921	Japhetic	Georgian, 67.7%; Armenian, 11.6%	3,722,252	2,362,801	27,027	Transcaucasus	Tbilisi
ABKHAZIAN ASSR	1921	Japhetic	Abkhazian, 27.8%; Georgian, 33.5%	303,147	Abkhaz. 61,963	3,358	Transcaucasus	Sukhumi
ADZHAR ASSR	1921	Japhetic	Adzharian, 53.7%; Georgian, 14.5%	179,046	61,260	1,080	Transcaucasus	Batumi
SOUTH OSSETIAN AR	1922	Iranian	Ossetian, 69.1%; Georgian, 26.9%	111,501	372,557	1,428	Transcaucasus	Stalinir
ARMENIAN SSR[3]	1920	Japhetic	Armenian, 84.7%; Turkic, 8.2%	1,346,709	2,261,207	11,661	Transcaucasus	Erivan
AZERBAIDZHAN SSR[3]	1920	Turco-Tatar	Turkic, 63.3%; Armenian, 12.4%	3,372,794	Azer. 2,390,374	33,345	Transcaucasus	Baku
NAKHICHEVAN ASSR	1924	Turco-Tatar	Turkic, 84.5%; Armenian, 10.8%	138,528	Azer. 2,390,374	2,277	Transcaucasus	Nakhichevan
NAGORNO-KARABAKH AR	1923	Japhetic	Armenian, 89.1%; Turkic, 10%	180,063	2,261,207	1,659	Transcaucasus	Stepanakert
KAZAK SSR	1936	Turco-Tatar	Kazak, 57.1%; Russian, 19.7%	6,458,175	3,256,193	1,066,533	Central Asia	Alma-Ata
UZBEK SSR	1924	Turco-Tatar	Uzbek, 76%; Russian, 5.6%	6,601,619	5,090,116	160,095	Central Asia	Tashkent
KARA-KALPAK ASSR	1932	Turco-Tatar	Karakalpak, 39.1%; Kazak, 27%	436,995	195,211	79,631	Central Asia	Turtkul
TURKMAN SSR	1924	Turco-Tatar	Turkmen, 72%; Uzbek, 10.5%	1,317,063	853,009	189,033	Central Asia	Ashkhabad
TADZHIK SSR	1929	Iranian	Tadzhik, 78.4%; Uzbek, 17.9%	1,560,540	1,201,399	55,497	Central Asia	Stalinabad
GORNO-BADAKHSHAN AR	1927	Iranian	Iranian, 87%; Kirghiz, 13%	41,769	41,019	25,784	Central Asia	Khorog
KIRGHIZ SSR	1936	Turco-Tatar	Kirghiz, 66.6%; Russian, 11.7%	1,533,439	920,231	78,624	Central Asia	Frunze
TOTAL POPULATION[4]				202,087,877				
TOTAL AREA[5]						8,701,491		

* Prepared and copyrighted by Corliss Lamont.

[1] It is to be noted that all the chief peoples of the Soviet Union overflow to some extent the boundaries of the territorial divisions bearing their names. Thus each main division has within it a minority or minorities other than the predominant one. *National origin* does not necessarily coincide with *nationality*. Because the territory of the Tuva AR became part of the U.S.S.R. only in 1945 and therefore was not included in the 1926 Soviet census, the data for that territory are from sources outside the census.

[2] This column does not include the approximate totals for the following national groups in the Soviet Union: the Poles, 1,000,000; the Germans, 1,495,854; the Japanese, 400,000; the Greeks, 300,419; the Bulgarians, 260,242; the Koreans, 189,577; the Chinese, 31,124; the Kurds, 48,195; the Arabs, 22,898; the Assyrians, 21,233; and a number of the smaller peoples.

[3] The three republics of Georgia, Armenia and Azerbaidzhan first united in 1922 in the Transcaucasian Soviet Federated Socialist Republic, which then became one of the four original Union republics of the U.S.S.R. In 1936 this federation was dissolved and its three constituent members became Union republics in their own right.

[4] Totals of area and population are reached by adding figures for the 16 Union republics, abbreviated as "SSR."

APPENDIX IV

ECONOMIC AND CULTURAL PROGRESS, 1933–1938 *

The following data indicate the improvement in the standard of living of the workers and peasants during the period 1933 to 1938, inclusive:

1. The national income rose from 48,500,000,000 rubles in 1933 to 105,000,000,000 rubles in 1938.

2. The number of workers and other employees rose from a little over 22,000,000 in 1933 to 28,000,000 in 1938.

3. The total annual payroll of workers and other employees rose from 34,953,000,000 rubles to 96,425,000,000 rubles.

4. The average annual wages of industrial workers, which amounted to 1,513 rubles in 1933, rose to 3,447 rubles in 1938.

5. The total monetary incomes of the collective farms rose from 5,661,900,000 rubles in 1933 to 14,180,100,000 rubles in 1937.

6. The average amount of grain received per collective farm household in the grain-growing regions rose from 61 poods in 1933 to 144 poods in 1937, exclusive of seed, emergency seed stocks, fodder for the collectively-owned cattle, grain deliveries, and payments in kind for work performed by the machine and tractor stations.

7. State budget appropriations for social and cultural services rose from 5,839,900,000 rubles in 1933 to 35,202,500,000 rubles in 1938.

From the standpoint of the cultural development of the people, the period under review has been marked by a veritable cultural revolution. The introduction of universal compulsory elementary education in the languages of the various nations of the U.S.S.R., an increasing number of schools and scholars of all grades, an increasing number of college-trained experts, and the creation and growth of a new intelligentsia, a Soviet intelligentsia—such is the general picture of the cultural advancement of the people. Here are the figures:

RISE IN THE CULTURAL LEVEL OF THE PEOPLE

	Unit of measurement	1933–34	1938–39	1938–39 compared with 1933–34 (per cent)
Number of pupils and students of all grades	thousands	23,814.0	33,965.4	142.6
Of which: In elementary schools	thousands	17,873.5	21,288.4	119.1
In intermediate schools (general and special)	thousands	5,482.2	12,076.0	220.3
In higher educational institutions	thousands	458.3	601.0	131.1
Number of persons engaged in all forms of study in the U.S.S.R.	thousands	.....	47,442.1	.....
Number of public libraries	thousands	40.3	70.0	173.7
Number of books in public libraries ..	millions	86.0	126.6	147.2
Number of clubs	thousands	61.1	95.6	156.5
Number of theaters	units	587.0	790.0	134.6
Number of cinema installations (excluding narrow-film)	units	27,467.0	30,461.0	110.9
Of which: With sound equipment ..	units	498.0	15,202.0	31 (times)
Number of cinema installations (excluding narrow-film) in rural districts ..	units	17,470.0	18,991.0	108.7
Of which: With sound equipment ..	units	24.0	6,670.0	278 (times)
Annual newspaper circulation	millions	4,984.6	7,092.4	142.3

* Joseph Stalin, *Leninism: Selected Writings* (New York: International Publishers, 1942), pp. 455–457.

NUMBER OF SCHOOLS BUILT IN THE U.S.S.R. IN 1933-38

	In towns and hamlets	In rural localities	Total
1933	326	3,261	3,587
1934	577	3,488	4,065
1935	533	2,829	3,362
1936	1,505	4,206	5,711
1937	730	1,323	2,053
1938	583	1,246	1,829
Total (1933-38)	4,254	16,353	20,607

APPENDIX V

STATE BUDGET OF THE U.S.S.R. FOR 1945 *

The state budget for 1945 which the Council of People's Commissars of the U.S.S.R. submits for your approval provides for the allocations needed to cover war expenditures, an increase in expenditures on restoration work in the liberated areas and for the further development of the national economy and culture of the Soviet Union.

The revenue and expenditures under the state budget of the U.S.S.R. for 1945 has been set at 305,300 million rubles. The revenues are 37,300 million rubles, or 13.9 per cent greater than in 1944, while the expenditures are 42,300 million rubles, or 16.1 per cent higher.

In the state budget of the U.S.S.R. for 1945 which has been submitted for your approval, expenditures for financing the People's Commissariats of Defense and the Navy have been set at 137,900 million rubles, which makes up 45.1 per cent of the expenditures under the budget this year.

Expenditures under the state budget for financing the national economy have been set at 64,600 million rubles, as against 49,000 million rubles in 1944, or an increase of 31.8 per cent. This considerable increase of expenditures on financing the national economy is one of the characteristic features of state budget of the U.S.S.R. for 1945. The above total appropriations are distributed among the various branches of the national economy as follows (in thousands of millions of rubles):

Item	Expenditure in 1944 (preliminary data)	1945	Increase in %
Total for national economy	49.0	64.6	31.8
Of which:			
Industry	27.3	35.9	31.5
Agriculture	7.0	9.2	31.4
Transport and communications	7.7	9.8	27.3
Trade and state purchases	1.2	1.7	41.7
Public utilities and housing	1.8	2.9	61.1

The increased expenditures for financing the national economy in 1945 are due in the main to the growth of allocations for capital construction and first and foremost for reconstruction in the liberated areas. The financing of capital investments increases from 29,000 million rubles in 1944 to 40,100 million rubles in 1945. Budget appropriations for capital

* Excerpts from report of People's Commissar of Finance of the U.S.S.R. at Eleventh Session of the Supreme Soviet of the U.S.S.R., April 24, 1945, as published in *Moscow News*, April 28, 1945.

investments are set at 31,200 million rubles. . . . Almost half of the 40,100 million rubles earmarked in 1945 for capital investments is to be routed into restoration work.

One of the most important construction tasks of 1945 is the restoration and reconstruction of heavy industry in the liberated areas, in the first place of the southern coal and iron and steel producers. Large funds are assigned also for the restoration of transport, machine and tractor stations, housing and public utilities. . . .

The state budget of the U.S.S.R. for 1945 also provides for an increase in expenditures for social and cultural measures. These expenditures will increase from 51,100 million rubles in 1944 to 66,100 million rubles in 1945, or by 15,000 million rubles. Appropriations for the various social and cultural measures are distributed as follows (in millions of rubles):

Item of Expenditure	Expenditure in 1944 (preliminary data)	1945	Increase in %
Education	20,440	28,591	39.9
Public health and physical culture	10,210	13,194	29.2
State social insurance	3,856	5,202	34.9
State grants to mothers of large families and unmarried mothers	872	1,407	61.3
Social welfare	15,686	17,695	12.8

. . . Expenditures for maintaining state administrative bodies in 1945 are planned at 9,500 million rubles, of which 3,100 million rubles come under the Union budget and 6,400 million rubles under the state budgets of the Union republics. Expenditures for the state administrative apparatus increase by 2,200 million rubles as compared to 1944, chiefly for the maintenance of administrative bodies in the districts liberated from the German invaders. . . .

The state budget of the U.S.S.R. for 1945 is the first in wartime to include the budgets of all the Union republics with all their territory. . . .

The state budgets for the various Union republics for 1945 are presented as follows (in millions of rubles):

Union Republic	Expenditure in 1944 (preliminary data)	1945	Increase in %
R.S.F.S.R.	23,556	28,588	21.4
Ukrainian S.S.R.	5,355	9,124	70.4
Belorussian S.S.R.	720	2,377	230.1
Azerbaijan S.S.R.	971	1,183	21.8
Georgian S.S.R.	1,223	1,456	19.0
Armenian S.S.R.	572	650	13.6
Turkmenian S.S.R.	417	516	23.7
Uzbek S.S.R.	1,719	2,160	25.7
Tajik S.S.R.	498	651	30.7
Kazakh S.S.R.	1,437	1,885	31.2
Kirghiz S.S.R.	407	562	38.1
Karelian-Finnish S.S.R.	153	288	88.3
Moldavian S.S.R.	170	540	217.7
Lithuanian S.S.R.	169	728	330.8
Latvian S.S.R.	156	792	407.7
Estonian S.S.R.	130	698	436.9
Total	37,653	52,198	38.6

APPENDIX VI

FIVE–YEAR PLAN OF THE U.S.S.R. FOR 1946–1950 *

The peoples of the Soviet Union were able to switch over to peaceful labor as a result of a great historic victory—the smashing of Hitlerite Germany and the defeat of Japanese imperialism.

This victory could have been achieved only on the basis of the preliminary preparation of all the country's material resources for active defense. The material prerequisites of our victory were created on the basis of the consistent policy of the industrialization of our country and the collectivization of agriculture.

The gross output of large-scale industry (in stable prices) in 1915–1917 in Russia amounted to 33,000 million rubles. In the period from 1942 to 1944 (in the main in the eastern regions of the country) it amounted to 361,000 million rubles, i.e., it increased nearly elevenfold. The output of marketable grain increased correspondingly by two and one-half times. The average annual railway freight traffic grew by 3.4 times.

During the First World War practically no tanks or planes were built in Russia; in the U.S.S.R. during the last three years of the Great Patriotic War more than 30 thousand tanks and self-propelled guns and some 40 thousand planes were built annually.

The average annual production of guns in Russia during the last three years of the First World War was about 3,900; in the U.S.S.R. during the last three years of the Great Patriotic War some 120,000 guns, that is, more than 30 times as many, were built.

In Russia during the last three years of the First World War there were manufactured about 8,900 light and heavy machine guns annually; in the U.S.S.R. during the last three years of the Great Patriotic War, some 450,000 machine guns, or more than 50 times as many, were manufactured annually.

In Russia, during the last three years of the First World War, 1,050,000 rifles were produced annually; during the last three years of the Great Patriotic War in the U.S.S.R. five million rifles and tommy guns, that is, almost five times as many, were produced annually.

During the last three years of the First World War, Russia annually produced about 6,200 mortars; in the U.S..S.R. during the last three years of the Great Patriotic War, 100,000 mortars per year, or more than 16 times as many, were produced.

The annual production of shells, bombs and mines increased respectively from 16,300,000 in the last three years of the First World War to 240,000,000 in 1944, that is, almost fifteenfold.

Such were the results of the development of the productive forces on the basis of socialist production, revealed in the period of the Great Patriotic War, in spite of the temporary occupation of a considerable part of Soviet territory containing highly developed industry and agriculture.

The Union of Soviet Socialist Republics is confidently marching forward along the road of the further consolidation and development of the socialist system. It fears no economic crises, depressions or unemployment. It is consistently reconstructing the national economy and increasing the rate of rehabilitation and development, on the basis of the State Plans, which in the Soviet Union have the strength of laws of economic development.

In future, too, the U.S.S.R. will continue to develop economic relations with foreign countries, while maintaining the well-tried policy of the Soviet Government aimed at ensuring the technical and economic independence of the Soviet Union.

* Report of Nikolai A. Voznessensky, Chairman of State Planning Commission, before the Supreme Soviet of the U.S.S.R., March 15, 1946.

I

MAIN TASKS OF THE FIVE–YEAR PLAN

The main economic and political task of the Five-Year Plan for 1946–1950 is to rehabilitate the affected districts of the country, restore industry and agriculture to the prewar level and then considerably to surpass this level. Accordingly, the Five-Year Plan for the Restoration and Development of the National Economy comprises the following tasks:

FIRST, to increase industrial output by nearly 50 per cent compared with the prewar level, ensuring the rehabilitation and development of heavy industry and railway transport in the first place.

SECOND, to achieve the growth of agriculture and industry producing consumer goods, to ensure the material welfare of the peoples of the Soviet Union and to create an abundance of main consumer goods in the country.

It is necessary to surpass the prewar level of national income and national consumption, and to abolish the rationing system at the earliest possible date, replacing it by highly developed Soviet trade.

Special attention is to be paid to the development of the production of consumer goods and to raising the living standards of the working people by means of the steady reduction of commodity prices. These tasks call for the consolidation of the monetary circulation and of the Soviet ruble.

THIRD, to ensure further technical progress in all branches of the national economy of the Soviet Union, as the prerequisite for a powerful rise of production and of labor productivity. For this purpose we must in the nearest future not only come level with, but also surpass, the achievements of science beyond the borders of the U.S.S.R.

The history of our country knows many innovators and revolutionaries in science and technology, who made discoveries of world importance. It is sufficient to mention Popov, outstanding phyicist and inventor of radio which to this day continues to revolutionize science and forms the basis of the most modern radio location technique; Mendeleyev, the world's greatest chemist, who discovered the Periodic Law—the basic law of chemistry—which to this day helps scientists to discover the secrets of atomic energy; Zhukovsky, who laid the theoretical foundations of modern aero-dynamics and aviation; Tsiolkovsky, who developed the theory of reactive movement, which forms the basis of modern reactive movement technique, and who anticipated similar researches abroad.

Provided proper assistance is rendered to our scientists, Soviet science will be able to surpass the latest achievements of science beyond the borders of the Soviet Union.

FOURTH, to ensure a high rate of socialist accumulation of capital and to provide for centralized capital investments in the rehabilitation and development of the national economy during the next five years to the amount of 250,000 million rubles, and to provide for the launching of restored and new enterprises valued at 234,000 million rubles.

Along with rehabilitation of the national economy in the affected districts, the Five-Year Plan provides for the further development of the national economy in all the Union Republics and economic districts of the U.S.S.R. As a result of the execution of the plan of capital construction, the basic funds of the Soviet national economy will not only be restored but even increased in 1950 to 1,130,000 million rubles (in stable prices), that is, eight per cent above the prewar level of development of basic funds in the entire territory of the U.S.S.R.

To accomplish the program of capital construction, we must create a powerful building industry and ensure an annual margin of increase of about 12 per cent in the volume of capital construction.

FIFTH, our task is to raise further the defensive power of the U.S.S.R. and to supply the armed forces of the Soviet Union with the most modern military equipment. The Soviet people wish to see their armed forces even more strong and powerful, in order to guarantee the country against any accident and to safeguard peace.

In the East and West the historical boundaries of the Soviet Union have been restored. From now on, in the East, Southern Sakhalin and the Kurile Islands will no longer serve as a means of isolating the Soviet Union from the ocean or as a base for a

Japanese attack on our Far East, but as a means of direct access of the Soviet Union to the ocean and as a base for the defense of our country from Japanese aggression. From now on the free and democratic Polish State is no longer a base for German attack on our western frontier, but our ally in defense against German aggression.

Comrade Stalin has warned us, however, that "in days to come the peace-loving nations may once more find themselves caught off their guard by aggression, unless of course, they work out special measures right now which can avert it." (Stalin's speech on November 6, 1944.)

One should not forget that monopolistic capitalism is capable of breeding new aggressors. To avert new aggression it is necessary to disarm the aggressive nations completely, to place them under military and economic control and to have in the United Nations organization an organ which will guard world peace and security and will be capable of defending peace and opposing new aggression.

We must strengthen the armed forces of the Soviet Union; we must work tirelessly to provide them with the most modern equipment and to strengthen further the military and economic power of the Soviet State.

Ensuring the rehabilitation and development of the national economy in the Soviet Union, the Five-Year Plan at the same time continues the course of development of Soviet society outlined by the Eighteenth Congress of the Communist Party of the Soviet Union and temporarily interrupted by Hitlerite Germany's treacherous attack on the Soviet Union.

This course envisages the completion of the construction of a classless socialist society and the gradual transition from socialism to communism. It envisages the solution of the main economic task facing the U.S.S.R.—that of overtaking and surpassing the main capitalist countries in respect of economy, i.e., in regard to industrial production per head of the population.

II

PLAN FOR PRODUCTION, BUILDING AND RESTORATION

In regard to the main economic and political tasks of the new period of peaceful development of the U.S.S.R., the Five-Year Plan defines the tempo and the level of production for 1946–1950.

A. INDUSTRY

The gross output of the entire industry of the U.S.S.R. in 1950 is fixed at a sum of 205,000 million rubles (at 1926–1927 prices), i.e., 48 per cent above the prewar level, while in districts affected by occupation the prewar level will be exceeded by 15 per cent. In the period of 1946–1950 we must ensure an annual absolute increase of production by 15,600 million rubles. The rate of growth of the output of means of production somewhat exceeds that of the output of articles of consumption.

In the iron and steel industry, on the growth of which depends the restoration and development of the entire national economy of the Soviet Union, it is planned to increase the output of pig iron to 19.5 million tons, and of steel to 25.4 million tons. That is to say, the output of iron and steel must increase to 35 per cent above the prewar level.

To restore and develop the iron and steel industry, 45 more blast furnaces, 180 more open-hearth furnaces and converters, 90 more electric furnaces and 104 more rolling mills will be put into operation.

The output of non-ferrous and rare metals will be increased so as completely to satisfy the requirements of the national economy by means of home production alone. Compared with the prewar level, the output of copper will increase 1.6 times, that of aluminum 2.0 times, magnesium 2.7 times, nickel 1.9 times, lead 2.6 times, zinc 2.5 times, tungsten concentrates 4.4 times, molybdenum concentrates 2.1 times, tin 2.7 times. The production of new rare metals will be developed at a similar or even more rapid pace.

In the fuel industry, in 1950 the output of coal will be increased up to 250 million tons, or by 51 per cent above the prewar level. The mechanical equipment of the coal industry will increase three or four times compared with the prewar period.

During the five years, coal mines with an aggregate capacity of 183 million tons, 277 coal washing plants with an aggregate capacity of 184 million tons, and 26 plants for the production of coal briquettes with an aggregate annual capacity of 10 million tons of briquettes, will be launched.

New branches of the fuel and power industry will be created and developed, such as the production of synthetic liquid fuel to an amount of 900 thousand tons a year, and the gas industry producing 11,200 million cubic meters of gas per year.

Oil output will increase up to 35.4 million tons, which is 14 per cent above the prewar level. The share of the eastern districts of the Soviet Union in the total oil output will increase from 12 per cent in 1944 to 36 per cent in 1950.

In the sphere of electrification, the Plan provides for increasing the output of electric power to 82,000 million kilowatt hours, which is 70 per cent above the prewar level. Within five years, power stations with an aggregate capacity of 11.7 million kilowatts will be launched, including 3.3 million kilowatts provided by large and small hydro-electric power stations.

In the engineering industry the Plan provides for doubling the production of machinery and equipment in 1950 compared with the prewar level, while the production of equipment for the metallurgical industry will increase 3.7 times. The output of automobiles will increase to 500 thousand per year, or 3.4 times. The production of locomotives will increase 2.4 times, that of tractors 3.6 times, and that of electrical equipment 2.5 times.

In the chemical industry, production will increase in 1950 to 1.5 times the prewar level. The output of synthetic rubber will be doubled, that of paper will increase by 65 per cent compared with the prewar level.

The Five-Year Plan provides for the rapid rehabilitation and development of the timber and building material industry.

As regards the output of foodstuffs and consumer goods, the Plan provides for an annual increase of 17 per cent, in order not only to reach but to surpass the prewar level.

In conformity with the plan of growth of industrial production, the volume of capital investments in Soviet industry in the next five years is fixed at 157,500 million rubles. In the period of 1946–1950 we must restore, build and launch about 5,900 State enterprises, including 3,200 in the war-ravaged districts, small enterprises not included.

To ensure the realization of the capital construction program, the Five-Year Plan provides for the utmost strengthening and development of the building industry and an increase in the output of building machinery. The program of construction and assembly work for the next five years is estimated at a sum of 153,000 million rubles.

To carry out this Plan it is necessary to ensure wide mechanization of construction work. The Five-Year Plan provides for a thorough mechanization of labor processes, especially in the iron and steel, timber and fuel industries, and for an increase of labor productivity in industry during 1946–1950 by 36 per cent as compared with the prewar level.

This is to be achieved by means of increasing the amount of mechanical equipment per worker by approximately 50 per cent, by means of a wide program for raising the grades of workers, engineers and mechanics, and by full utilization of the eight-hour working day.

The further raising of the technical level of the national economy and the mechanization of labor is to be based on a highly developed engineering industry, equipped with a sufficient quantity of highly productive machine tools.

The Five-Year Plan provides for increasing the number of metal cutting machine tools in the U.S.S.R. to 1,300,000, i.e., approximately 30 per cent above the number of machine tools in the United States in 1940.

This is the most important foundation of the technical and economic independence of the Soviet Union and of further technological progress in all branches of the national economy.

Along with the extensive mechanization and electrification of production, we must ensure the development of new branches of technology and production, such as:

(a) gasification and combined electro-chemical utilization of solid fuel, which replaces, by the distribution of gas through pipes and of power by wire, the transportation of enormous quantities of fuel;

(b) the use of electrical technology in the production of light and nonferrous metals, alloyed steels and chemical products, and in the treatment of metal;

(c) the production of synthetic materials—artificial liquid fuel, synthetic rubber and plastics, synthetic fiber, leather and alcohol;

(d) the introduction of oxygen in various industrial processes, first of all in the iron and steel and chemical industries;

(e) the transmission of direct high-tension current over long distances;

(f) the production of modern instruments, in particular for radio location and for use in the national economy;

(g) the development of reactive technique and the use of engines of new types producing new speeds and capacities;

(h) research work on problems of atomic energy for the needs of industry and transport.

To ensure further technical progress it is necessary to expand existing, and to create new experimental plants, designing bureaus and scientific research institutes, and to give every material encouragement to the work of scientists, engineers and technicians in the sphere of science and invention.

B. AGRICULTURE

In agriculture, the Five-Year Plan provides for the rehabilitation and further development of soil cultivation and animal breeding in order to surpass the prewar level of agricultural production in the U.S.S.R. as a whole.

If the gross agricultural output in 1932 (in the First Five-Year Plan) is taken as 100, then in 1937 (in the Second Five-Year Plan) it amounted to 153; in 1940 (in the Third Five-Year Plan) to 177; and in 1950 it will amount to 225. By the end of the five years, the gross grain harvest will increase to 127 million tons i.e., 7 per cent above the 1940 level.

As regards industrial crops, the gross yield of sugar beet will increase to 26 million tons, i.e., 22 per cent above the prewar level; the raw cotton yield will increase to 3,100,000 tons, i.e., 25 per cent above the prewar level; the flax yield to 800 thousand tons, i.e., 39 per cent above the 1940 level; and the yield of sunflower seed to 3,700,000 tons, i.e., 11 per cent above the prewar level.

In livestock breeding the Five-Year Plan provides for the restoration of the prewar herds of cattle, sheep, goats and pigs, and envisages an increase within five years in the number of horses by 46 per cent, of cattle by 39 per cent, of sheep and goats by 75 per cent and of pigs by 200 per cent as compared with 1945.

The cattle herds of the collective farms will increase to 25.9 million head, i.e., 29 per cent above the 1940 level; the number of sheep and goats will increase to 68.1 million, i.e., 62 per cent; and of pigs to 11.1 million head, i.e., 35 per cent above the 1940 level.

To ensure the rehabilitation and further development of agriculture, the Five-Year Plan provides for a considerable increase in the supply of tractors, agricultural machinery and mineral fertilizers to agriculture. Within five years agriculture will receive 720 thousand tractors (reckoned on the basis of 15 horsepower units) as against 512 thousand tractors supplied under the Second Five-Year Plan. The countryside will receive agricultural machinery to the value of 4,500 million rubles (at stable 1926–1927 prices), as compared with 1,900 million rubles under the Second Five-Year Plan.

The Five-Year Plan provides for the growth of the irrigated area by 656 thousand hectares (1,620,976 acres) and of the drained area by 615 thousand hectares, (1,519,665 acres.)

Along with the further mechanization of agricultural production, electrification will be continued on a larger scale. The Five-Year Plan provides for the construction in the villages of small hydroelectric stations with an aggregate capacity of one million kilowatts. This ensures electrification not only of machine and tractor stations and of State farms, but of many thousands of collective farms as well.

C. TRANSPORT

To ensure the outlined program of material production and construction work, the Five-Year Plan provides for an increase in the freight turnover of railway, water and automobile transport from 483 million ton-kilometers in 1940 to 657,500 million ton-kilometers in 1950, i.e., 36 per cent above the prewar level.

The Plan provides for the capital restoration of the railways in the formerly occupied districts, the construction of new railway trunk lines and the technical re-equipment of railway transport to ensure its steady work, especially under winter conditions.

In accordance with these tasks, the Five-Year Plan provides for increasing the number of locomotives of the country's own production by 6,165 steam locomotives, 555 electric locomotives and 865 diesel locomotives, as well as an increase in the rolling stock by 472 thousand freight cars.

, Along with the capital restoration of the railway network in districts affected by invasion, new railway lines totaling 7,230 kilometers (4,510 miles) will be constructed, including 3,550 kilometers (2,200 miles) in Siberia. Electrification will be applied to 5,325 kilometers (3,310 miles) of railways, including those in the Kuznetsk Basin—Urals direction.

The Five-Year Plan provides for the capital investment of 40,100 million rubles for the restoration and development of railway transport.

As regards water transport, the Five-Year Plan provides for an increase of river transport freight traffic by 38 per cent and of sea transport freight traffic by 2.2 times in 1950 as compared with the prewar period.

In 1950 the building program for ocean-going vessels will be 2.5 times as great, and the river shipbuilding program will be four times as great as in 1940.

The Five-Year Plan ensures the construction of a powerful Soviet fleet, as well as the restoration of existing, and the construction of new sea and river ports.

The development of highway transport will continue; the country's automobiles will be doubled as compared with the prewar period, and air transport will be rapidly developed.

D. REDUCTION OF PRODUCTION COSTS

The postwar reconstruction of the national economy requires the enhancement of the part played by economic levers in the organization of production and distribution, such as prices, money, credit, profit and premiums.

The systematic reduction of production costs is a law of socialist production. The total sum saved through reduction of production costs in industry, transport, machine and tractor stations and State farms as compared with the 1945 level will amount to nearly 160,000 million rubles in the period of 1946–1950.

III

PLAN FOR IMPROVING LIVING CONDITIONS

The peoples of the Soviet Union experienced incalculable material privations during the Patriotic War and made great sacrifices to ensure our country's victory. Improvement of the material, living and cultural conditions, worthy of a victorious people, is one of the most important tasks of the Five-Year Plan.

The growth of material production ensures a considerable rise in the national income, which in 1950 will surpass the prewar level by 38 per cent.

In 1950 the number of workers and employees occupied in the Soviet national economy will reach 33,500,000. The total payroll of workers and employees occupied in the national economy will increase in 1950 to 252,000 million rubles as against 162,000 million rubles in 1940.

The average annual wages of workers and employees occupied in the national economy will grow parallel with the growth of labor productivity, and in 1950 will surpass the 1940 level by 48 per cent.

The Five-Year Plan provides for an increase in State expenditure for the cultural and material needs of the working people in town and countryside (State expenditure for urban construction not included) to 106,000 million rubles in 1950, i.e., 2.6 times as much as in 1940.

In 1950, the number of elementary seven-grade schools and secondary schools will increase to 193 thousand, i.e., to the prewar level, and the number of pupils to 31,800,000. The number of students in higher educational institutions will increase to 674 thousand and in special secondary schools, to 1,280,000.

It is planned to increase the number of children in kindergartens to 2,260,000 in

1950, i.e., double the 1940 figure. Orphans of the Patriotic War will be fully taken care of at orphanages at the expense of the State.

The number of hospital beds will increase in 1950 to 985 thousand as compared with 710 thousand in 1940; and the number of places in permanent nurseries to 1,251,-000 as compared with 859 thousand in 1940.

The network of rest homes and sanatoriums for workers, peasants and intellectuals will be completely restored and medical treatment for disabled ex-servicemen is ensured.

The number of cinema installations will increase in 1950 to 46,700 as compared with 28 thousand in 1940. All theaters, clubs and public libraries in town and countryside will be completely restored.

Within five years it is planned to invest 42,300 million rubles in housing construction and to put into use 72,400,000 square meters of State-owned living floor space in towns and workers' settlements.

The retail trade turnover of State and cooperative stores will increase in 1950 to 275,000 million rubles, i.e., 28 per cent above the 1940 level. The prewar level of per capita consumption of basic foodstuffs and consumer goods will not only be attained but even considerably surpassed.

The Five-Year Plan provides for the abolition of the rationing system and the change to highly developed Soviet trade. It is planned to abolish the rationing of bread, flour, cereals and macaroni in 1946, and rationing of all other goods in 1946 and 1947.

The development of Soviet trade on the basis of the abolition of rationing and a steady reduction of commodity prices will strengthen currency circulation and will greatly increase the significance of the Soviet ruble in the country's entire economic life.

IV

DISTRIBUTION OF PRODUCTIVE FORCES

With regard to the distribution of productive forces in the Union Republics and the economic districts of the U.S.S.R., the Five-Year Plan proceeds from the necessity of rehabilitating the districts affected by the invasion, of developing further the national economy of all the Union Republics and economic districts, and of bringing industries supplying raw materials closer together with regions of consumption.

In connection with this task the Five-Year Plan provides for an increase of capital construction in all of the Union Republics and economic districts of the U.S.S.R., especially in Siberia and the Far East.

Of the total volume of capital investment in the national economy of the U.S.S.R., 115,000 million rubles are allocated for the rehabilitation of the districts affected by the invasion, and about 135,000 million rubles for the development of the national economy in other districts of the country.

In Moscow, Leningrad, Kiev, Kharkov, Rostov, Gorky and Sverdlovsk the construction of new enterprises will be restricted. The Five-Year Plan provides for the construction of industrial enterprises in new districts and towns possessing the requisite fuel, power and raw material resources.

In the districts of the U.S.S.R. which were under the temporary rule of the fascist bandits, we face the task of restoring demolished towns and villages, industry, transport, agriculture and cultural institutions, and of creating normal living conditions for Soviet citizens delivered from fascist slavery.

During the Patriotic War, thousands of industrial enterprises were already partly restored in those districts, as well as more than 1,800 State farms and three thousand machine and tractor stations, 85 thousand collective farms, about six thousand hospitals and more than 70 thousand schools.

An area of 17,900,000 square yards of living floor space has been restored in the towns and 1,260,000 houses have been rebuilt in villages formerly occupied by the enemy.

However, only the smaller part of the restoration work required has been carried out in the districts of the U.S.S.R. affected by enemy occupation.

The main tasks of the Five-Year Plan in the rehabilitation of the districts of the Russian Federation and of the Ukrainian, Byelorussian, Lithuanian, Moldavian, Latvian, Estonian and Karelo-Finnish Republics affected by occupation are as follows:

FIRST, to attain the prewar level of industrial output and a further development of
the national economy on the basis of thorough mechanization of labor and the introduction of the most modern technique. This means that within five years the industrial production in these areas must be increased 3.9 times, the output of coal 2.9 times,
pig iron 5.1 times and power 4.4. times.

SECOND, to restore the network and carrying capacity of the railways, waterways and
motor transport to ensure the attainment of the prewar level and a further increase
in trade turnover, for which purpose we shall have to increase railway freight traffic in
the affected districts 2.3 times and river freight 6.5 times within five years.

THIRD, to restore agriculture, which implies in the districts listed above an increase
in the production of grain by 87 per cent, in the yield of sugar beet by 3.2 times, and
in that of sunflower seeds by 73 per cent in the next five years; while the cattle herds
must increase by 52 per cent and the number of pigs by 220 per cent.

FOURTH, to rebuild the towns and villages demolished by the invaders, dwelling
houses in the first place, which calls for putting into use a living floor space of 33,-
200,000 square meters (Government owned alone) within five years; a rise of the
people's standard of living, with a simultaneous growth of labor productivity; the
restoration of the retail trade turnover of State and cooperative stores, which will require the turnover to become 2.2 times as great within five years; the restoration of
the prewar network of schools, cultural and public health institutions. . . .

V

SPEED OF ECONOMIC PROGRESS

After the termination of the First World War and the Civil War, it took the
U.S.S.R. about six years to restore industrial production to the prewar 1913 level. The
Five-Year Plan envisages the restoration of industrial production in the Soviet Union
to the prewar 1940 level by 1948, while by the end of the five-year period this level
will be greatly surpassed.

Thus, we intend to carry out industrial restoration twice as rapidly as after the
termination of the First World War and the Civil War.

The industry of the Urals and Siberia is of paramount importance for speeding the
pace of the restoration of our national economy.

In 1945 the industrial output in the Urals was more than three times as great as in
1940; the pig iron output had nearly doubled, the coal output had more than doubled
and power production had doubled.

The industry of the Urals and Siberia is the pride of Soviet industry and our task
is to strengthen and develop it in every way.

We have everything necessary to carry out the rehabilitation of our national economy
at a rapid pace. We have reared the necessary cadres, cadres of Soviet intelligentsia.
The peoples of the Soviet Union have grown culturally and passed through the historical
school of socialist construction.

The industrial base in the eastern and central districts of the U.S.S.R. has grown
and gained strength.

Exploiting classes have been eliminated in the U.S.S.R. and an unparalleled moral and
political unity of the peoples of the Soviet Union has been achieved. The trust and
prestige enjoyed by the Communist Party and the Soviet Government, headed by our
leader, Comrade Stalin, are exceptionally high. In this lies our strength and the earnest
of victory.

We shall have to develop production in industry, agriculture, transport and construction at a rapid pace. To slow the pace of rehabilitation and further development of
the national economy of the U.S.S.R. would mean to fall behind, and those who
fall behind are beaten. This is why we must achieve the pace of development envisaged
by the Five-Year Plan.

Guided by Lenin's and Stalin's precepts, forbidding any complacency after the achievement of victory, we must call upon workers, peasants and intellectuals to give all
their strength to the cause of the earliest rehabilitation and further development of
our national economy, the raising of the material and cultural standards of life of the
Soviet people. . . .

APPENDIX VII

STATE AID FOR MOTHERS AND CHILDREN *

The Presidium of the Supreme Soviet of the Union of Soviet Socialist Republics resolved on July 8, 1944, as follows:

On increasing State aid to mothers of large families and unmarried mothers.

1. To establish that State allowances are to be granted to mothers of large families (whether the husband is living or not) on the birth of the third child and of each subsequent child, instead of the existing procedure of granting State allowances to mothers of six children on the birth of the seventh and of each subsequent child.

2. Payment of State allowances to mothers of large families is to be effected as follows: On the birth of the third child to a mother with two children, a single grant of 400 rubles. On the birth of a fourth child to a mother with three children, a single grant of 1,300 rubles and a monthly allowance of 80 rubles. On the birth of a fifth child to a mother with four children, a single grant of 1,700 rubles and a monthly allowance of 120 rubles. On the birth of a sixth child to a mother with five children, a single grant of 2,000 rubles and a monthly allowance of 140 rubles. On the birth of a seventh child to a mother with six children, a single grant of 2,500 rubles and a monthly allowance of 200 rubles. On the birth of the eighth child to a mother with seven children, a single grant of 2,500 rubles and a monthly allowance of 200 rubles. On the birth of a ninth child to a mother with eight children, a single grant of 3,500 rubles and a monthly allowance of 250 rubles. On the birth of a tenth child to a mother with nine children, a single grant of 3,500 rubles and a monthly allowance of 250 rubles. On the birth of each subsequent child to a mother with ten children, a single grant of 5,000 rubles and a monthly allowance of 300 rubles.

Monthly allowances to mothers of large families are to be paid beginning with the second year of the child's life and continuing until the child reaches the age of five.

Mothers with families of three, four, five or six children at the date of issue of the present Edict will receive allowances under the present Article for every child born after the publication of the present Edict.

Mothers with families of seven or more children at the date of issue of the present Edict retain the right to receive large family allowances according to the procedure and in the amounts set forth in the decision of the Central Executive Committee and the Council of People's Commissars of the U.S.S.R. of June 27, 1936, namely, for the seventh, eighth, ninth and tenth child, 2,000 rubles each annually for five years from the day of the child's birth, and for each subsequent child 5,000 rubles in a single grant and 3,000 rubles each annually for four years, beginning with the child's second year. For every child born after the publication of the present Edict allowances will be paid in accordance with and in the amounts set forth in the present Article of the Edict.

In determining State allowances for large families, children killed or missing on the fronts of the Patriotic War are to be included.

3. To establish allowances for unmarried mothers for the maintenance and upbringing of children born after the publication of the present Edict in the following amounts: 100 rubles monthly for one child, 150 rubles for two children and 200 rubles for three or more children.

State allowances to unmarried mothers are paid until the children attain the age of 12.

Unmarried mothers with three or more children are entitled to allowances issued in accordance with Paragraph 2 of the present Article, in addition to the allowances provided for under the present Articles.

Upon her marriage an unmarried mother retains the right to the allowance provided for under the present Article.

The mother who received alimony for children born prior to the publication of the present Edict retains the right to receive alimony until the children come of age, but is not entitled to receive the allowance provided for under the present Article.

Mothers of children born in 1944, prior to the publication of the present Edict, who

* Edict of Supreme Soviet of U.S.S.R. on the Increase of State Aid for Mothers and Children. Embassy of the U.S.S.R. *Information Bulletin,* July 25, 1944.

have not been receiving alimony are entitled to the allowance provided for under the present Article.

4. If an unmarried mother wishes to place her child in an institution for children, said institution is obligated to accept the child which will be maintained and brought up fully at the expense of the State.

The mother of the child has a right to reclaim it from the institution and to bring it up herself if she so desires.

While the child is in the institution, no State allowance is to be paid.

5. To increase single grants paid from the social insurance funds and the mutual aid funds of producers' cooperatives, for newborn infants, from 45 rubles to 120 rubles, facilities to be extended for the purchase by the mother of layettes for this amount.

On increasing the privileges for expectant mothers and mothers, and on measures for extending the network of institutions for protecting mother and child.

6. To increase maternity leaves for women factory workers and office employees from 63 to 77 calendar days, 35 days before and 42 days after childbirth, with payment during this period of the State allowance in the amounts fixed heretofore. In the event of an abnormal birth or the birth of twins, post-natal leave is to be extended to 56 calendar days.

Managers of enterprises and institutions must grant expectant mothers annual vacations, which must be timed to precede or follow maternity leave.

7. After four months' pregnancy, women are not to be given overtime work at enterprises and institutions, and women with infants are to be exempted from night work throughout the period of nursing.

8. To double additional food rations for expectant mothers beginning with the sixth month of pregnancy and for nursing mothers during four months of nursing.

9. Managers of enterprises and institutions must render aid to expectant mothers and nursing mothers by issuing additional food products from auxiliary farms.

10. To reduce by 50 per cent fees at kindergartens and nurseries for the accommodation of children of parents with three children and with monthly earnings up to 400 rubles, with four children and with monthly earnings up to 600 rubles, with five or more children regardless of earnings.

11. To instruct the Council of People's Commissars of the U.S.S.R.:

(a) To approve the plan for the organization in Republics and Regions of additional mother and child centers, and also of special rest homes for needy unmarried expectant mothers, as well as for nursing mothers in ailing health; inmates of such rest homes to perform light tasks compatible with the state of their health.

(b) To approve the plan for the extension of the network of children's institutions under the People's Commissariats and other departments, to provide accommodations for all children in need of such service, at the same time to provide for the extension of the network of medical consultation centers for children, and of milk kitchens, of nurseries for infants and evening accommodations at kindergartens and maternity institutions in areas liberated from the German invaders.

(c) To provide for the obligatory organization at enterprises and institutions where women are employed in large numbers, of nurseries, kindergartens and special rest rooms for nursing mothers.

(d) To make it obligatory for the People's Commissariats in their plans for industrial construction to provide for the building of children's institutions (nurseries, kindergartens, mother and child rooms) with accommodations sufficient for all children of women employed at the given enterprise and in need of such services.

(e) To approve measures for the considerable extension of the output of clothing and footwear for children, toilet accessories for children, and the like, both for children's institutions and for sale to the general public, as well as for the extension of the chain of workshops producing children's clothing and shops catering to mother and child. . . .*

On the tax on single men and women and citizens with small families.

16. In modification of the Edict of the Presidium of the Supreme Soviet of the U.S.S.R. of November 21, 1941 "On the tax on single men and women and childless

* Clauses 12–15 relate to awards for mothers of large families.

citizens of the U.S.S.R.," the tax will henceforth be levied upon citizens who have no children and on citizens who have one or two children: for men over 20 and up to 50 years of age and for women over 20 and up to 45.

17. The tax is to be levied in the following amounts:

(a) Citizens paying income tax will be taxed to the extent of six per cent of their income in the absence of children, one per cent if they have one child and one-half per cent if they have two children.

(b) Collective farmers, individual farmers and other citizens of households subject to the agricultural tax will be taxed to the extent of 150 rubles annually in the absence of children, 50 rubles annually if they have one child and 25 rubles annually if they have two children.

(c) Other citizens having no children will be taxed 90 rubles annually, those with one child 30 rubles annually and those with two children 15 rubles annually.

18. To exempt from the tax:

(a) Servicemen of the rank and file, sergeants and petty officers.

(b) Army and Navy officers of units and organizations on active service.

(c) Wives of servicemen specified in points (a) and (b) of the present Article.

(d) Women receiving allowances or pensions by the State for the upkeep of children.

(e) Citizens whose children have been killed or reported missing on fronts of the Patriotic War.

(f) Men and women students of secondary and higher schools up to 25 years of age.

(g) Invalids belonging to the first and second categories of invalidity.

On changes in laws on marriage, family and guardianship.

19. To establish that rights and obligations of husband and wife provided for under the Code of Laws of the Union Republics on marriage and family, re guardianship, accrue from legally registered marriages only.

Persons who have been married de facto prior to publication of the present Edict may legalize their relations by registering the marriage and stating the actual period of their conjugal life.

20. To abolish the existing right of a mother to appeal to the court for the purpose of establishing fatherhood and claiming alimony for the upkeep of a child from a man to whom she is not legally married.

21. To establish that upon the registration of the birth of a child whose mother is not legally married, the child is given the mother's surname and any patronymic the mother might indicate.

22. The registration on passports of marriages, indicating surnames, names and patronymics and year of birth of the other party to a marriage, as well as the place and time of registration of marriage is obligatory.

23. To establish that divorces are to be effected publicly through the courts. At the request of husband or wife a divorce in certain cases on the decision of the court may be heard in camera.

24. The following procedure is to be followed when petitioning for dissolution of marriage.

(a) A petition for the dissolution of a marriage is to be submitted to the People's Court, giving reasons for the divorce as well as the full name, date of birth and address of the other party to the marriage; when filing the petition for divorce, the sum of 100 rubles is to be paid.

(b) The court summons the party against whom the petition has been filed, to acquaint him or her with the contents of the petition, to ascertain the motives for the divorce, as well as to establish witnesses to be summoned during the court proceedings.

(c) Announcement of the filing of a petition for divorce is to be published in the local newspaper at the expense of the party filing the petition.

25. The People's Court is obliged to establish the motives for the filing of a petition for the dissolution of a marriage, and to take steps to reconcile the parties, for which purpose both parties must be summoned, and in case of necessity witnesses as well.

In the event of failure by the People's Court to reconcile the parties, the petitioner has the right to file a petition for the dissolution of the marriage with the higher court.

A decision regarding the dissolution of a marriage may be passed by the Regional and city courts or the Supreme Court of the Union or Autonomous Republic.

26. The Regional, territorial and city courts or the Supreme Court of the Union or Autonomous Republic which decide that the marriage should be annulled, must:

(a) Settle the question of the custody of the children between the parents and determine which of the parents is to defray expenses for the maintenance of the children and to what extent.

(b) Establish a procedure for the division of property whether in kind or in respective proportions between the parties.

(c) Restore to each of the divorced parties their original surnames if they so desire.

27. On the basis of the court decision, the civil registry office draws up the certificate of divorce, makes a corresponding entry in the passports of both parties and charges one or both parties, at the decision of the court, a sum ranging from 500 to 2,000 rubles.

28. To instruct the Supreme Soviets of the Union Republics to make, in accordance with the present Edict, the necessary changes in the legislation of the Union Republics.

29. To instruct the Council of People's Commissars of the U.S.S.R. to draw up statutes covering the procedure for the payment of allowances to expectant mothers, mothers of large families and unmarried mothers in accordance with the present Edict.

30. To instruct the Council of People's Commissars of the U.S.S.R. to adopt measures regulating the procedure of registration of marriages, births, etc., providing for the introduction of a solemn procedure for which suitable premises properly furnished are to be set aside, and for the issue to citizens of certificates duly drawn up.

31. In accordance with criminal legislation in force, the State prosecuting organs are to prosecute those guilty of performing illegal abortions, of forcing women to undergo abortions, of insulting and humiliating the dignity of mothers and of refusing to pay alimony for the upkeep of children.

Index